M000203578

INDEPENDENT QUEERS

LGBTQ EDUCATORS IN INDEPENDENT SCHOOLS SPEAK OUT

This book is dedicated to the brave student who called me up to say, "Mr. McAdoo, I am like you; I am gay." In the days following this declaration, we talked about what that meant in the context of his school, but ultimately his struggle with his sexual orientation led him to stay at home, depressed and afraid to go to school. I was unable to convince school officials that we, as educators, were responsible for playing a role in validating this student. This book is an apology and acknowledgment of the suffering that students endure when a community of teachers and leaders ignore and deny the existence of LGBTQ youth.

Today, that student is a proud, openly gay man. I celebrate and honor him—his INDEPENDENCE—his QUEERness—and all QUEERS in INDEPENDENT schools. Speak out!

www.mascotbooks.com

Independent Queers:
LGBTQ Educators in Independent Schools Speak Out

©2019 Dr. Philip D. McAdoo. All Rights Reserved. No part of this publication may be reproduced, stored in a retrieval system or transmitted in any form by any means electronic, mechanical, or photocopying, recording or otherwise without the permission of the author.

Some names or identifying details may have been changed to protect the privacy of individuals.

Author photograph on dust jacket by KL Moore Photography

For more information, please contact:
Mascot Books
620 Herndon Parkway #320
Herndon, VA 20170
info@mascotbooks.com

Library of Congress Control Number: 2018903953

CPSIA Code: PRFRE1118A
ISBN: 978-1-68401-939-7

Printed in Canada

INDEPENDENT QUEERS

LGBTQ EDUCATORS IN INDEPENDENT SCHOOLS SPEAK OUT

DR. PHILIP D. McADOO

CONTENTS

Preface: Challenging the Norm—William   1

Introduction: Sexual Orientation, Teaching, and Me   3

LGBTQ Teachers and Social Acceptance   8

Finding LGBTQ Voices   33

Lower School
   Robert   45
   Sarah   51
   Steven   55
   Joseph   62
   Anthony   68
   Linda   73
   Betty   77
   Michael   81
   Margaret   89

Middle School
   William   93
   Mark and Paul   98
   Joshua   104
   Jessica   110
   David   115
   Barbara   120
   Matthew   128
   Donald   132
   Patricia   138
   John   143

Upper School

Kenneth 148
Jennifer 153
George 159
Christopher 164
Thomas 168
Nancy 173
Edward and Andrew 178
Richard 188
Kevin 198
Olivia 202
Brian 210
Lisa 215
James 220
Daniel 228
Mary 232

Administration

Elizabeth 239
Charles 245
Dorothy 249
Karen 257

Discussion and Implications 265

Appendix 284

Bibliography 285

PREFACE

CHALLENGING THE NORM

William

They asked me to be Grand Marshal. Gloria sent out this list and said, "You know, look, we'd love for somebody to be Grand Marshal. Any volunteers?" And so, I thought about it. I'm like, "What the fuck, why not?" So, I sent her an email and I'm like, "I'll do it." Her email back was, "Are you serious?" I said, "Yes." Five minutes later, she sends an all-school email. Everybody stop! No more volunteers. We have a grand marshal. And I'm like, "Well, she's really going with it."

So then, I'm like, "Well, what do I have? What sort of costume do I have?" And, literally the week before, I am having no luck coming up with any sort of costume. What does a grand marshal wear? I went to costume shops. I went all over. I can't find anything. Well, what can you do? I was like you can do stuff with hair (because I have none) and shoes. I'm like all right.

I go online and I order a size 15, Lucite six-inch pumps, platforms. So, I order them and they come in and I try them on, and I'm like, "Oh, my God." Then I try them on and I'm like, "Damn, I'm going to do this. I can do this. All right." Well, they're the shoes, now what? Hair, hair, hair: let's go get a wig. So, I found this kind of this huge, blonde Afro wig. That's great. Now I've top and bottom, but what happens in between? I said to myself, "Well, wear your tux bands! I own a red smoking jacket, wear a 50s straight tie, just camp it up." So, I just really camped it up. I had big earrings, big dangly earrings. I did fake nails, I'm painting my nails. I was not in drag, but I was gender bending.

I was walking...and I realized, as I was doing it, that here I was walking down the hall after I got dressed that morning. The kids were speechless. And they, sort of like Moses and [the Red Sea], like parted. These are kids who know me, and after they realized who I was, they were still—they were stopped. They were just like, what do we say? It was at that point that I realized this is scary for some of these kids. Then I go out and I get in front of the cars for the lineup and they're like, "Oh, my God." And some of my boys came [up to me] and were like, "Love it, love it!" Others of them were like, "How dare you?" Some of the girls came by and were like, "How are you wearing those shoes?" And I'm like, "Take lessons from me, sweetheart. Talk to me before prom."

Then the music started. I'm like, "Well, here goes." So, I started walking. As I got closer (because I was [a distance] away), people were like, "Oh!" Or they were like, "Oh, my God," then they go crazy. I don't understand those reactions. I'll be quite honest with you, I don't understand them. It's so not remarkable for me. I know that's going to sound weird. Because my point was to get the cheers going. "Cheer! This is homecoming, let's do it!" I never intended to break new ground. I never intended to challenge any norm.

INTRODUCTION

SEXUAL ORIENTATION, TEACHING, AND ME

My introduction to Black feminist literature in college was my first experience of self-acceptance as a Black gay man. I felt completely affirmed by the experiences of these Black women and found an abundance of literature that allowed me to define myself as a Black gay man. Until then, I did not have the language to begin the process of self-affirmation. Incorporating the work of Black feminist authors into my process was not difficult, because I could relate to the pain of being silenced and ignored. My transformation began to occur when I was able to acknowledge the power of self-definition: the power to define ourselves as straight or gay, woman or man, or as someone who has suffered at the hands of those who deemed themselves entitled to interpret others' reality. As Collins (2002) notes, "By insisting on self-definition, Black women question not only what has been said about African-American women, but the credibility and the intentions of those possessing the power to define" (p. 42). So, when naming, blaming, and projecting happen outside of who we are as self-determined people, we are able to stand inside of who we are, self-identify, and say, "That is not who I am."

I am a teacher. I began my career in education in the New York City public school system. As a gay man, I was cautious about how my work with young men could be perceived. My work yielded a basketball mentor program, an arts exchange initiative, and a global educational outreach program for inner-city students. Given the nature of what I was trying to teach the young men—self-respect, advocacy, and equity—to remain silent about my sexual identity felt somewhat disingenuous.

Being a teacher, I was reluctant to "come out." Rasmussen (2004) describes coming out as a lifelong process of "becoming aware of one's sexual orientation or gender identity" (p. 144) and disclosing this information to others. My experience of school cultures was that of traditional gender norms, heteronormativity (heterosexual norms), and homophobia. I assumed that sharing my homosexual identity—fed by experiences I had seen, heard, and read about— meant my sexual orientation would distract my students from learning and deter my colleagues from engaging with me.

As I transitioned into independent schools, I worked hard to use my life as a teaching resource. Drawing from my personal and professional challenges, I conscientiously taught students and colleagues alike about the experiences that minorities often face. I felt safe and protected in my school setting because—as in most independent schools—there was a clear and stated diversity mission of acceptance and tolerance. I defined and evaluated my effectiveness as an administrator, teacher, coach, and mentor in terms of my relationships with my students, their families, and my colleagues. My professional demeanor and integrity were critically important to me, and I went to great lengths to establish collegial and constructive relationships. But, slowly that sense of safety and security began to change as I encountered increasing bureaucracy, homophobia, and limitations within the independent school setting.

During the aftermath of a gay teacher being arrested for possession of child pornography, I experienced an insensitive homophobic rant directed at me by a student—the headmaster's son. The implication was that gay teachers had an intrinsic perversion for young boys and male colleagues. When I brought it to the attention of the head of discipline, he was equally concerned and made provisions to see that a proper form of discipline would be applied to the student. Within moments, the same school that praised and awarded my creativity, innovation, and dedication now had questions and concerns about me, which I suspect evolved from homophobia. At this time, I thought about my newly adopted son and my students. I thought about the kind of father I wanted to be and the kind of teacher and leader that I had become. More importantly, I thought about all the LGBTQ teachers who put their lives, families, and reputations on the line every day, just to be able to do what they enjoy doing: teaching children.

I designed this study as a quest for authenticity in education. Given my experiences as an "out" gay teacher, I wanted to explore other LGBTQ teachers' processes of coming out and how they negotiated their sexual orientation and identity within the educational contexts, philosophies, and practices of independent schools. The purpose was to use this research to construct a model of teacher identity development and advocacy for lesbian, gay, bisexual, transgender, and questioning (LGBTQ) teachers and students.

Rationale and Significance

Diversity has become a bullet point on a list of challenges facing independent schools, schools which are defined as in charge of their own governance. Commonly referred to as private schools, independent schools are governed by a board with religious and financial freedoms.

Hall & Stevenson (2012) highlight that principals, board members, and other leaders of independent schools are being charged with creating more inclusive learning environments, but Brosnan (2012) notes that many independent schools are struggling to define *diversity*. In spite of this, schools are making progress in recruiting faculty and students from a range of social, racial, cultural, and socioeconomic backgrounds. In 2013, the Gay, Lesbian and Straight Education Network (GLSEN) reported that many schools have incorporated sexual orientation into their nondiscrimination policies and regularly offer training to staff about LGBTQ issues. The findings of a report on the state of independent schools regarding LGBTQ issues were startling, concluding that "anti-LGBT language remains rampant" (p. 104) on independent school campuses.[1] Thus, nondiscrimination efforts, while commendable, appear far from effective in producing the same gains for LGBTQ educators that have been achieved within the LGBTQ community in society at large.

Scholars and authors have written extensively about LGBTQ students, their coming out processes, and the challenges they face. And at a grassroots level, schools and national organizations such as the Anti-Defamation League (ADL) and GLSEN work to provide safe spaces for LGBTQ youth. Although there is still much more to learn about the experiences of LGBTQ students, far less has been written about the adults at school who often feel obligated yet powerless to help them—namely, LGBTQ teachers.[2]

Gays and lesbians are starting to be more open about their sexual orientation.[3] In the late 1990s, the editors of *The Harvard Educational Review* dedicated an entire issue to "out" people in education.[4] Eisen and Hall (1996) added that societal changes in the perceptions and experiences of sexuality have left many people with reflections, research, and ideas to share. Various forms of inquiry have opened the lives of LGBTQ people in positive ways. Meezan and Martin (2009) offered a collection of resource materials dealing with the LGBTQ population in various contexts for study. And qualitative research studies have brought to life stories related to sexual orientation, habits, and behaviors of gay people in education and public school settings.[5] However, much less insight is available for LGBTQ teachers in independent school settings.[6]

---

1   Jennings, 2004

2   Birden, 2005; Epstein, 1994; Graves, 2009; Jackson, 2007; Kissen, 1996

3   Blount, 2006; Jennings, 1994; 2005

4   Eisen & Hall, 1996

5   Maxwell, 2012

6   Brosnan, 2012

Research Question

The primary focus of this study was how LGBTQ teachers in independent schools view the relationship between their sexual orientation and their identity as teachers. This study presents a critical analysis of the experiences of LGBTQ teachers in independent school settings that were researched using qualitative data gathering methods. This study was guided by the research questions below:

Primary research questions. Do LGBTQ teachers in independent schools view their sexual orientation as informing their teacher identities? If so, in what ways?

Secondary research question. How do LGBTQ teachers in independent schools perceive the relationship between their sexual orientation and their identity as teachers?

1

LGBTQ TEACHERS AND SOCIAL ACCEPTANCE

There is a growing body of literature calling attention to LGBTQ people in education, but literature that specifically describes the lives and experiences of LGBTQ teachers in independent schools is limited. This study will examine the experiences of LGBTQ teachers in independent schools and how their sexual orientation informs their identity as teachers.

Overview

LGBTQ people have always had a presence in history. Boswell (1980) provides a clear perspective on religious response to homosexuality up to the 14th century. He points out that no compelling reasons exist to support the notion that homosexuality and heterosexuality are incompatible, and he explains that gays and lesbians had equal social status until the 11th century. However, Duberman (1991) notes that between the mid-12th and mid-14th centuries, attitudes about homosexuality began to change dramatically for the worse. Katz (1985) reports that in 1566 in St. Augustine, Florida, a man was sentenced to death because he was gay: the first recorded execution related to the issue of social acceptance of homosexuality in the United States.

Lauritsen and Thorstad (1974) note that the modern gay rights movement began in Germany in 1869. Magnus Hirschfeld, a German educator, founded the Scientific Humanitarian Committee—the first gay liberation organization—to ensure that the oppression of homosexuals was recognized as a form of discrimination. This organization paved the way for acceptance of gays and lesbians. However, with the rise of Hitler and the Nazi regime, homosexuality continued to be criminalized. Fischer, Imi, Färberböck, and Munro (1994) describe how gays and lesbians were taken to concentration camps and identified by pink triangles, and lesbians were forced to wear black or red triangles in order to identify them as political prisoners. When Allied forces finally liberated the camps, gays and lesbians were not released with the other detainees. They were sent to German prisons in violation of German Penal Code Paragraph 175, which outlawed homosexuality but had been widely ignored prior to Hitler's uprising, and homosexuals remained imprisoned until 1968 when Paragraph 175 was abolished.[7]

Back in the United States, during the 1950s, the Mattachine Society and Daughters of Bilitis, the first national organizations for gay people, was founded.[8] Weiss and Schiller note that, prior to the formation of these advocacy groups, gays and lesbians were seen as isolated in big cities with little known about their ways of life. The newly formed organization provided support for gays and lesbians and marked the beginning of the acceptance of gays and lesbians in the United States.

The 1960s saw gay rights at the forefront of conversations across the United States.[9] Cain (1993) reports:

> Most lesbian and gay rights activists cite June 27, 1969, as the beginning of the modern gay liberation movement. On that evening, when the New York police raided the Stonewall Inn, a gay bar in Greenwich Village, something unusual happened. The patrons, mostly gay men, resisted police harassment, sparking three days of riots known as the Stonewall riots (or, the Stonewall Rebellion). Gay solidarity throughout the country generated many similar demonstrations of gay pride. (p. 1580)

---

7   Plant, 1986

8   Weiss & Schiller, 1988

9   Weiss & Schiller, 1988

The Stonewall riots have a significant place in the struggle for civil rights for gays and lesbians. Cain (1993) maintained that the long-argued catalyst for the gay rights movement was one of many events.

This modern gay movement is considered "the quintessential identity movement."[10] The movement's origin can be traced to the formation of the Mattachine Society in Los Angeles, the concentrated litigation effort in Washington, D.C. against the federal government, and the growing resistance to police raids of gay bars and gay social events in San Francisco in the 1950s and 1960s.[11] Marcus (1992) notes that Stonewall planted the seed for gay organizations on U.S. university campuses, as students challenged administrations and sexual orientation found a platform in education and the law.

During the 1990s, more gay people began holding positions of power in the workplace than they had prior, often without trying to conceal their sexual identities.[12] This decade saw the growth of gay business and professional networking groups, elected officials, entrepreneurs, and local and national celebrities. Gay individuals proved adept at working together to challenge discrimination they experienced at home, at school, at work, and from their elected representatives.[13] Fleischmann and Hardman explained how the political surge of Black and female leaders in Atlanta led to the formation of strategic alliances with LGBTQ groups within the area and in neighboring cities and states, as well as with straight allies—families, friends, coworkers, and elected officials.

Despite racial segregation and religious fundamentalism, gay people have been able to live productive and fulfilling lives.[14] By the end of the 20th century, cities in the United States had some of the largest lesbian,

---

10   Bernstein, 1997, p. 532

11   Weiss & Schiller, 1988

12   Duyvendak & Krouwel, 2009

13   Duyvendak & Krouwel, 2009; Fleischmann & Hardman, 2004; Yoshino, 2007

14   Jackson, 2007

gay, bisexual, and transgender populations.[15] Many of the trends and forces that had shaped the country throughout the century—urban development and suburban expansion, race relations, business, and transportation—continued to have an impact on the way gays and lesbians lived, as well as the landscape of LGBTQ movement.[16]

The gay movement continues to expand in the 21st century with the growing public support for same-sex marriage. There has been a steady increase in support for same-sex marriage since 2004, when Massachusetts became the first state to legalize it.[17] On page one of their report, Powell, Quadlin, and Pizmony-Levy say, "Same-sex marriage has become legal in 33 states covering over two-thirds of the U.S. population. In 22 of these states, the move to marriage equality occurred as a direct result of court decisions." Support for same-sex marriage is expected to grow as the Supreme Court continues to rule in favor of the rights of LGBTQ individuals.

The Struggles of LGBTQ Teachers

Research on sexual orientation, the coming-out process, gender norms, homophobia, and legal perspectives of LGBTQ people in education helped to guide this study. The literature discusses several factors that affect the experience of LGBTQ teachers, such as sexual orientation, stigma, safety, social patterns, and cultural patterns.[18] These factors prove to be critical components of constructing a conceptual framework for LGBTQ teachers in independent schools.

---

15   Duyvendak & Krouwel, 2009

16   Doan & Higgins, 2011; Duyvendak & Krouwel, 2009; Fleischmann & Hardman, 2004; Walther, 2015; Yoshino, 2007

17   Powell, Quadlin, & Pizmony-Levy, 2015

18   Birden, 2005; Irwin, 2002; Kissen, 1996; Yoshino, 2007

Research has found that gay teachers have had to navigate their sexual orientation within the heterosexual matrix of education.[19] Birden states, "Heterosexism has been broadly defined as the belief that heterosexuality is inherently superior to non-heterosexuality in its various forms" (p. 6). Many gay people go back and forth between heteronormative and homonormative identities; some choose to reveal their sexual identity, and others remain not "out" about their sexual orientation.[20] Evans (2002) adds to the research by highlighting the presence of both overt and subtle forms of homophobia in education. The concept of homophobia is linked to the way homosexuality is defined and experienced in the world.[21] Education often perpetuated heterosexuality in the context of established gender roles.[22]

Redefining Gender Norms in Education

Historically, gender roles and norms have led to a heightened scrutiny of single male and female teachers.[23] The continued suspicion of homosexuality has forced some teachers out of the classroom. For example, in the early 20th century, as homosexuality was being viewed by the general population as something that could be taught, Blount (2006) notes that school administrators began to target single male teachers at same-sex schools. School officials viewed unmarried female teachers with less concern because there was less stigma associated with women in the classroom. Society had been conditioned to think that a woman would more likely seek the affection of another woman to "reduce loneliness" than seek sex.[24]

---

19   Birden, 2005
20   Yoshino, 2007
21   van Dijk & van Driel, 2007
22   Epstein, 1994
23   Blount, 2006; Griffin & Ouellett, 2003
24   Blount, 2006, p. 29

Albert Kinsey published a report on male sexuality in 1948 and a second report on female sexuality in 1953. These precedent-setting studies of male and female sexual activity continued to ignite homophobia in the educational system, even with Kinsey's conclusion that homosexuality was "perfectly natural."[25] Public awareness and concern over homosexuality continued to grow as "efforts to cleanse the educational system of all suspected homosexuals were in full force."[26]

In 2006, Blount wrote about the history of LGBTQ teachers being controlled by school communities and their resistance to it. Blount (2006) provides detailed accounts of how schools have historically attempted to control the sexuality of their workers. She described the gender, identity, and other mistreatment of LGBTQ teachers and educators:

> Educators who identify as gay, lesbian, bisexual, or transgender have begun pressing for the right to claim these identities openly in spite of powerful social opposition. This marks a critical development in the gender identification of schoolwork, as cross-gender behaviors and characteristics have been linked in the popular mind with homosexuality and all of its attendant taboos since the late 1920s.[27]

This push for acceptance is helping to redefine gender norms in education.

---

25   Lugg, 2003
26   Brunner, 2013, p. 163
27   Blount, 2006, p. 84

The Challenges of Heterosexism and Homophobia

Heterosexism is the assumed norm in most aspects of our culture.[28] A range of research points to heterosexism as one of the biggest challenges facing LGBTQ teachers.[29] According to Chambers (2003), heterosexism is a set of attitudes, beliefs, and practices that regard heterosexuality as the normal or preferred sexual orientation. M. Warner (1993) coined the term *heteronormativity* in referring to the complex social, legal, and cultural systems that construct the normalcy of heterosexual standards. These heteronormativity codes and norms are embedded in educational discourse, and they project images of the teacher identity as heterosexual.[30]

According to Brunner and deLeon (2013), heteronormativity dictates how gay individuals negotiate their sexual identity. As Sumara (2008) notes, "living in a heterosexist culture means that persons are assumed to be heterosexual unless some evidence to the contrary is presented" (p. 44). He then describes individuals who identified as "other than heterosexual" as living in "enforced heterosexuality" situations.[31] Donelson and Rogers (2004) acknowledge that heterosexuality is the assumed sexual identity in most school settings, and that some LGBTQ teachers choose to conceal their sexual identities at school as a result.

In addition to the fear of navigating heterosexual norms, research supports homophobia and homophobic actions as points of concern for LGBTQ teachers. Van Dijk and van Driel (2007) examine the factors contributing to school-based homophobia and offer accounts from researchers around the world of widespread prejudice, discrimination, stereotyping, and violence against LGBTQ youth and adults in school

28   Howarth, 2004; Warner, 1993
29   DePalma & Jennett, 2010; Epstein, 1994; Irwin, 2002; Sumara, 2008
30   King, 2003
31   Sumara, 2008, p. 44

settings. The contributors emphasize the importance of challenging homophobia and inequalities and of transforming the institutional culture of school. Additionally, they offer effective and creative methods to address homophobia such as LGBTQ policies and updated school curricula.

Although the gay community has benefited from the legacy of the civil rights movement, personal danger and financial loss have been cited as reasons for gay men and women to hide their sexual orientation and remain silent in their roles in education.[32] Kissen (1996) refers to homophobia as "the last acceptable prejudice in America," meaning that homophobic and derogatory rants are common in schools and in our culture, oftentimes going unchallenged. Drawing on the parallel to the Black Civil Rights Movement, Foster (1997) outlines the importance of being able to speak truth in education and in learning environments where minorities without equal rights are present. Many teachers choose to hide their sexual orientation in their everyday school lives, often resulting in feeling marginalized and silenced.[33] Some may choose to accept their status by adopting heteronormative behaviors and "altering facts about [their lives], changing the names of places and people in order to appear straight."[34] Yoshino (2007) observes that the desire for authenticity is a common human need of expression. People who come out as gay after they have started teaching struggle to incorporate their identities into their profession.[35]

Jennings (2005) found that LGBTQ teachers often navigate oppressive conditions inside and outside of their school communities. In his research on LGBTQ teachers and the cultures of schools, Jennings (2005) identifies common variables that affect teachers' abilities to negotiate difficult work conditions, including identity, visibility, stu-

---

32 Fleischmann & Hardman, 2014; Harbeck, 1992

33 Ferfolja & Hopkins, 2013

34 Kissen, 1993, p. 44

35 Kissen, 1993

dent-teacher relationships, and the coming out process. Jennings's (2005) collection of personal stories and struggles of LGBTQ teachers highlight the dimensions of homophobia that teachers face in school settings.

The Process of Coming Out

Coming out and being open about one's personal life and identity are difficult for LGBTQ teachers.[36] Many LGBTQ teachers choose to conceal their sexual identity, but being out has broad ethical significance.[37] Boswell (1980) states, "Gay people are for the most part not born into gay families. They suffer oppression individually and alone, without benefit or advice or frequently even emotional support from relatives or friends" (p. 362). He further notes that gays and lesbians find themselves the object of social tensions and hostility from the heterosexual majority. As a result, according to Jackson (2007), coming out involves an awareness and acceptance of a non-normative sexual orientation.

Several studies have been highly influential in the development of research on teachers' coming out in the classroom. For example, Russell (2014) documents the experience of gay teachers in an in-depth qualitative study. Many of the participants in her research study grew up without any visibly gay or lesbian teachers. One participant states that she believed that coming out was critical in order "to be an effective teacher, to connect to students, to be honest and real about who [she] was" (Russel, 2014, p. 146).[38] She adds that in her ten years of teaching as an out lesbian, she encountered few out teachers and found that "very problematic" (Russel, 2014, p. 146).[39]

---

36   DeJean, 2008
37   Gregory, 2004
38   Russel, 2014, p. 146
39   Russel, 2014, p. 146

Kissen (1996) examines the experiences of more than 100 gay individuals in education who worked as teachers, librarians, counselors, social workers, and administrators. Kissen's research explores the conditions that cause gay teachers to feel isolated and marginalized. Fear of harassment, threats, and loss of employment are identified as major areas of concern. For example, one teacher says:

> I have this fear about having parents go to the school board complaining that they have heard that Mr. Marshall is gay, that he's teaching our kids...Some of the parents I work with, probably their fundamentalist beliefs are against homosexuality. They might be outraged at the idea that the school district would hire a homosexual.[40]

This and other stories highlight the struggles that teachers face when coming to terms with their sexuality and identity in an assumed heterosexual environment. Rofes (2000) completed a self-study of his experiences as an out teacher who identified as a gay man. He found that he was confronted daily with his two identities as a teacher and a lover, noting:

> I might check my answering machine at home on a Sunday afternoon and there will be a student calling with questions about White racial formations or the purpose of public education for the following day's mid-term examination. The next message might be from my lover who is calling to inform me he will be late for dinner as he is meeting his boyfriend for a late-afternoon romp.[41]

---

40   Kissen, 1996, p. 78
41   Rofes, 200, p. 441

Rofes offers a direct examination and an honest approach to challenging the freedom of expressing his sexuality and his commitment to creating resistance to institutionalized forms of oppression. He admits to the advantage of having worked within the privileged geography of big cities like Boston and San Francisco, where the setting is more liberal and open-minded. Many teachers, however, find themselves unable to manage the risk of the emerging identities that become evident when teachers struggle with the right to teach as their complete selves.

Defining Teacher Identity

The literature suggests that teacher identity is varied.[42] As Poole (2008) declares, "Teachers teach who they are" (p. 30). A teacher understanding and being comfortable with his or her identity is important to being an effective teacher.[43] Palmer states that "good teaching cannot be reduced to technique; good teaching comes from the identity and integrity of the teacher" (p. 10). The research of Sfard and Prusak (2005) presents ways that teachers construct their identities and highlights how teachers come to understand the personal and cultural messages that influence the perception of themselves in the classroom. DeJean (2008) argues that self-identity can have a significant impact on teachers and their work in the classroom. DeJean (2008) stresses the use of literacies for teachers to build greater understanding of their individual identities as well as a critical awareness and respect for the identities and values of others. That type of effectiveness in the classroom requires what DeJean (2008) calls "critical self-awareness and radical honesty" (p. 70).

The role of teachers has historically been informed by societal expectation and defined by religious and hegemonic institutions.

---

42   Johnson et al., 2014; Mayo, 2008
43   Palmer, 2010

Akkerman and Meijer (2011) emphasize teacher identity as "involving 'sub-identities' as being 'an ongoing process of construction' and as 'relating to various social contexts and relationships'" (p. 310). They define teacher identity as "an ongoing process of negotiating and interrelating multiple I-positions in such a way that a more or less coherent and consistent sense of self is maintained throughout various participations and self-investments in one's (working) life."[44] "I-positions" are presented as a way for teachers to define themselves and self-reflect on identity. Based on the understanding of teachers' personal narratives and how teachers themselves make sense of their identities, Akkerman and Meijer add that teachers have multiple identities connected to subject knowledge, self-realization, and personal expectations of being a teacher.

Akkerman and Meijer (2011) echo a postmodern theory that "identity is no longer seen as an overarching and unified framework but, instead, as being fragmented along with the multiple social worlds that people engage in" (p. 309). Gee (2001) focuses on "contextually specific ways in which people act and recognize identities, which allows for a more dynamic approach than the sometimes overly general and static trio of race, class, and gender" (p. 99). Gee further explains that identity development is social and historical, but people's trajectories are individual and "fully socially formed and informed" (p. 111). Gee shares a similar view of post-modern society, where the "emphasis has moved from individuals and the identities that seem to be part of their individuality to the discursive, representational, and semiotic processes through which identities are created, sustained, and contested" (p. 113).

---

44   Akkerman & Meijer, 2011, p. 318

The Impact of Sexual Orientation on Teacher Identity

Mayo's (2008) research highlights the complexity for teachers of having to negotiate various aspects of their identity. For example, Mayo comments on the relationship dynamics gay teachers have with their students, in addition to the relationships they form with their colleagues. The research points to challenging the status quo and being open about identity as critical components to combat the veiled acceptance and fear that gay teachers face concerning their sexual orientation in education.[45]

Kissen (1996) concludes that gay teachers enter the profession for the same reasons as other teachers. Many perceive themselves as connected with their students and the subjects they teach and even describe teaching as a calling. In Kissen's (1996) research, one participant states, "I always saw teaching as an extension of other things that are really at the center of myself. It's a spiritual activity, it's a very musical activity, and it's totally integrated into the deepest places of me."[46] However, as Sanlo (1999) notes, the difference in the experiences of gay teachers is that many gay and lesbian educators go to work each day with the fear that their sexual orientation and identity will be discovered.

Sexual Orientation and Identity Development Models

Several models have been established to describe the sexual orientation development process. Cass (1979) establishes an identity model that argues that all people move through six stages in a specified order to develop a full sense of self-identity in relation to sexual orientation: (1) identity confusion, (2) identity comparison, (3) identity tolerance,

---

45   Birden, 2005; Epstein, 1994; Kissen, 1996
46   Kissen, 1996, p. 10

(4) identity acceptance, (5) identity pride, and (6) identity synthesis.

Troiden (1989) proposes a four-stage model of homosexual identity development, including: (1) sensitization, (2) identity confusion, (3) identity assumption, and (4) commitment. Troiden introduces three key concepts—self-concept, identity, and homosexual identity—as integral components of identity development. Troiden's model is a fusion of multiple theories of identity formation that describe how people who see themselves as homosexual and adopt corresponding lifestyles recall having acquired their homosexual identities.

Jackson (2007) claims that exploring the nature of identity is important when examining how gay teachers perceive themselves in an educational setting. Jackson's (2007) study finds that "the more gay teachers integrated their full selves into their teaching, the more student-centered their teaching became" (p. 173). Jackson's (2007) gay teacher identity model provides a necessary backdrop for understanding how internal and external factors impinge upon homosexual teachers' identities and influence their professional practice.

In addition to internal and external factors, school culture, and social norms, research supports the continual nature of coming out and identity development as key parallel processes in gay and lesbian teacher identity development. Evans (2002) examines the experiences of four LGBTQ-identified teachers in and outside of their school settings to highlight the effects of language, learning, sexuality, and culture on LGBTQ teachers as they navigated the social orders of school systems and the complexities of sexual orientation and identity development. Evans asks, "What happens when one's sense of self interacts with a new role of identity? And what happens when a preservice teacher is a sexual minority (lesbian, gay, queer), an identity historically at odds with teacher?" (p. 5). Evans presents a compelling case for how sexual orientation identity affected the work of teachers. She concludes:

The knowledge that social categories help us to understand one another, but also limit understanding, may help us hold open to changes in the other and thus the self. If we hold open to the possibility that categorical overflow may one day manifest within a person as unintelligibility, we may be able to be in relation with one another in richer ways—ways that allow for more ways of being in the world that do not categorically insist on rigid, dichotomous identities.[47]

The Intersection of Race, Gender, and Sexual Orientation

Kimberly Crenshaw (1995) first conceived the concept to address the identity and social structures of women of color. Later, the concept would be expanded to include frameworks for the intersections of race, gender, sexual orientation, and other inequalities.[48] Collins (1998) acknowledges intersectionality and the work of Crenshaw in her framing of Black feminist theory and the racial and gender discrimination experienced by Black women. Similar to Crenshaw, Collins (1998) argues that race, gender, class, ethnicity, and sexuality are often experienced through shared patterns of oppression and are crucial to understanding the concept of identity.

Robinson (1999) argues that the process of coming to terms with sexual orientation can create commonalities in experiences across race and gender identities, and highlights privilege and oppression as crucial to understanding self-identity. In a similar study, Richardson and Taylor (2009) champion intersectionality to reflect analytical structures that allow race, gender, and sexual orientation to interact. Richardson (2007) uses the term to describe the interconnectedness between gender and sexual orientation, and argues that "gender intersects with sexuality so fundamentally as to negate the possibility of

---

47 Evans, 2002, p. 184
48 Collins, 1998; Crenshaw, 1995

abstracting either one" (p. 464). In her research, she called for "theoretical frameworks that allow more complex analyses of the dynamic,
historically and socially specific relationship between sexuality and
gender" (p. 464). She concludes with the hope that additional research
will be conducted to recognize the fluid intersections between race,
gender, sexual orientation, and multiple identities.

Protection of Teachers' Sexuality in Classrooms and Courts

Several court cases have documented that gay teachers across the
country have been sanctioned or dismissed for a wide range of behaviors connected to sexual orientation. The 2003 Supreme Court decision
in was an important victory for gays and lesbians.[49] The judges struck
down the Texas law that targeted same-sex partners and that stated
same-sex sodomy was "deviant sexual intercourse."[50] The ruling was
a necessary step toward de-stigmatizing same-sex relationships and
the cultural association of gay men engaging in criminal sexual acts.[51]

The courts began to deem laws against same-sex relationships as
unconstitutional when no evidence substantiated how teachers' sexuality had any bearing on their ability to teach. However, school board
members still sought to exclude gay teachers by citing immorality statutes.[52] In the case of (1975), for example, Portwood notes that James
Gaylord was fired when he responded truthfully to his employer when
asked if he was gay. The termination was upheld when colleagues and
a student objected to his presence in school, stating that his presence
"would be disruptive given the then-public knowledge of his sexual
orientation" (p. 126).

Gays and lesbians, despite certain social changes, have had a diffi-

---

49   Tribe, 2004
50   Kennedy, 2003, p. 1
51   Tribe, 2004
52   Portwood, 1995

cult time being accepted and have often faced termination on grounds of immorality.[53] Cain offers some common descriptions of cases involving gay teachers that highlight the legal gains and challenges at the federal and local levels. Heatherly (1985) documents cases that involved balancing individual rights to privacy and equal protection against the interests of the government with respect to homosexual conduct. Heatherly's case highlights the law regarding the constitutional rights of homosexuals in educational and military contexts. In another case, Schneider-Vogel (1986) points to the unchanged conservative restrictions society has placed on teachers' personal lives, which have resulted in statutes allowing termination for immorality. In support, the (1990, p. 93) reported:

> School authorities must consider more than their conception of "appropriateness" in employing faculty members; their policies and attitudes toward any minority group or minority viewpoint instruct students of the viability of First Amendment protections and of the constitutional principles being taught. If gay and lesbian teachers are summarily excluded or stigmatized in the school systems, such disregard for the fundamental principles of fairness and equal protection mandated by the Constitution would teach students to "discount" important principles of our government as mere platitudes.

Teachers' Sexual Orientation in Independent Schools

Scholars believe that independent schools were socially constructed to produce a specific class-oriented result.[54] The cultural identity of the students and leaders of independent schools have been historically

---

53 Cain, 1993
54 Anderson, 1988; Datnow & Cooper, 2000; Decuir & Dixon, 2004; Ladson-Billing & Tate, 1995

efficient, reliable, and predictably White, with a long-standing track record of high enrollment and demand.[55] Datnow and Cooper (2000) add that, at the time most independent schools were being established, influential White businessmen governed the schools and led the communities. The school model was extremely effective for the bureaucratic organization of the school and social capital, and the structure of the socioeconomic divide in the community ensured a sustained level of status for the school and its attractiveness to upper-class Whites.[56] This educational culture maintained a legacy of prominence built on segregation and years of tradition.

Independent schools are "defined as private, non-parochial schools and include the most prestigious and privileged of private schools."[57] According to the National Association of Independent Schools (NAIS) (http://nais-schools.org), there are over 1,500 independent schools in the United States. In 1996, the so-called Principles of Good Practice for Equity and Justice in Schools were passed by the NAIS with the intention to create bias-free environments and address issues of equity and justice.[58]

Independent schools are important areas in which to study the experiences of LGBTQ teachers because of the autonomy that allows self-governed, principled values and attitudes to shape the consciousness of the school community (Hall and Stevenson, 2007; Riddle, 1996).[59] Most independent schools have committed themselves to diversity and inclusion, presenting these commitments in their mission statements, on their school websites, and in their strategic plans. Many have established standing committees on diversity and have used diversity as a tool to recruit a range of faculty members, while

---

55 Decuir & Dixon, 2004
56 Datnow & Cooper, 2000
57 Hall & Stevenson, 2007, p. 2
58 Hall & Stevenson, 2007; NAIS, 2014
59 Hall and Stevenson, 2007; Riddle, 1996

others have also established diversity leadership positions. Despite taking these steps, many independent schools are unable to sustain their original achievements or to make further progress toward their goals of inclusive learning communities.[60] Many have a seemingly unapologetic devotion to family, church, and tradition as they try to reflect the fundamental values that represent the "heartland of America."[61] Sears also acknowledges that this resolute sense of worthiness has been known to leave people to navigate their sexuality with a sense of fear and shame and in what Riddle (1996) describes as the "hostile or repressive environments that exist at the school" (p. 38).

Jennings (2005) notes that homophobia remains prevalent in independent schools and argues that teachers often adopt a code of silence. Jennings found that blatant homophobia and fear of backlash from students, peers, parents, and bosses were common reasons that teachers kept silent. The irony is that the words frequently appear on websites and in strategic plans of elite independent schools. Extant research corroborates that teachers who are open about their sexual orientation often have to manage their sexuality given fears of possible termination from their teaching positions.[62]

Independent schools have been charged by the NAIS to create sites where people of different genders, races, classes, and sexual identities can come together to work across and learn from differences. Yet research has pointed to a "widespread under-estimation of the prevalence and significance of homophobia in schools" that often leads to LGBTQ teachers feeling silenced and overlooked, with little they can do to challenge school policies.[63,64]

---

60   Riddle, 1996

61   Sears, 1989, p. 422

62   Birden, 2005; Jackson, 2007

63   van Dijk & van Driel, 2007, p. 23

64   DePalma & Jennett, 2010; Graves, 2009

Conceptual Framework

Researchers addressing LGBTQ issues have begun to focus on key concepts and complexities when examining the lives of LGBT people.[65] Jackson (2007), Birden (2005), and Meezan and Martin (2012) provides detailed examinations of current methods and theoretical frameworks for conducting research with lesbian, gay, bisexual, transgender, and queer or questioning (LGBTQ) populations in education. Analysis from the scholarly field of LGBTQ studies informed the conceptual framework of this study of the experience of LGBTQ teachers in independent school settings. Pre-existing theories point to the integration of identity, sexual orientation, and acceptance to combat the multiple strands of sexuality, such as heterosexual norms, fear, shame, and advocacy.[66] The work and theories of two researchers were instrumental in the design of this study and in the focus of the research questions—namely, Troiden (1989) and Jackson (2007). Their work provides clear guidelines for researchers who want to influence the lives of LGBTQ people.

---

65   Meezan & Martin, 2012

66   Birden, 2005; Epstein, 1994; Jackson, 2007

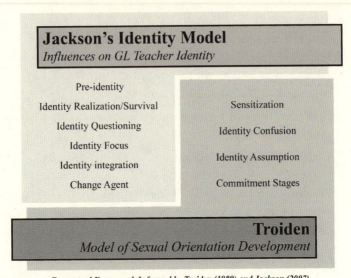

Conceptual Framework Informed by Traiden (1989) and Jackson (2007)

Figure 1. Conceptual Framework

As depicted above, Troiden (1989) proposed four stages of individuals' homosexual self-identity development. Stage one typically occurs before puberty. Individuals are under the assumption that they are heterosexual, with little thought given to their sexual orientation. At this point, individuals are likely to have experienced a resistance to heterosexual ideals that can later lead to acknowledging childhood feelings of marginalization. Troiden (1989) describes this as "characterized by generalized feelings of marginality, and perceptions of being different from same-sex peers" (p. 197).

Equating gender-appropriate behavior with heterosexuality and reflecting on early childhood experiences begins the process of transitioning into stage two. In this stage of adolescence, individuals begin to struggle with heterosexual expectations, conflicting feelings, and behaviors that could be considered homosexual. Troiden (1989) notes, "The hallmark of this stage is identity confusion, inner turmoil, and uncertainty surrounding their ambiguous sexual status" (p. 199). This stage of homosexual identity formation leads many to adopt "stigma management strategies," such as denial, avoidance, and feelings of bisexuality.[67]

Many men and women transition into stage three during late adolescence with unresolved stigma management issues. At this stage, individuals begin to seek out other gay and lesbian individuals, organizations, and social groups as a means of accepting their sexual orientation. Troiden (1989) refers to this important phase of identity disclosure as "coming out" and says, "The earmarks of this stage are self-definition as homosexuals, sexual experimentation, and exploration of the homosexual subculture" (p. 204). Stage four is when individuals accept their homosexual identity as a committed way of life. According to Troiden (1989), that commitment has "both internal and external dimensions" (p. 208). Internal dimensions include:

- The fusion of sexuality and emotionality into a significant whole;
- A shift in the meanings attached to homosexual identities;
- A perception of homosexual identity as valid self-identity;
- Expressed satisfaction with the homosexual identity; and
- Increased happiness after self-defining as homosexual.[68]

External dimensions include:

- Same-sex love relationships;
- Disclosure of the homosexual identity to non-homosexual audiences; and
- A shift in the type of stigma-management strategies.[69]

---

67   Troiden, 1989, p. 204
68   Troiden, 1989, p. 208
69   Troiden, 1989, p. 208

In this study, Troiden's model of homosexual identity development proved to be central to the process of understanding the complexities of sexual orientation as the participants reflected on their awareness at various stages.

In a study examining gay and lesbian identity among teachers, Jackson (2007) claims it was important to explore the nature of identity to examine how gay and lesbian teachers perceive themselves in an educational setting. Jackson (2007) posits a six-stage gay teacher identity development concept to show how internal and external factors impinge upon homosexual and teacher identities, as well as how they influence individuals' professional practice. They are described as the following:

1. Pre-identity: before the person is aware of one's own identity
2. Identity Realization/Survival: awareness of one's own identity along with acceptance of society's stereotypes
3. Identity Questioning: cognitive dissonance between self and society's stereotypes leads to questioning of society's stereotypes
4. Identity Focus: emphasis on pride in that particular aspect of identity
5. Identity Integration: integrating that aspect of identity with rest of self
6. Change Agent: empowering others to change their views about themselves and others in regards to that identity aspect[70]

Jackson's (2007) research finds that the gay and lesbian teacher identity development process "was facilitated and inhibited by several factors, both internal and external" (p. 2). She finds that the gay and lesbian teachers included in her study had to manage their personal

---

70   Jackson, 2007, p. 78

and professional lives at various stages.[71] Internally, that often means dealing with acceptance of self, and externally that often translates into seeking the acceptance of others, both personally and professionally.

Troiden's (1989) sexual orientation identity development model and Jackson's (2007) gay and lesbian teacher identity theory parallel each other and merge into a gay teacher identity development paradigm that this study used as a framework to explore the shared experiences of gay and lesbian teachers in independent schools. Using their work, I focused on the following major aspects of the stages of sexual orientation and gay and lesbian teacher identity development: identity, gender norms, heteronormativity, homophobia, and coming out.

This study probes how those aspects coexist, where they overlap, and how LGBTQ teachers manage the complexities of the intersection of their personal and professional identities. Sexual orientation, stigma, safety, and social and cultural patterns are other factors that are considered with interconnectedness as part of the overall guiding questions of the study—namely: How do LGBTQ teachers perceive their sexual orientation as informing their identity as teachers in an independent school setting?

---

71   Jackson, 2007

Significance of This Study

Researchers have pointed to blatant homophobia and fear of back-lash from students, peers, parents, and bosses as reasons for gay and lesbian teachers to keep silent about their sexual orientation in school settings.[72] Evans (2002) noted that the topic of gays and lesbians in education deserves exploration because of the lacking educational literature that speaks to the experiences of LGBTQ who are teachers or to the identities they bring with them into the classroom. In his book, Irwin (2002) documents the stories of gay men, lesbians, and transgender people working in the education system to explicate the issues they face. Donahue (2008) also describes the complex nature of continuous identity development and coming out for gay and lesbian teachers.

Self-identity can have a tremendous impact on the work of teachers, mentors, and friends. Irwin (2002), Donahue (2008), and Jackson (2007) all note that homophobic discrimination in the workplace oftentimes causes gays and lesbians to suffer in the silence of not identifying as homosexual, leaving coworkers and associates to rely on grossly misguided stereotypes to depict what it means to be gay or lesbian. Given these myriad contextual factors and issues, this study seeks to deeply understand the experiences of LGBTQ teachers in independent schools through engaging with their stories as they relate to the sexual orientations, habits, and behaviors of queer educators in education.

---

72   Ferfolja & Hopkins, 2013; Gregory, 2004; Jackson, 2007; Kissen, 1996; Takatori & Ofuji, 2007

2

FINDING LGBTQ VOICES

The number of LGBTQ educators in independent schools is not known. Lesbian, gay, bisexual, and transgender, or LGBT, has been used to categorize and identify sexual orientation in general society, literature, research, and various organizations. For the purpose of this study, I chose to recruit only participants who identified as "out" and openly LGBTQ.

Research suggests that not all teachers will be open about their sexual orientations, and some will find it difficult to discuss the topic "on the record" (Graves, 2009; Jennings, 2005; Kissen, 1996). Selecting individuals who can provide the information needed to answer the guiding research questions is a critical consideration in participant selection decisions (Maxwell, 2012). For this study, an applicable purposeful selection process was used because it allowed for the deliberate selection of times, settings, and individuals who were relevant to questions in and goals of this research (Miles, Huberman, & Saldaña, 2014).

I determined that the focus of this study would be on LGBTQ teachers who were open and out about their sexuality and had a vantage point of self-knowledge. Presumably, more could be learned about the relationship between their sexual orientation and their teacher identities as the teachers recalled the stages of their processes of coming out, acceptance, and visibility in their personal lives and within school settings.

Participant Selection and Selection Criteria

A national network of diversity professionals at various independent schools acted as a resource for soliciting study participants. In addition, individuals were asked to participate through an email solicitation with the NAIS listserv, an electronic mail service. There were 40 participants who participated in the study. The participants were self-identified, openly LGBTQ teachers from varying independent schools across the country of various ages and ethnicities, and with a range of teaching experience. Once potential participants initiated contact and expressed interest, I followed up with an introduction, an overview, and detailed information about the expectations for participating in the qualitative research study. Finally, consent was obtained from potential participants to be a part of the pool of actual participants.

Data Collection

Interviews. This study used interviews as the process of data collection. Interviews were conducted between June 10, 2014, and September 3, 2014. Each interview lasted from 30 to 90 minutes with 25 interviews conducted via Skype, an online video service, and the remaining 15 interviews in person. The interviews were conducted with the goal of discovering how LGBTQ teachers in independent schools viewed the relationship between their sexual orientation and their identities as teachers.

The interview questions and prompts for this study were designed to accomplish the research goals by focusing on the experiences of LGBTQ teachers in independent schools. Each interview focused on the following themes:

- Teacher identity: Sexual orientation
- Openly LGBTQ: Race and gender
- Independent school setting

These themes were important to explore during the interviews with LGBTQ teachers because of their influence on self-identity. Smith, Flowers, and Larkin (2009) describes the qualitative research interview as a conversation with a purpose. This approach gave participants an opportunity to (1) express their thoughts, (2) share their perspectives, and (3) explore their feelings on the sensitive issues of sexuality and identity. The flexibility of open-ended questions allowed for exploration of a variety of viewpoints related to the research topic. In addition, at the conclusion of each interview, each participant had time to present additional information that did not come up during the session. I intentionally designed the interview questions to elicit details of the perceptions that LGBTQ teachers had of their experiences in independent schools.

Terms of reference. The operational definitions for words and terms for this study were provided by GLSEN (National School Climate Survey, 2013). GLSEN is an LGBTQ network founded as an independent school initiative that now serves as a national political and educational resource. This glossary of terms proved to be helpful in framing the conversation and creating an understanding of this important topic.

The following words and phrases appear throughout the study:

Bisexual. A person who is emotionally or physically attracted to two genders, such as a person attracted to some male-identified people and some female-identified people.

Cisgender. A person whose gender identity and expression are aligned with the gender they were assigned at birth.

Coming out. The ongoing process that LGBTQ people go through to recognize their own identities pertaining to sexual orientation or gender identity and gender expression, and to be open about these identities with others.

Dyke. A derogatory term directed at a person perceived as a lesbian. It is oftentimes used against women who are gender nonconforming, with the assumption being that their gender nonconformity implies a sexual attraction to women. Many lesbians (of all gender expressions) have reclaimed the term.

Fag/Faggot. A derogatory term directed at a person perceived as a gay man. It is oftentimes used against men who are gender nonconforming, with the assumption being that their gender nonconformity implies a sexual attraction to men.

Gay. A person who is emotionally and/or physically attracted to some members of the same gender. The term often refers to a male-identified person who is emotionally or physically attracted to some other males. Gay should not be used as an umbrella term to refer to all lesbian, gay, bisexual, and transgender people; the term LGBTQ is more accurate and inclusive.

Gender. A set of cultural identities, expressions, and roles—codified as feminine or masculine—assigned to people based upon the interpretation of their bodies and, more specifically, their sexual and reproductive anatomy. Because gender is a social construction, it is possible to reject or modify the assignment made and develop something that feels truer and more just to oneself.

Gender binary. A socially constructed system of viewing gender as consisting solely of two categories, male and female, in which no other possibilities for gender are believed to exist. The gender binary is inaccurate because it does not take into account the diversity of gender identities and gender expressions among all people.

Genderqueer. A person who has a gender identity or gender expression that does not conform to the gender this person was assigned at birth. People who identify as genderqueer may or may not also identify as transgender.

Gender expression. The multiple ways (e.g., behaviors, dress) in which people may choose to communicate gender to themselves or to others.

Gender identity. How an individual identifies in terms of their gender. Gender identities include but are not limited to being male, female, androgynous, transgender, genderqueer, or a combination thereof.

Heterosexism. A system of oppression that benefits straight and heterosexual people at the expense of LGBTQ people. Heterosexism may take the form of homophobia, biphobia, bias, and discrimination towards LGBTQ people.

Homophobia. Applies to attitudes, bias, and discrimination in favor of heterosexual sexuality and relationships. It includes the presumption that everyone is heterosexual or that male-female attractions and relationships are the norm and therefore superior. It is the belief that everyone is or should be straight.

Homosexual. A person who is emotionally or physically attracted to some members of the same gender. Many people prefer the terms lesbian or gay instead.

Identity. Identity is how we understand ourselves, what we call ourselves, and often whom we connect to and associate with. Each of us has a unique diversity of social identities based on our sexual orientation, gender identity, race, ethnicity, socioeconomic status, religion, and other important personal qualities. These identities develop over time, intersect with each other, and help give meaning to our lives.

Lesbian. A person who is female-identified and emotionally or physically attracted to some other females.

LGBT or LGBTQ. An umbrella term referring to people who identify as lesbian, gay, bisexual, or transgender. Sometimes the acronym is written as LGBTQ, with the "Q" referring to those who identify as queer or questioning. The acronym can also include additional letters in reference to other identities that do not conform to dominant societal norms around sexual orientation and gender identity and expression.

Queer. An umbrella term used to describe a sexual orientation, gender identity, or gender expression that does not conform to dominant societal norms. While it is used as a neutral or even a positive term among many LGBTQ people today, historically queer was used as a derogatory slur.

Questioning. A person who is in the process of understanding and exploring what their sexual orientation or gender identity and gender expression might be.

Sexual orientation. The inner feelings related to whom a person is attracted emotionally or physically in relation to their own gender identity. People may identify as asexual, bisexual, gay, lesbian, pansexual, queer, straight, and many more.

Straight or heterosexual. A person who is emotionally or physically attracted to some members of another gender (specifically, a male-identified person who is attracted to some females or a female-identified person who is attracted to some males).

Transgender. A person whose gender identity or expression is not aligned with the gender they were assigned at birth. Transgender is often used as an umbrella term encompassing a large number of identities related to gender nonconformity.

Data Analysis

Smith, Flower, and Larkin (2009) described the initial phase of interview analysis as the process of entering the participant's world. I listened to the interviews while reading the transcripts in order to become immersed in the participants' stories and to make sure that the data were transcribed properly. In this phase of analysis, each participant received a copy of the transcription and was given the opportunity to verify the transcript, check for errors, clarify anything that I might have misinterpreted, ask questions, or expand upon any of the data. This detailed analysis led to the construction of themes that emerged from participants' perceptions of the impact of their sexual orientations on their identities as teachers in independent schools. Each transcribed interview was stored in a secure, password-protected file.

Each participant was assigned a pseudonym as outlined in the IRB-approved study consent form. Names were obtained from the official Social Security website (http://ssa.gov/oact/babynames/decades/century) listing of the Top Names Over the Last 100 Years and were assigned randomly to each participant. One participant made a special request for her name to be "Olivia," and that request was honored. School names were replaced by three-letter initials, starting with A and continuing through the alphabet, with the last two letters as "IS" for "independent school" (e.g., AIS, BIS, CIS). New school names were randomly assigned. Participants were also assigned to a region based on the location of the state where they lived and worked. I developed an analytic profile for each participant as a part of the initial data collection process. This profile included basic background information such as name, age, teaching experience, and biographical data about teaching experience and the school setting. Table 1 highlights the participants' basic background information, whereas Tables 2–5 show the gender, racial identity, region, and number of states represented by each participant.

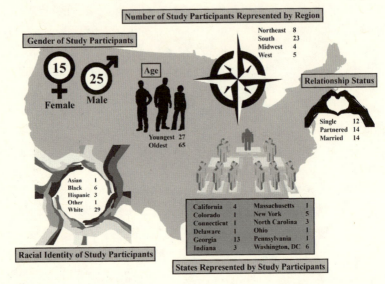

Figure 2.

Table 1. Background Information of Study Participants

Name	Interview	School	Relationship Status	Age	Race	Gender	Grade Level	Region
Kenneth	Skype	ZIS	Single	40–46	Other	Male	7–12	NE
Elizabeth	Skype	AIS	Partnered	30–39	White	Female	7–12	MW
Mark	Skype	BIS	Married	30–39	Asian	Male	7–12	S
George	Skype	WIS	Partnered	20–29	White	Male	7–12	MW
Brian	Skype	MIS	Married	40–49	White	Male	Pk–6	S
Christopher	Skype	CIS	Single	20–29	White	Male	7–12	S
Thomas	Skype	DIS	Single	30–39	White	Male	7–12	W
William	In person	EIS	Married	40–49	White	Male	7–12	S
Joshua	Skype	BAIS	Single	30–39	White	Male	7–12	NE
Nancy	In person	AAIS	Partnered	30–39	White	Female	7–12	S
Jessica	Skype	FIS	Single	40–49	White	Female	7–12	W
Robert	In person	GIS	Single	30–39	Hispanic	Male	Pk–6	S
David	Skype	HIS	Single	40–49	Hispanic	Male	7–12	S
Sarah	In person	HIS	Partnered	40–49	White	Female	Pk–6	S
Edward	In person	AAIS	Married	60–69	White	Male	7–12	S
Barbara	Skype	IIS	Partnered	20–29	White	Female	7–12	NE
Matthew	Skype	JIS	Partnered	30–39	White	Male	7–12	S
Charles	Skype	KIS	Single	40–49	White	Male	7–12	NE
Richard	In person	LIS	Married	30–39	White	Male	7–12	S
Paul	Skype	BIS	Married	30–39	White	Male	7–12	S
Steven	Skype	XIS	Single	20–29	Black	Male	Pk–6	NE
Joseph	In person	LIS	Partnered	40–49	White	Male	Pk–6	S
Kevin	Skype	CAIS	Married	40–49	White	Male	7–12	S
Olivia	Skype	MIS	Partnered	40–49	White	Female	7–12	S
Mary	In person	NIS	Married	40–49	White	Female	7–12	S
Andrew	In person	AAIS	Married	40–49	White	Male	7–12	S
Jennifer	In person	OIS	Single	50–59	White	Female	7–12	S
Lisa	Skype	DAIS	Married	20–29	White	Female	7–12	NE
Anthony	Skype	PIS	Single	30–39	White	Male	Pk–6	S
Linda	Skype	QIS	Partnered	30–39	Black	Female	Pk–6	MW

Table 1. Background Information of Study Participants (cont.)

Name	Interview	School	Relationship Status	Age	Race	Gender	Grade Level	Region
Anthony	Skype	PIS	Single	30–39	White	Male	Pk–6	S
Dorothy	In person	RIS	Married	30–39	Black	Female	Pk–6	NE
Donald	Skype	MIS	Married	30–39	White	Male	7–12	S
James	In person	SIS	Single	40–49	Black	Male	7–12	S
Betty	In person	YIS	Partnered	20–29	White	Female	Pk–6	S
Michael	In person	YIS	Married	40–49	White	Male	Pk–6	S
Karen	Skype	AYIS	Partnered	40–49	Hispanic	Female	Pk–6	NE
Margaret	Skype	TIS	Partnered	40–49	Black	Female	Pk–6	W
Patricia	Skype	QIS	Partnered	30–39	Black	Female	Pk–6	MW
John	In person	HIS	Partnered	40–49	White	Male	7–12	S
Daniel	Skype	UIS	Married	40–49	White	Male	7–12	W
Total Participants		40						

Table 2. Gender of Study Participants

Male	25
Female	15

Table 3. Racial Identity of Study Participants

Asian	1
Black	6
Hispanic	3
Other	1
White	29

Table 4. Number of Study Participants Represented by Region

Northeast	8
South	23
Midwest	4
West	5

Table 5. States Represented by Study Participants

California	4
Colorado	1
Connecticut	1
Delaware	1
Georgia	13
Indiana	3
Massachusetts	1
New York	5
North Carolina	3
Ohio	1
Pennsylvania´	1
Washington, DC	6

Independent Queers

Who I am as an LGBTQ educator is central to how I approached this study. My status as a gay man who has taught in an independent school was crucial to gaining the trust of the participants. My intention was not to impose my assumptions, limitations, definitions, or biases on the emergent data, but to engage fully with the research and to design a study that was meaningful and helpful to the plight of LGBTQ voices in independent school settings, as well as to the greater LGBTQ community.

This book consists of stories of self-identified, out LGBTQ men and women. Their stories represent the emerging narratives that speak to the experiences of LGBTQ teachers and queer voices in independent schools, as they work to find the balance between what they share, how they share, and the impact of sharing on their identity as teachers.

3

LOWER SCHOOL

Robert

I feel I have professional goals for myself, and I don't think that I'll ever be able to live them out in an independent school because of the fact that I am gay.

Education has always been very important in my family. My grandmother didn't get to finish her education overseas in a third world country. My mother stressed the importance of education for my future, and I've always loved children.

What I enjoy most about working with the children is that I am very open to all of their needs. I like to individualize my attention to the students, and I particularly look at the students that are struggling and the students that are excelling, and I cater to them. They're the ones who need the most support, whether they're going up or they need a challenge, they need a little more enhancement in the curriculum, that's specifically what I look at, the individual student one-on-one.

I think there are some things that in my personal life and identity I cannot bring into the classroom. There are some things that I have to keep to myself, particularly because I'm working with third grade students, and in the school that I'm working in there are lots of my own personal identities that I put on the back burner.

One of the hardest parts of working in education is knowing that there is a stigma attached to being a male teacher, and on top of that being a gay male teacher. There's a stigma from administration and parents, they immediately think, "Okay, this isn't right, something is not going to work here." Or, "Do I have to be on guard?" I think a big part of that is because of the stereotypes that are associated with being a gay male.

My coming out was a very bad experience. I basically just brought it up to my family, and I did not hear from my family for three years, because it was not acceptable to them for religious reasons. There was no contact, no communication for three years. Finally, we started breaking down the barrier and started talking, and now we have a pretty good relationship even though it's not spoken of a lot, it's known and it's become accepted.

My uncle, who was my mother's brother, actually reached out to my mother and said, "This is not the way it should be between a mother and son." She refused to make communication, make contact with me, and he said, "Well, then if you lose him, you lose me as well." She didn't want that to happen, and so that's when it started to change. I was very close to him, I am very close to him to this day. Even though he's my uncle, he sees me as his little brother, we grew up together, so he's very protective of me.

What I've always told people, is that I don't have a problem with who I am in my sexuality, but if you have a problem with it then you need to deal with it. When I meet someone I never mention the fact that I'm gay. If it comes up in conversation and it's appropriate then I may make mention of it, but it's not something that I initially tell people. The only times I've ever spoken to people about it is if I'm working in close contact with an associate or an assistant and I know that we're going to be working relatively close. I make it a point to let them know that this is who I am as an individual, and you may not see it in the classroom, but it's important for you to know because we will get personal if we work together, and so I need you to understand and be accepting of that, and if not accepting at least just understand that this is who I am and this is my perspective.

I honestly have not had the opportunity to be open or out as a gay male in a lower school. I've never mentioned it to any of students or the parents. I think some parents suspect, and they really want to know and they try to find clues, but they will never ask. With the administration I know that, especially at the school that I'm at now, it's been questioned round about they've tried to find out and search and prodded, but have never asked me specifically.

Well, I know of a colleague who came up to me and said, "Administration was asking about your sexuality." I said, "Well, can you give me a little more detail?" The question that was asked to her about me was, "Is he a gentle man?" The word gentle meaning gay. The response that she gave was he is a very gentle man, he's a gentleman, and that was it. I don't know if they picked up on the fact that I was gay.

I really don't talk about my sexual orientation at all. If it's not with my associate, occasionally we'll have personal conversations; she shares a little bit about her life and I'll share a little bit about mine. Other than that, I can't mention it. I think working with the younger children, when it gets really uncomfortable is when, for example, a student comes up to me and says, "Oh, so and so said I was gay." Then I have to approach it and confront the student and say, "Okay, well what does that word mean?" So, that gets a little uncomfortable because I don't know what they're taught at home, and I'm not sure if they have had conversations. Usually if the child comes up to me and says, "What does gay mean?" I'll say, "Well, that's a conversation for your family." I wouldn't want to approach that conversation and go against whatever is being taught at home. That's probably the hardest part of it, of working in an independent school.

The other part of that is that I think I feel I have professional goals for myself, and I don't think that I'll ever be able to live them out in an independent school because of the fact that I am gay. Next year there will only be two males in the lower school, and I'm one of the two. I'm also the only male that will be in the classroom. The first thing that children say to me when they walk into the classroom is, "I've never had a man teacher." A lot of the times it's usually the girls that are very afraid, because they're not quite sure how they'll get along with a male teacher. The boys were always very excited, because they think I'm going to come in and be like their dads and just be very athletic and easy to talk to, which is usually the case. I think a lot of the times the parents, who usually are the female parents that are involved in the children's education, they are a little stand-offish at first.

When I think about it, there's the three-strike rule. Here I am, a gay Latino with dark skin. When they see those three things in one person it can be intimidating in an environment like the one that I'm in right now, where it's not really the norm. I think a lot of times people have a hard time relating to someone who is from a different ethnic background or has a different perspective in life. They are very familiar with the people who are in their communities. One thing that happened this year was that one of the families came to me and requested a meeting. The very first thing that they said was, "We are a very conservative family." I didn't quite know what to make of that. I thought maybe they were suggesting that I was very liberal or it had to do with my ethnic background and maybe what they thought my political standings were. It was just a very broad and awkward statement that was made and I didn't quite know how to approach it.

There is a lack of diversity here. There's a lack of diversity in the faculty, and there's lack of diversity in the student body. I think it's very homogeneous, it's very Caucasian. There's not a lot of veering from that. I'm always surprised that [when] I walk into the school, there are not a lot of people that can relate to who I am. The students, I don't think, can relate just by looking at me or just because I'm gay; there's no way. I think a lot of them have not had experiences with someone like me, and the parents as well. Sometimes I think that the parents choose this school because they don't want that diversity, and they specifically want this homogeneous setting for their children.

This year we had some boys in the lower grades who wanted to be cheerleaders, and they were told that they could not be cheerleaders because that was for girls. One of the parents got involved and said, "Well, if my child wants to be a cheerleader than he should have the opportunity. We need to re-examine these gender roles as they are." The gender roles are very specific. I know that when there are announcements made from the principal, it's always about someone getting married, nothing else is mentioned other than that. When we've had staff meeting as well, it's very evident that they'll talk about male and female pairings. Sometimes they veer off the actual conversation that we're supposed to be having, and they'll talk about a female teacher dating a male, or a boyfriend-girlfriend engagement, but they've never asked questions about me or my personal life, nor would I expect them to.

I've never asked anyone about their sexuality, and nor would I want to because it's really none of my business. If they share, because they're just being a human being and want to be personal, then I would welcome it. Again, I've had colleagues who talk about different types of relationships that they have, and I just have never felt comfortable enough to open up and say, "This is the relationship I'm in." Or, "This is what I'm working on now."

We did have a scandal a little bit earlier, a year ago, and that brought out a lot of homophobic thoughts. I saw different sides of my colleagues that I never thought I would see. One of the teachers was ordering child pornography on the internet and was convicted. I think the conversations following that whole scandal were about gay men in the workplace. I felt that I was being monitored a lot closer after that. I do know that some of the teachers in my division started talking about how it's a sickness. There was some talk about gay men, but it just felt that it was really an unfair stigma that was being attached. Just because of one person's actions, everyone who was gay was suffering through it.

There is this other part of it. I feel if I'm here, and while I'm here, why not be an example? Be that voice, why not be that? Just represent the other perspective that's not being represented. I think it's important for the children to see that. I think I've changed a lot of opinion and changes a lot of minds. I think when parents and children come in and they see, and know a little bit about me, from the beginning of the year to the end of the year, they see a completely different person. They have changed opinions, and they've changed their minds and their perspectives, just because of who I am and what I do in the classroom with their children.

Sarah

*The messages are that gay and straight are welcome.
The message that I get is, "Either way, you are honored."*

I think I am a facilitator. I think I am a role model. I think I am a communicator. I think I help bridge differences. I try to bring together a vast array of differences in what doesn't seem to be a very different kind of student body, but it is. When you're talking about learning, and you're talking about the weakness of someone, it brings a great deal of baggage, and I manage baggage.

My father did not have anyone who was watching over him as a youngster. He had learning issues that were never identified, and I knew I didn't want that to happen to children who were poor or children who were disadvantaged. I knew I wanted to be in the helping profession, but I didn't know which way I wanted that to go. I wanted to be a physical therapist, and that's what I am. I'm a clinical director. Then they asked me to come on board at school. My learning specialist piece encompasses everything because it's teachers, it's kids, it's adults, it's family, it's systems, it's administrators and helping everything for those who have no voice.

I have a completely different viewpoint now that I have a little person at home. It wasn't quite as emotional before. Of course, you connect in an emotional way, but having a little person, you think how would you want someone who's advocating for her to act in this space at this time. Before, I was like, "Yeah I got it. I'll just take care of whatever." Now, I think of my daughter walking into school and being sad, or being scared, or being whatever—how would I want her support staff to help her? How would I want her support staff to help her? I never thought of that before. Before, it was just like I just do this. I'm awesome at it. Now, it's, "No, this is somebody's little girl, somebody's little boy." Even if you're a 12th-grader, you're somebody's little boy.

It was easier for me to be out here because I was away from my parents and away from people who knew me. I was in a new place, so everyone getting to know me was like, "Oh Sarah, who's gay, like whatever." It would've been different if I was home. I just selected certain people in my life that I told I was out to, and everyone was amazing. My father was fine. My mom was not, but now she is and she really journeyed. She's fine now. The coming out with just my friends was okay. I have it built up in my head this big thing, and they're like, "If you're happy, awesome. Are we going to get together Friday? Who's bringing pizza?"

My mom did not want me to be gay. Then she didn't want to tell anyone. Then she thought there was shame in that. Then she was like, "What if I'm not a part of your life?" And I said, "Well, you are going to miss out on stuff." Once she met my partner who I have now...we've been together for 12 years...immediately everything was fine.

My partner and I are not married. She's my partner. Because of the Georgia statutes at this time, we find it a little silly to go through with something at home in New York to come back and be unrecognized. We find it a fruitless exercise. We don't need anyone to recognize our love and our family. Especially in our home state, it's not going to change anything anyway. It doesn't really matter. Plus, we don't even care, really.

It is interesting...I think about race and sexual orientation a lot. This school has really helped shape my knowledge of how much privilege I have just by being a white person. By being in Georgia, and New York... we don't talk about race. It's just as segregated as it is here. Here it's speak nicely not segregated. At home in New York, we also don't talk about it; we just don't. Here, there's a lot of talking about it, but people are too nice to be mad and too busy to hate. There's a lot of talking, but there's still just explicit racism everywhere. I think Ferguson is a perfect example of that.

If I was walking down the street, I would not have gotten shot. There's no way. I think even if I was brandishing a firearm, I still don't think those cops would've shot me, I really don't. I'm like where is Ferguson? I pulled it up on Google Maps, and I really looked at it. The names, like Johnson's...they had all these names, and I'm like, I can perfectly picture that I, white Sarah, would have never been walking down those streets, but that is that young man's universe, and he was shot, on his street in his world. He was shot because he's Black. That makes me more aware of my whiteness.

The messages I get in my school community are that gay and straight are welcome. The message that I get is, "Either way, you are honored and we want you for being smart. We don't want you for color or this or that. We want you because you are going to be an amazing part of uplifting this whole place. Whatever that comes in, gay, straight, Black, White, whatever it comes in, it comes in, but we want you for what you are going to bring to this facility." Does that make sense?

I'm quite sure the headmaster did not know that I was gay when I was hired. Well, I don't know. It didn't matter though. I know it would not have mattered. If he had been told, "The new person we're thinking of hiring, she has a same-sex partner," he would've shrugged either way. He probably would have been more annoyed that I'm a Yankees fan than anything else, just because he's from Boston, and I will never cheer for the Boston Red Sox, never. That's probably the thing that would piss him off the most, but that would be it.

I was at a birthday party the other day, and a person of color was talking to me. She was like, "Oh, did you see *Maleficent*?" I'm like, "Yeah, I saw it with my partner." I was with another friend, who is a really good friend, and she's from Norway. So we have someone from another continent who is not American, a person of color who is American and a person of color, and me. She, the person of color, said, "Oh, you mean your husband?" We were at the birthday party, and my partner was right there. I said, "No, my partner." [She understood and] her jaw hit the ground. Then she righted herself, but it was this long, awkward bizarre exchange. The rest of the day, I was super-nice and super-smiley and super-whatever, and she was very unfriendly to my partner the rest of the birthday party. My partner didn't know that happened. We got the out of the jeep. I was like, "John's mom was being so weird with me. Do we know her?" I was like, "Mmmm-hmmm." It was all very interesting. That's the first time that has happened.

Coincidentally, her son John, during lunch said something like, "Well, I don't care about your two moms," which was taken as a bullying threat. There had to be talks to the whole class, and all these people had to be pulled in, and it was this whole thing. My partner and I were like, that wasn't that big of a deal. It became this huge thing. I was just like, "Can we pretend like he didn't say that? It's no big deal." That kid had to write an apology. I mean...here, where I work, that shit doesn't happen.

And that is what I like about my school. What I like is that every day, I come in and I help push a boulder a little farther, or I help bridge a gap. It's diverse. It's different. I talk to lots of people. I'm in tons of classrooms. I'm all over the place. I'm not just sitting behind a desk doing one thing. Every day, my schedule is different. I have to be flexible. I have to be a leader, but be a listener too. I have to be sympathetic, but I have to be strong. I have to be a bunch of different things. I like that a lot. I enjoy that a lot. This is such a unique place, and I know that it's very unique.

Steven

> *When we talked about it, they sort of regretted not having done it earlier because they knew full well—and I knew that they knew, and they knew that I knew that they knew, but none of us had the courage to say it out loud.*

I think that I'm sort of a bubbly person inside and out of the classroom. I bounce around in the classroom as much as I do in my head. Whether it's talking [in class] about various random things that we come upon or when I'm doing something with some research for the class, I have twenty million tabs open because there's so much stuff online. And I think that I kind of have a little bit of trouble when there's dead silence in the classroom. I'm working on being comfortable with silence. I like it when there's a lot of action and a lot of stuff being done in the class. And that sort of matches who I am.

I attempted to come out in seventh or eighth grade to a close friend of mine who had told me that I was too young to know. Both of his parents were psychologists or therapists, and so I sort of believed him in a way, if I do remember. My mom, she had many gay friends, many gay colleagues. She works in a language department, just sort of the gayest department in the school, so I've always been exposed to gay people, but they were always adults so that sort of made me think, "Maybe there's a certain age to come out," or "it's not set yet." I sort of shoved it to the back of my mind and didn't come out officially until 10th grade to my close friends. I started attending my school's GSA that was run by my best friend, and then I came out to my parents the summer before going to college.

It was really intense. I mean, it was nerve wracking. They asked me, and I found a journal recently between 10th and 11th grades where I had chronicled all the possible ways I was going to tell them. I just could never muster the courage, despite the fact that I knew nothing bad would happen. I was just scared, I guess, or nervous. I'm happy that they came forward and asked me.

When we talked about it, they sort of regretted not having done it earlier because they knew full well...and I knew that they knew, and *they* knew that *I* knew that *they* knew, but none of us had the courage to say it out loud. And the first couple of days after I said it out loud, the dust settled, I guess. There wasn't that much dust, but I was able to take it back into my own hands and say, "Hey, about what we talked about, this is really how I'm feeling. This is who I am." They were very, very supportive and still are.

Being out and openly gay means that when someone asks me if I have a girlfriend, I don't have qualms about saying I don't date girls or that I'm gay. It's walking around with the assumption that everyone assumes I'm gay. It makes my life easier [because I] don't have a problem if someone assumes [I'm gay]; I'm okay.

And then I try not to hide my sexuality in most circumstances and situations, though at times it can be hard. Like when dealing with people of older generations, when meeting people for the first time. I mean, coming out is an ongoing process, and it always takes a bit of energy every time you're going to have to confront how vocal you have to be about your own sexuality.

I've been actually really blessed with my school community. Of the 15 or so male teachers in the elementary and middle schools, 10 of us are gay.

So it's a pretty large percentage and not all of them are out to their students. Not all of them are necessarily openly gay in the classroom, and I would actually count myself in that group. We can talk about that, but we are all open and out to our colleagues and the administration. I have been doing a lot of work with LGBT diversity issues in school. I run the faculty GSA and we're hopefully going to start a middle school GSA this year. Starting last September, until this December, we're focusing on gender and sexuality diversity as our diversity theme for the school, and so I've been helping out with the diversity coordinator to sort of implement certain things and get conversation started in schools. I have come out to a group of students when I spoke to a middle school affinity group. I came out to them. So that was mostly sixth, seventh and eighth graders.

Actually, it was the second time that I'd come out to a group of students. The first time I was asked by the ethics class, or whatever it was, that was the assigned class for eighth graders to talk about my experiences as an out adult, and I was able to do that to two groups of eighth graders. None of those groups I directly taught, but that was interesting. I sort of had to do a little bit of preparation and focus on what I wanted them to take away.

Talking to the affinity group, which involved younger students as well as some of my students, was easier than I thought it would be. I wanted to make sure that I was doing it in a way that was confident, not showing any sort of hesitation or insecurity about it. As a science teacher, I haven't yet taken the opportunity to come out to my students in class, which is something I struggle with. And there are times when it comes up and I've shied away. The most glaring example that I can think of is the annual blood drive in our school for community service. For the past couple of years, they did actually come into our school and use our gym for the day, and some of my students ask if I'm donating blood, and I can't. It's usually the second graders that ask that, and I just turn beet red and can't think of the vocabulary that I would want to use. I hate that I have to think so consciously about how to say this, and I really don't think it would be that much of a problem to have to talk about why. Why can't I, as a gay man, donate? Well, because of AIDS and the government. But, it is very liberating to have many other gay faculty, and it's really nice to not have to pretend anything. I feel really supported by administration, which makes a huge difference in how I can operate, especially with helping the school do work with

GSA and LGBT diversity issues.

When I came out to my grandmother very recently, her biggest fear about my being gay, the reason why she had an issue with it was because she was afraid that I would lose my job. You know, in her generation, that's kind of what happened, and I assured her, "No, actually my job sort of pays me more to be gay, and I get a stipend to do diversity work and run GSA and coordinate these things." She was like, "Oh. Oh! Okay. All right." It's sort of been cool. Yeah, so I'm lucky in that sense.

All the other elementary and middle school science teachers are males, so I don't think it's anything abnormal for the students. I'm sure it reinforces stereotypes that science and math are male realms. I work with the IT teacher and the computer teacher, and we celebrate Ada Lovelace Day in October, which is a recognition of women in science, technology, engineering and math in the beginning of the year. So, I try to do some things that sort of debunk that. I don't know if being a man gives me any more confidence in the classroom or doesn't because teaching nowadays is seen more as a woman-dominated field, especially in the ages I teach. I think it also—bringing it back to the fact that there are so many men in the elementary school and middle school here—it helps to sort of normalize that.

Being gay and being Black, I'm much more conscious of things. I'm as conscious as the young students are. I feel like if it's not directly related to you as an adult, you start to tune things out, and the students pick up on this. For example, all the brown faces and black faces are in maintenance or in the kitchen. We do have a few brown faces in the high school administration, which is great, but in the elementary and middle school, I am one of two Black male teachers.

I had a really interesting conversation last year. It must have been a seventh grade boy. It just so happened we had an hour of time and the other kids, who were supposed to show up, were on a field trip or something. And we just got to talking so candidly about race. He is the only Black boy in his grade of 40 kids, and there's one other Black girl, but they've sort of taken two very different paths. The girl has tried really hard to be part of the White girl group, and she has a tricky time doing that with the White boys. Because of that, they [the boy and the girl] can't really be friends. They can't find support or strength in each other. And he had mentioned that seeing me, as a young Black person at the head of a classroom, has impacted him, and that was the first time that I had heard that vocally from a student. You hear that from other adults...when they see someone like me in front of the classroom, that's so powerful for them, but to hear that from another student, that sort of shook me a little bit. I don't know. In a good way, but it was powerful and it stuck with me.

So, my race and sexual orientation intersect all the time. The diversity coordinator and I love that word, intersectionality. It's our favorite word. Let's just throw it out there and love and embrace it because it applies to really everyone, but my identities are three very prominent ideas that very rarely intersect, all three of them. Sometimes gay males are the spokespeople for the LGBT movement, but they're gay White males. Black males are what you hear about in the statistics, but gay Black males are often brushed under the rug or not really spoken about in a public way.

I really hate when people not of my race and gender or sexual orientation tell me that the Black community is very homophobic. It really irks me so bad because I feel it's such a blanket statement that is sidestepping so many issues that come with that. I don't know. And I hear that a lot. I hear that so often that two very important parts of my identity should not be together and that is so troublesome. It irks me because a lot of the anti-gay rhetoric that I've heard on a very public and media scale comes from White politicians or White religious groups or Black-hate YouTube commenters.

It just seems like not a productive conversation, and it just sort of completely hides the beauty of the LGBT voices of the Harlem Renaissance, for example, or how so much of what is cool in LGBT mainstream vocabulary and culture comes from queer people of color spaces and histories. All of the words that Ru Paul's Drag Race has made cool did not come from, whatever, like the vanishing society or something. It came from the Christopher Street Piers in the '90s, you know?

At school, we are in the midst of an identity crisis. There have been instances when the administration has been hesitant about certain things because of the fear of...the fear of gay people, so it's more like an instance that happened a year ago, or two years ago. A teacher decided to come out to his third grade class with a Read Aloud that he had picked up when he and I went to a conference in Atlanta that was held by the National Gay & Lesbian Task Force. We picked up these books and were so glad to bring them back. He had been teaching for 13 years and had never fully divulged his sexuality to his class. And he said, "You know, this conference has so inspired me. This is the year I'm doing this." So he read the book to the kids, and they talked about it and he came out to them, and the reaction was actually just like, "Okay." It was fine. They were great, and it was a really important moment for him.

When telling our division head, her first reaction was, "Oh, I wish you would have told me you were going to do that in case parents called and I could tell them 'Oh, this is happening,'" or whatever. I dug down, knowing who she is and what happened, and knew what she was really saying was she was afraid of the backlash. She wished that she'd had warning so that she could maybe even preemptively tell them this is what's going to happen. Treating something like that, like a very special episode, is what we are actively trying to avoid when talking about these issues in school, but I wish that she had said, "That's awesome! Good for you, and whatever happens, we'll support you 100 percent! This is so cool. Glad you did that." But that's the first thing that came out of her mouth.

I feel like in a school setting, and our school setting in particular, the parents are often scapegoated as an excuse to stop whatever we're doing. One teacher got her sixth graders to make up signs to put around the stairwell that said, "Don't say gay!" Or "That's so 'gay' meaning 'stupid.' Don't say that." I think at one parent's questioning, the administration pulled her in, took down the signs, told her that was not appropriate, blah, blah, blah. It's mixed messages, honestly.

There's not been hatred of gay people. There have not been physical or verbal attacks. I know that the word "gay", as in "that's so gay" or whatever is being thrown around. I'm sure that students are calling each other gay. It's hard for me to tell if it's more playful than hurtful, but I know that that language is being used in the hallways and what-ever, but in terms of more institutional or systematic homophobia in the school, I'm hesitant to say that that really exists.

I think in my particular circumstances of being gay; I've been very blessed in my life to have supportive people sort of every step of the way. My friend was supportive in high school. My family was sup-portive in college. My college peers were supportive. My faculty and my administration are supportive now, so I'm sort of very lucky, and I'm sure one of the very few people who have an easy ride with this the whole time.

I love everything. I love being in front of the classroom. I love connecting with students. I love to explore cool topics and interesting things. I love being in a school community and watching kids learn and grow. My seventh graders that I had last year were my fourth graders in my first year at the school and my fifth graders I had my second year at the school, so I had them again all grown up. I love that. I love the challenge. I love the camaraderie of the faculty. I love...I don't know...I just love it all.

Joseph

I guess that's what it means me to be out—that you can talk about your life and be who you are without worrying about the repercussions. I think that's what it means to me to be out: I get to be who I am and to be an example for kids.

I grew up as a pastor's kid. When I was a little boy, when I was in third grade, fourth grade, fifth grade, I wanted to be a minister. When I got to be an adolescent, I realized I was having mixed feelings about being gay. I realized I needed to figure out something. My mom was always encouraging me to be a teacher or something like that because the idea of becoming a doctor was way beyond my parents' ideas of what I could do.

When I got in high school, I became really involved in the school marching band. I did choreography, riffles and flags, and dances and all that stuff. I started envisioning my life as this somebody who taught school and worked with the bands and that kind of thing.

I never imagined I would have a life with a partner and all that stuff. Growing up in the Midwest, I didn't know anybody gay. I didn't know any gay kids. I didn't know any gay girls. There was one man who I remember he worked at Kroger with my mom. I remember the store moved to a new location when I was probably in fifth grade or fourth grade. I remember looking for him but not knowing what I was really looking for or why; I just remember hearing people refer to something. He was gay.

I've never really fit into a mold, like when I was in high school, to survive in small-town Indiana. We are lots of different colors, and I could hang out with the potheads even though I wasn't doing that. I could hang out with the jocks because I knew how to talk sports. I could hang out with the cheerleaders because I used to be a cheerleader. I was in student government, so I knew those kids, and my best relationships were in band. I learned how to read situations really well.

I taught in inner-city schools in Indianapolis for four years. They rode me like crazy, but I was a good teacher and they knew it. They also liked it if I didn't follow the rules exactly. My kids were happy and my kids did well. Then, by the fate of God, I ended up in a coffee shop and met a woman. She said, "I teach at this school and there is an opening you should apply." And so I went.

There was a new head of school, and he was from out east and went to private school. His dad worked at medical school at Harvard and all that whole thing. He came to Indianapolis to teach these people diversity. I interviewed and did all the stuff and jumped through all the hoops to get a job. Then I was like, "What the fuck do I do now? How do I live in this world?"

My best friend, who's been gone for 20 years, his mom and dad took me under their wing. They were financial advisor people. I would call them and say, "Oh my god. I have to go to this thing—what do I wear, how do I do it, how do I act?" I would say come over and she would just tell me everything, like this is that fork this is this fork. One time I met one of his mom's friends, and I put out my hand. My friend laughed and said, "You never put your hand out to a woman"—this was the late '80s—"If she extends her hand to you, then you shake her hand. If she doesn't then... you know, that's just not what you do."

I had someone who taught me so much about code that I was never exposed to. That's how I survived my first year, and my principal wanted people from all different walks in the school. I would go in there and say I don't know what to do with this...and he would just talk it through.

I left the Midwest and moved to England because my partner worked at a company. We moved to England and then we moved here and we separated. My identity outside of school... it's like I don't need to identify. I mean I am gay, and that's a really big part of who I am.

That's not the first part of who I am, and I would say that people say I am...funny, kind, generous to a fault, amazing listener [laughs].

As a teacher, I want the kids to think about multiple perspectives. They are third graders, and I don't expect them to know what it means to be gay and to understand that much at that age about family dynamic. But, let's make sure the kids know. We do talk about all kinds of families, and there are kids whose parents are same sex couples and stuff.

I don't really talk about my private life a lot except for in third grade ways, meaning I talk about my dog, I talk about my brother, I talk about when I saw a snake when I was walking the dog and I was scared to death and ran in the house. They don't deal with things like doing laundry and going to the grocery store. The roof is leaking—that's not a third grade trouble. They don't ask me if I'm married. Occasionally maybe once a year it comes up, and I'll say, "No I'm not," and that's all I ever say about it. Nothing else ever comes from it.

When I applied here, the head of school looked at me and goes, "We are going to get all kinds of people in here." That's how I knew that it was okay for me to be there. When I was at the other school, I had an interview with the head of school and the first question that he asked me was, "So, are you out?" I said, "Yeah. But why are you asking that?" and, he said, "You came out to people during your interview." I said, "People asked me why I moved here, and I told them my partner works here. I didn't come out to them—they assumed, but I didn't do that." He said, "Do you feel comfortable? We want you to feel comfortable."

I said, "I will not live in the closet in this community. If I'm at the Performing Arts Theater...if I'm walking down the street with my partner, we might be holding hands because this community is a pretty safe place to do that. I won't hide, so it needs to be known that that can happen." They were like, "That's fine."

My personal identity does impact my work, and the fact that I don't see edges very well. How is reading different from writing because don't they interchange? I feel that's who I am too. At my current school, I feel like they really want everything to be in a box, in a section, in a package. What I feel I'm learning and practicing is to be like this is my job: I come here and I do my job and I go home. This is my job, whereas at my old job it was more of my life and more like a huge part of my life, and I spent gobs and gobs of time planning and organizing. Now I'm like I'll just do this lesson tomorrow, and I will be doing okay, and I'll go home.

I hope I'm getting better at compartmentalizing all that stuff because I don't feel it's valued. I think as a person, I don't really see edges very well, you know? I don't see that official role. "This is *your* role with this, and this is *your* role..." I guess I am fluid, which gets back to the whole thing about high school, which is that I could run with different groups and could do different things and be different people yet still be who I am.

I remember being five or six, having feelings when somebody was saying, "Boys don't like other boys." Watching soap operas, I said "so and so" is cute. I never really saw that as my identity, and so I had a really hard time in school because I grew up in the Midwest. A lot of people accusing me and calling me names and hurting me. I never knew what that meant or what that was or how that took shape.

My official coming out was when I told my friend Sarah at a party sophomore year in college. I said, "Sarah I think I'm gay." And this is after hanging out with Sarah a couple of years...and Sarah met my girlfriend and all that stuff. She was like, "That's fine no big deal."

There was a book that came out in the mid-80s about coming out to your family. When I was in college, I had friends who were sociology majors, and they were all getting their PhDs. When I was in school, my friends were all graduate students, so I didn't really hang out with undergrads a lot. Those people were really, really smart and they just kept giving me books, giving me books. One thing that stuck in my head [from that book] was it takes people about seven years to fully open up.

The last piece for me was when to come out to my family. I needed their love and support. My mom had the conversation and my mom said, "Joseph, we love you and we will always support you. I don't understand, and I may not agree, but we are always going to love you and support you." I looked at my mom and said, "Mom, I read this book, and it said that you need to give your parents seven years to be able to be comfortable with it." Within three years my partner was coming home for Christmas and slept in the same bed that kind of thing. And they are fine with it. They sent the birthday cards and birthday presents, and the first time my partner came home with me with my family, we walked into the house and no one spoke to me because they wanted to make sure they were including him. They wanted him to know that he was welcome and none of my family members spoke to me.

I came out when I was at junior college. I was at home for a while, then I went back to college and when I went back, I made the decision: no more lying, no more pronoun changing…none of that! This is the way it is from here on out. That was in 1989, and I haven't changed pronouns or that stuff since. When you are on a plane and you don't know who the person is you're talking to and you just start talking to them…I guess that's what it means to me to be out: you can talk about your life and be who you are without worrying about the repercussions.

Being openly gay and having lived this life makes me see kids who are struggling, those kids who have learning disabilities who can't understand it the way other kids understand it. It means that I can be who I am. I get to be me. Just having this conversation makes me realize that coming out is a continuous process, especially for those of us who grew up in a time when there were no models.

Being nine years old and self-identifying as a gay man, it like mortifies me, even though I think it's a really good thing, but I would have been only nine years old and that would have been a big problem. I think it's a continual life-long process of being comfortable with who we are. I think this conversation has helped me realize that my next level at my current job is to make sure that my partner is included in my narrative about my life. When we are talking about writing and personal narratives and talking about challenges that we face and stuff like that, I am not going to leave him out to make life easy. I will say, "We…'we' went to California."

This year at the end of a parent conference, I had a parent say, "Can I talk to you about something?" I was like, "Sure," and they were like, "Our son and the kids are saying that you are gay, and my child doesn't know what that means. We wanted to talk to him about it, and we wanted to make sure you were okay with that." I was like, "Of course. You are the people who should be doing that, not me." She shared what she said to her child. She said, "Well, remember when we saw Mr. Joseph at the grocery store, and you saw a man with him? That is who he lives with, and that's who he loves, and that's who he spends time with." Then I was like, "That's beautiful." I think doing that and being that way is what's really important.

Anthony

My mother told me she would rather be shot in the head and dead than to know I was gay.

I was singing opera, and then I moved here, actually for a relationship that didn't work out. I moved here and needed a job, so I started teaching. I never thought I'd be teaching little kids, and that's what I did when I came back to it. I thought I'd be a college teacher, or high school at the youngest. But, I don't know, there's something about this age.

Every part of me comes to the table as a teacher. I'm just who I am. At my first job, just so you know, I was not out. It wasn't that I couldn't be out, but there was nothing stated in their mission that made me feel okay. Whereas here, my interview was a lot about me being gay because of where they were in the South.

I think a lot of that has to do with the school I'm at because it's so celebrated. We have gay pride, pre-K through 12. I don't know how much you know about our school. I'm the head of the faculty/staff GSA and the middle school GSA. Of course, just like anyone, I have my personal life and then my teaching life, but as far as my sexuality is concerned, I don't feel like there's a difference. I don't know how to explain it.

I feel like I probably realized I was gay, at maybe 11 or 12 years of age. I always had little crushes on guys at church and the older youth group and things like that. Now, being a teacher, especially in this age group, I realize that, developmentally, what I was processing was a really legitimate crush that then, as I went through puberty, turned sexual. I think when I actually went through puberty, which was seventh and eighth grade, then it was sexual, and that's when I really knew I was gay.

I was being fed information that was negative by my family and my community. Being in that area, my grandfather's a minister...I think that made me hyper-aware that I was gay, and I kept thinking I would wake up and not be gay. At the same time, I'm a singer, and I rode and showed horses, jumpers...two of the things where you have a lot of gays. At the same time, I didn't know anyone out, because they knew the way my family was...kind of an interesting twist, I think.

If I fast-forward really quickly, my family, including my grandfather the minister, show how time can change a lot. When I was living at home, my mother found a note someone had wrote me. She was cleaning my room, which she never had done, so there was obviously a suspicion. My mother told me she would rather be shot in the head and dead than to know I was gay. We talked about this. That was a pretty significant moment in my life because it was, of course, upsetting.

My coming out process was not good. They wanted to send me to Christian counseling. I went once, and I said, "I'm wasting your time and my parents' money." I said, "I know who I am, and I just need to deal with this, with my coming out process."

I had a boyfriend, several boyfriends, along the road. There was one point when I was with someone, and I transitioned from my grandfather's church to a mega-church, a really huge church. My sister and I sang on TV all the time, as soloists and as a duo. The church found out I was gay because I was out at the university (but not out at church). I was in the music program at the school, and someone in the church chorus saw this. Anyway, long and short, the church kicked me out. I feel like that's part of a coming-out process, because I had to be able to deal with rejection. They said, "Anthony is living in sin with another man." The leaders of the church called me in, and I decided I wasn't going to deny it. They said I was no longer welcome. It was especially hard. Most disappointing thing for me was my mother and my sister sang with me there, as well. We were supposed to sing that Sunday, as a trio, and I wasn't allowed to. Then I had to go and tell my mom and my sister what had just happened and to change their plans. That was hard. Sometimes you block things out in your mind because you remember this is kind of traumatic. I remember them saying, "Well, we knew this would happen someday." Not, "I'm sorry"—there was no comforting.

I temper my behavior wherever I'm at. I live in the city. We have a lot of gay people; I'm completely comfortable here. But then if I'm home, in North Carolina, or with my partner in Virginia, I gauge who I am and how I need to be. I would love to say that being out means you're out and comfortable, no matter where you are in the world, but I think that, for my own safety...if I were truly out, I wouldn't care what anyone thinks. But I want to be respectful of my family and the fact that they're not as comfortable with my being out with certain people as they are with others. I feel like I'm truly out, but let's just say that when I go to a restaurant in Virginia with my partner and his mom, we don't hold hands. We're not affectionate. I change behavior. Does that make sense? But, again, if someone asked me, I would not deny that I'm gay.

At my school we celebrate gay pride. During the gay pride assembly, I stand up as an out teacher. I don't feel like I've ever had to come out to someone here. There's never been any type of a negative reaction, but a lot of that has to do with the way our school has been established and the mission of the school. We have a lot of same-sex parents.

My principal for middle school was a lesbian when I started. She's retired since. She told me, and I believe it to this day, that the most important thing for our students is that they have out, positive role models. As I reflect, I didn't have any of that, especially going through the middle school years, when you're thinking about your sexuality, your identity, and all those things.

When you are out—when you don't feel like you have to hide anything, especially such a core part of your identity—I just think it changes your teaching. I know that when I did my student teaching in the undergraduate school, I was actually out. It was an arts magnet school, and there were a lot of openly gay high school kids, because it was an artsy school. Then, when I started teaching at a private school that was religiously based here, I didn't feel as...I don't know how to explain the comfort level, except that you just don't feel fully yourself. It's not even like you have to tell people you're gay, but you still feel like you're hiding something somewhere.

I just feel like I'm more honest. Maybe it's because of the personal shame I felt early on for being gay and that being a part of rejection, or the fact that I'm in a school where it's celebrated and where it's definitely not something to be shameful about; in fact, you feel lifted up. There's almost a pride that makes you feel so supported and lifted up. I feel like I have so many cheerleaders behind me. I'm trying to figure out how to articulate it. I think if anyone has what they perceive to be a deep, dark secret, which, for me, being gay was (because of the way I grew up and the messages I was sent), it's great knowing I don't have to fear someone finding out because everyone already knows.

I think being gay and out raises my awareness, I assume. I may be wrong. I think my awareness is raised for any of those kids I know that may be questioning. We've had some kids who, for example, in third grade changed their names from a more feminine to a gender-neutral. I try not to use gender pronouns like, "Boys, get your books. Girls, get your books," or things like that. I'm very protective of those kids, I think, for those who may be questioning their identity or where they fall on a gender spectrum. I think that they know I'm someone they can come to. I don't know how directly in my actual teaching of a lesson that comes out, but in my connection with students and how I know my students, that is very important. Very important.

It's amazing how many high school kids come out at the high school. I knew, there was a kid from second grade who I just knew was going to be gay. I didn't really know how I knew, but a lot of the teachers knew, and he came out in the high school. It was something that he always felt safe. He says, "I always felt safe around you, but I didn't know why." I think it was because I'm a gay man. I think my girls feel there's something very safe about the man who is gay as their teacher when they're 13 and 14. That make some sense?

Right now, there were no people of color as eighth-grade advisors. I was the only gay person. It was very interesting how the dance teacher, who's an eighth-grade advisor, had almost all of the black boys and I had almost all of the black girls (although not exclusively because there were more). The reason I'm saying this is that I asked one of my fellow teachers, who's black, "Why?" He said, "The parents wanted you because they feel safe with you. They know their girls feel safe with you." I don't know if that's true or not, or how it came out. I don't know if that should be a compliment or not. I guess it can provide a certain amount of safety for some of my students. I don't know.

Linda

This is who I am. This is not a phase, or something that you did or anyone did. This is just ... I just fell in love with this person.

I don't wish to become someone else when I go to school. I feel like it's exhausting for me to try and take masks off and click them back on, and if you're having a bad day or something, to not let that be shown. I don't feel like I need to share all the details with the kids, but I do feel like it's important for them to see if I'm struggling and that is normal and that's okay; this is how you deal with it. Because I don't feel like a lot of kids get that necessarily from home as much anymore. In our culture, for some reason, it seems like you have to be perfect. I need to be able to do all these things and not be tired, and not be grouchy, and still make it to this party, or whatever, you know?

I grew up Apostolic, so I feel like I learned at a very young age that I had to keep certain parts of me hidden in order to be accepted. So that whole process was really difficult. I wish that I could have done it differently. Basically, it was a really big argument that occurred at a family function between my mother and me because she was speculating, and I wasn't ready to tell the truth. It just blew up, and that's how it [coming out] happened for me. I was seeing someone, and there were just questions that I wasn't ready to answer because I was afraid, I think, of a response.

I've always been this person who was idolized and put on a pedestal, and so there was some fear about being knocked off of it...being perceived differently. And things that I had heard my family members say about others—it just didn't seem like a good idea ever. [Laughs]. My mother was asking a question: "Who is this person to you?" For me, it was the tone of the question that caused me to not want to respond, because it was very hostile, in my opinion. So, I just froze. I didn't have the language, really, to explain to her what was going on because I had never really had a conversation like that with anyone. What does that even look like? This was before Upworthy and YouTube videos. So I really didn't have a framework of how to have that conversation

Very close family members reacted negatively to me coming out; others reacted very positively. Usually, it was a generation gap. You know, the older generation had an issue [laughs]. The younger generation was like: "We love you, and we don't care, and you're still you." But I had some difficulty with my mom and my aunt. I felt almost as if they were praying it away or something. Little did they know that I had already tried that [laughs.]

My aunt has passed since. We came to an understanding, I think. We didn't necessarily speak about it, but it wasn't something that kept us from spending time together and loving each other. My mom and I have had discussions since then, and I think she needed to do some work on her own, and she needed to have a growth experience for her to be able to understand where I was coming from. I don't think that she'll ever fully understand, but at least now I feel like she's doing a better job of taking her own ego out of it. Seeing it as something that she did wrong, or didn't do, or whatever. Something that happened in my childhood and whatnot. I don't think she's at that place anymore.

Since my partner and I have been together, she [Mom] has really come around. She came and stayed at our house, which she wouldn't even walk into for years. She asked about her. She has pictures of the girls at her house, and whatnot. So, I feel like that relationship has been strengthened. I really had to say, "This is who I am. This is not a phase, or something that you did or anyone did. This is just … I fell in love with this person, and that's what it is for me, right now." Honestly, I wouldn't be who I am if this wasn't a part of me. I think she really needed to understand that piece of the puzzle: "I wouldn't be this person that you love so much if this wasn't who I was."

Me being gay is no secret, I don't think. All the faculty and staff know, unless you just don't know me at all, which could be the case for a few people [laughs]. I've never been the type of person to broadcast. That doesn't matter, sexuality or whatever else. I'm not hiding it at all.

With the students, I have been a little more hesitant to really be open and whatnot. That's changed in the last year, especially with the older kids. You teach what you need to learn yourself, I guess. So, I had a big growth experience in the last few years. Posing questions to the kids, like, "Okay, so what do you do if your family values you finding someone to love, but as soon as you bring someone home, they're not comfortable with them?" [Laughs.]

Everyone knows. It isn't something that is being hidden, but I'm not one to really say: "Hey!" You know? They're fine! They're so fine. Actually, this past year, I shared a lot more. I shared my coming-out story with one of my classes, and they were all really emotional: "I can't believe that happened to you!" and "Thank you so much for sharing with us." I don't exactly remember what the conversation was about, but it went there, and so it was just really on my heart to just tell them the truth, so I did.

It was very interesting to watch, because there were only 14 kids in that class. It was very interesting to watch the reactions of them individually because I could see some of them really having a hard time understanding how someone [laughs] could react that way to their child, and I felt like some of them were, "Man, if that was me, how would that affect me?"

Some of them were pretty emotional. You could see that it was bothering them.

Some of them I think, it just made them think differently. We have conversations in class about values and how when you're younger, you usually mirror the values that your parents have, because that's what you're learning. As you get older, that might start to shift as you become more cognizant and more aware of what's happening, and sometimes your parents don't develop [laughs] the way that you do, and how you handled that, and how you deal with it. So that was more likely what the conversation started as, and it led to "this was my experience."

I was fresh out of college when I got this job, and it was a complete accident. I was moving to New York City just for nothing, just to go. I got this job the day before school started, 10 years ago. So, at 22, I was really dealing with some serious insecurity about it. Then, my boss was an older White woman. She and her assistant, Administrative Assistant, and I, we're all in the same office—there are like six of us, but I'm by far the youngest [laughs]. So, I'm like the baby of the bunch. I'm literally as old as their daughters. After that incident that I was telling you about with my mom, I told them what happened, and it was then when those two women really became my mothers in a sense, and it was just like: "No, you're wonderful the way that you are. You're created this way for a reason. You have so many gifts and talents." They wouldn't let me feel anything other than proud of who I was, while acknowledging that I still had some shame that I was dealing with. It was just positive reinforcement for years.

I had to undo the first 22 years of my life and then start over and rebuild. It really took a falling out. My aunt wrote me an email and basically told me that I was going to Hell, but I still love you. [Laughs] I showed them that email, and they helped me draft a response and talk me through it. That was critical. That was probably one of the most significant experiences I've ever had in my life—in my adult life, it was the most significant—because I really became comfortable with who I was.

Betty

So, I never officially came out to my family. They just kind of figured it out. I didn't have one of those ah-ha moments.

I went to school for fine arts, and about two years in I felt a lot of pressure as an artist, like, "Oh, this is going to be a really hard career. I'm not going to make a lot of money." Self-doubt. Not thinking I was good enough. But I still really want to be able to be creative. I've always loved working with kids. I was always babysitting and stuff. So I'm like, "Oh, let me maybe go into teaching." So, I started taking arts integration classes, so my degree is actually in arts integration—that's drama, theater, dance, and music, all that into the regular school curriculum. That was kind of my way of figuring it out: "Oh, I can teach in a creative way," instead of just by the book like the common core kind of teacher...I didn't want that.

I am the nurturer. Maybe some people might see me as a little softy, but I want to hear every kid's voice. I want to make sure they are teaching me as much as I'm teaching them. I just feel like it's my second family being at school. I want every kid to feel welcomed.

I went to an all-girls Catholic school actually. My parents are not Catholic. I went to this school to get away from the kids I went to middle school with. So, I kind of like got to start over. It was like having a new identity almost. I was really boy-crazy, actually, for my first two years in high school. Then I met this girl. Actually, it was junior year, I think, when we finally met. We became really close friends, but I was like, "Oh, I know that there's more to this." And so we started dating.

I never officially came out to my family. They just kind of figured it out. I didn't have one of those ah-ha moments. I think my parents just observed my relationship with this girl and they're like, "Yeah, this is more than friends." And then I think eventually my mom probably read my diary or something [laughs]. And it was a little bit of an invasion of privacy, but the funny thing is actually, and I have no recollection of this. This summer, I was talking to my mom and she told me the story about how I came to her one day and asked her, "What would you do if Amy was gay?" That's my sister. She's six years older than me. And my mom kind of like looked at me and she said, "Well, it wouldn't matter. She loves who she loves." And I think that was probably my way of finding out how she would react to me coming out. But I never had to.

I think she ended up telling my dad, but he didn't like the girl-friend. He didn't like her, so he had a hard time with that part of it, but eventually they just kind of came around and said you know, "You love who you love, and as long as you're happy that's all that matters."

I'm not trying to be stereotypical, but because I don't come across as looking like a butch lesbian, most people are actually really shocked when they hear me say, "My partner" or "My girlfriend." And they're like, "You mean girlfriend? Like *that* kind of girlfriend?" But I think actually males give me that reaction more often than women do.

This school has been so supportive. I've never felt any kind of negative connotation towards it. Everybody I think that knows me personally—I've been here for three years—knows that I have a partner. Some of them have met her at functions and things like that. Like some of the new people that have come in probably don't know just because they haven't met me. I'm not going to go up and say, "I'm Betty, I'm gay." [Laughs.] I just kind of let it come naturally into a conversation.

I'm so fortunate to be at this school where we teach diversity to the kids. We have same-sex parents, and kids that are growing up not knowing that's really something different. I have kids that bring in books about gay families and we're reading those. It just feels like it's never been an issue. Like, for example, one of the girls I had last year had two moms. She was presenting her "all about me" poster. She came to me and said, "I have two moms." And I said, "Well that's really cool because if I had a daughter like you, my daughter would have two moms too." And she goes, "Oh, that's cool." [Laughs.] Just being able to make those connections is great. Because I know even though they are in kindergarten, they can still kind of feel like, "Oh, why don't I have a dad?" or "Why don't I have a mom?" Even if it's a single-parent family, I just don't want them to feel like that is going to change the way that we see them.

In kindergarten it's so important to get to know everybody. So, they all have a day where they present like a poster of pictures of their family and all of that stuff. So, on my poster I have a picture of my partner and our dog. They ask who she is and I'm like, "Well, I'm not married, but if I had a husband this would be my husband." That's kind of the way I have to explain it to them. But nowadays you'd be surprised. They're just like, "Okay!" It's no big deal. Some of them probably get it and some of them don't. Some of them are like, "Well, you can't get married to her." And I'm like, "Right. Not in Georgia." [Laughs.]

It's very diverse here. It's a very warm environment. Everybody knows everybody. I mean we call each other by our first name, including the kids. It just feels like we're all a big family or group of friends. Everybody gives each other hugs. I don't know, maybe I just stay neutral, and I don't get involved, but it doesn't feel like a drama-filled, gossipy sort of place.

I think our school does a really good job at breaking those gender norms. You can go into any classroom, I mean especially in the younger grades, and you'll see boys playing with dress-up clothes and wearing princess outfits. You'll see girls with a hard hat on and hammering. They're never told, "Oh, you should be playing with trucks" or "You should be playing with dolls." And the same goes I think even for the upper grades. I've experienced boys who maybe talk a little more feminine, and they're just allowed to be who they're allowed to be, and nobody's trying to tell them to be different. I just think our school is so open to thinking outside the box and we're always trying to find ways to teach kids tolerance. It's just a great place for that.

Michael

I knew I was gay...I would say probably when I was six years old. I just remember feeling different. Knowing that expressing what that feeling was was probably not the right thing to do, so I just kept it to myself.

I never would have thought I was going to be a teacher. If you had asked me up until mid-college, at least, I would have certainly said no. I have always been a very balanced academically. Always performed well in all my academics and nothing stood out to me as a strong talent or gift in any area. I was depending on college to lead me in that direction, but I still didn't get any feelings.

Sophomore year you need to declare a major. I chose general business because that was the easiest thing to do. I went through business classes still not really feeling it, but it had to be something. I got my degree in business from the University of Georgia. Then I worked in commercial real estate for a year and realized that I really, really hated business and corporate world: it isn't my thing. I packed up my little apartment Macon, Georgia, and headed back to UGA for grad school. Still a little uncertain about what that was going to mean.

I've always been into sports. I really enjoyed the notion of coaching, so that led me into asking what good majors would there be if you wanted to be a coach? Education being one of those.

I talked to several people on campus and decided I could do a masters in health and physical education at UGA, thinking coaching would be my thing. As I got into that field and enjoyed the health part, the physical education part, and the teaching and pedagogy classes. I really enjoyed that a lot. I got a grad assistantship through the athletic department with the women's basketball team. Once I was there, I was able to do that for three years in grad school, which was an awesome experience. There's a lot of teaching that goes on along the coaching lines of college athletics anyway.

I got a little disillusioned with the coaching notion as far as college athletics goes by the end, because it's kind of a mess. I decided that was almost as complicated as corporate business. I decided then that I really would love to teach. I found a job teaching primary school, physical education, in Madison, Georgia. I fell in love with teaching, and I stayed there for eight years. Then decided that I wanted to get out of the small town and come to Atlanta. That's where I landed. That's kind of what led me into teaching. It was a roundabout approach.

I try to be pretty low key. I stay low key. I enjoy a fairly small group of friends—really, really good friends. I like the spiritual nature of life and the journey that we're on, so I'll read those type of books. I like my quiet time. I need my "me time" a lot. Although I enjoy being with my friends, there's a good portion of time I spend in my head. That's kind of me.

I think being gay helps me see the kids more as individuals and respect where they are on their little journey in life because I did so much exploring and investigating on my own in various different parts of life. I know that it's a lot about perspective. My 25-year-old self saw things differently than my 45-year-old self. My journey through these changes. I think that I see that in the kids. I don't expect them to see the world the same way I do. I want them to be able to safely explore it.

I try not to be very black and white in class. There aren't a lot of wrong answers. I try to help them explore and figure out what they want to find. The answer may be wrong, but it's a chance to grow and see it differently, not sure if I'm putting those words together exactly right.

I knew I was gay…I would say probably when I was six years old. I just remember feeling different. Knowing that expressing what that feeling was…was probably not the right thing to do, so I just kept it to myself. I was a much more outgoing child. I remember from toddler age to up until that six- or seven-year-old kid who started realizing that I was a little different, and I felt like people looked at me a little differently. I didn't really like being looked at differently, so I learned to tone down my personality quite a bit. I still like that with 95 percent of the population—people that I'm around. I'm still pretty toned down.

I was raised in a very Christian environment. Religion was important. Probably like most families, it was a lot more talk than action. It was more the right and wrong things to do, but my family didn't necessarily follow through with the right and wrong things to do. They could certainly tell you what the right and wrong things to do were. I was a rule follower from early, early on. I wanted to please, and so I always did. In school and all the way through my teen years, never got in trouble, didn't do anything wrong.

In my teen years, that was when I got a little more confused: "Well, maybe I'm not gay, but maybe I am." There were little periods of time that I was trying to make it not true. That continued into college. I didn't date really. I had friends that I hung out with, but I was a little intimidated by the whole experience of trying to date girls, because that whole "doing the right thing" and "not being a liar." I felt that pretty strongly. I just never did give dating a super serious try. It was more superficial.

That continued into my 20s after I got out of college the second time (grad school). I was in a great little community I loved: I loved my school, I loved my kids, I loved all the people I was around. Except I didn't feel like I was being really true to myself. I felt not like I was really living a very authentic life. From the outside, everybody I'm sure thought, "That's pretty good. He's got a great life. Every thing's fine." But I didn't really feel that. At this point, I'd not dated, touched, kissed the opposite sex at all. That was probably about 26. I said, "That can't continue. I'm going to be myself, and everybody's going to hate me for it, but I can't keep pretending to be something that I'm not."

That's when I came out to my parents. My dad was like, "Oh, okay."

Completely fine with it. We never had a great relationship, so he was probably the one I least cared about having a reaction. My mom was upset for a couple of days, but in the end, she said she kind of knew it anyway. No big surprise. My sister was great; most of my family was fine. I was super close to my aunts and uncles growing up. They continue to be cool about it.

Because my family is still kind of small-town isolated, not very open minded, the relationship changed. I was no longer to them quite the same person. They're nice to me. I have one uncle who is kind of an ass anyway to everyone. He's just a bigot. He doesn't like anyone that is in any way different than himself. Whereas I don't care whether your Black, White, woman, whatever, he is the center of the universe. He's the one with the biggest issue. It's my mom's brother-in-law. He's not even blood related.

Overall, the relationships with my family changed. My mom, my dad, my sister, everything is fine. I just didn't feel quite as close to my extended family I guess. My grandparents were all dead at that point. That probably would have affected me more. I was super close to my grandmother. She probably would have been totally fine with it because she kind of raised me; I know she loved me more than anybody else. If mom can handle it, I'm sure she could have.

For my mom, it was more of a grieving process that she went through. She cried. She wasn't sure what it all meant. Probably the biggest thing it meant to her was that she wouldn't have grandchildren. At the time my sister didn't have any kids and swore she would never have kids. Mom thought I was the only shot at a grandkid. That made that a little bit worse for her. My first relationship, he was divorced and had a three-year-old girl. While we were together, Mom felt it. I think Mom felt a grandkid-like relationship with her. I think that kind of changed Mom's reality about the whole situation a little bit, and that I guess I could still have a grandkid even though he's gay.

Mom, I know, is still not super comfortable with some people around them knowing, but she's a whole bunch better. It's just been recently I think that she and my sister have felt it was not a big deal about me visiting with their friends in town. They are feeling better about the situation. I think the words my mom used is that she was "more concerned about what people would say about you."

In the end a lot of it, I think, whether she could articulate it or not, was also about what they would say about her. Because it's her small town. I wasn't around, and I didn't really care what they said about me. I get that. She lives it every day. I think she's kind of over it because Facebook changed a lot of all that. Now everybody knows. She's totally fine. My niece graduated from high school a few weeks ago, and my partner and I went to graduation and sat in the front row with my mom and my sister. My brother-in-law is the president of the board of the school where she graduated from, and he was on stage with the diplomas. Some of my friends came up and said hello. It wasn't such a big deal or it didn't seem like it was as big a deal to my mom and my sister as it would have been maybe five or ten years ago.

I don't have to necessarily hide any part of my life from anybody. I think I overcame that fear a lot earlier on than I would have thought. When I taught in Madison, Georgia, a small town, I couldn't imagine teaching in a school and being out. I said that to one of my friends, my teaching friend. She taught first grade, and she was a good friend of mine from college. She was one of the first people I came out to. I remember having a conversation with her about it: "I am out and I'm dating, and I have a boyfriend and a relationship. I'm not sure I can still teach school." I didn't know what that comfort level was going to be. I didn't want to be constantly defending myself or looking over my shoulder or whatever.

When I moved to Atlanta, I worked for a year in high school. It was a public school, I wasn't out at all. I lived in Grant Park. A job opened at the charter school there. I took that, and the principal was a lesbian and several of the teachers were gay. The whole community was very open minded. From day one there, I was out because I lived two blocks from the school. That was when I was with Steven. Steven and I had Chloe. We were out in the neighborhood and everybody knew. It was not a big deal. At that point I realized there were spaces, communities, that were accepting and it wasn't a big deal. I haven't thought about ever needing to keep that a secret since then.

If I'm in a conversation with a parent and something comes up about personal life or vacation, I will say "My partner and I." Or "Jeff and I" or whatever. I'm sure that being gay probably affects me a little bit. If it's a parent that I met before and I'm comfortable with, it's not usually a big deal. If it's someone I've not really been around much, I'm probably a little bit more guarded about what kind of personal information I'm going to tell. It's not necessarily for fear of any kind of retribution or anything; I think it's just more, "I don't know you well enough to share a whole lot about my life with you."

Coming into this school, I did feel like there is probably conservative little factions within this community. The beginning of the year, I said that if it's going to be the same as it was at my last school, I didn't have any intention of keeping a secret or lying to anyone if they ask. It's more about how much of your personal life do you want to share here again? I've gotten super involved with my last school. It made it hard for me to leave all of that. Part of it for me was how much of a family kind of relationship did I even want to have with these people? I wanted to just be work and then leave it here and have my life with my friends and everyone else outside of here. For me, I think it was more about that than about being gay. If that makes sense.

Now I have been tutoring. I know a couple of the kids in here know that I'm gay. A couple have met Jeff. One kid that I'd been tutoring from public school for two years actually enrolled here last year and ended up in my class. He knows that I'm gay. I had to go to their house. I remember meeting the parents. Mom is super Southern, seemingly maybe conservative and stuff. I just thought I really wanted to just keep it professional. I'll be tutoring. Mom would not have any of that. The third visit, I would tutor him and Mom would offer me wine and want to chat for 30 or 45 minutes or an hour if she could keep me there. About the third visit, during our chat after the tutoring session, she started talking about her uncle that she loved so much that lived in Key West and he died and he had AIDS. She was trying to make me know that she was totally cool with being gay because apparently, she suspected it to begin with.

I don't come right out and say it, but I'm sure that I make comments from time to time that any astute parent's going to pick up on. I intentionally don't sensor myself in that regard. I may not come right out and say "gay" or "I have a partner named Jeff," or whatever. Whatever she picked up on, she wanted to make sure that I knew that she was totally fine with it. That is really what I think her intention was—not to find out if I was gay, not to try to call me out or anything—I just think she wanted me to be a little more relaxed and know they were cool.

What age is it appropriate for me really to be sharing my personal life with them [the children]? I think that's something that I'm still trying to figure out. The state of society today, people are being more open-minded about gay relationships than ever, but it's really hard to know when it's okay to really share. I'm not sure if I were married to a woman how much of my personal life I would really share with a class of students anyway. I think there's a fine line of professionalism and how much you share about your outside life.

I have had a lifetime of embracing my feminine side. I got tagged early on as a kid as being a little flamboyant, which is why I had to tone it down a bit. Still toning it down, in a little bitty small town where everybody hunts and fishes and all that; I never was going to do those things. I don't care what they said, how many names I got called, I was never going to hunt or fish. Even though I toned it down, it was just to minimize the cruelty.

I have a student, who is a very complex child. There have been some times when I had worked with him, just seeing his reactions, wondering as an adult if maybe he's going to be gay too. I'm not sure. He's so all over the board, there's no way you could ever figure that out. One thing about Halloween around here is you can't wear masks. He is a planner, and he planned his Halloween, and he had his mask and everything. But he didn't get the message until the day before Halloween, mostly because he didn't hear it the two days before that. That afternoon, he's like, "Wait I can't wear my mask." He goes home, and he's upset about it when he got in the car. By the time he and his mom got home, he said he had a plan. He had been in a play at his other school the year before. He played a grandmother in total drag—the wig, the dress, everything. By the time he got home, he told his mom that was what he was going to do. She's like, "Okay, cool."

Then she texted me that night because she had been talking to a coworker at Georgia Tech. A coworker who's gay, and he said, "You can't let him go to school like that. He's going to be teased." She's like, "I don't think the school is like that. I think he can." She got to second guessing herself, so I get a text about 9:30 or 10:00 that night. She goes "This is the plan for tomorrow. That's going to be okay, isn't it?" I was like. "Yeah. I think it will be fine."

Sure enough, he comes in high heels, too. The most popular kid at school that day! No one said anything about it. He took his heels off, but the wig stayed on, and the dress, for football on the field. He definitely stood out. The adult comments made that day were not, "Oh my god, I can't believe he's wearing that." It was like, "Oh my god! That is so cool." To me that's kind of what the school environment is about...people that are different. That is what I am about.

Margaret

I feel teachers play this great role in kids' lives. We're adults that care about them and we show them ways of being adults. If I'm afraid to be out to my students, I don't know what kind of message I'm sending to them about what it means to be an adult in the world, so it's important to me.

I realized I wanted to teach when I was in graduate school studying Japanese literature. I primarily went to graduate school because I want to teach Japanese and Japanese literature. Then, I had crisis of faith and wondered why I was in graduate school. I put in for some time off and started subbing in middle schools and elementary schools and realized that I really love the teaching part, not so much the research part. I decided that I wanted to teach younger kids. It felt like I had more of an impact and that it was more relevant and that I could instill values to young children that were important to me. Also, the schools I was subbing at were schools I wished I had gone to. I was really excited by the opportunities that kids had in their learning environment, so I decided to teach middle school and elementary school.

I used to teach humanities and now I do tech, and those things are really important to me, but the thing that's most important to me is community building—creating a safe environment for students. I really put a premium on those things when I'm teaching. Content knowledge will come, I think, when kids feel safe and when they feel heard, so I would say my identity as a teacher is nurturing. I have a high expectation of my students, I want them to do well and be their best selves.

I identify as a parent, definitely as a Black woman, as gay: that's my identity outside of school. I really value my relationship with my partner, so that's really important. I'm a family person; I spend most of my time with my family. I guess I would say that. I feel I have a particular connection with my daughter right now. She's entering that time of her life, and I think she feels that way too. My partner is a preschool teacher or early childhood educator, so we feel we have covered the kid spectrum of life. I don't leave my identities at home when I go to school. I know that some teachers do to try to separate who they are outside of school from who they are at school. I have teacher friends who are gay and lesbian who don't bring that to their schools, but that's never a consideration for me. I'm always who I am, no matter where I am.

I think I had questions about my sexual orientation when I was in high school. I assigned myself the label asexual because I didn't feel the way that my friends obviously did about boys, and so I was like, "Oh, I must not be interested at all." When I got to college, I started identifying as bisexual, actually. I had two great friends who are also gay. We spent a lot of time together. I came out to my friends in college, but I didn't come out to my family until I was out of college.

My uncle died of AIDS, but he had never been out. That had a really big impact on me, and then a couple months later my dad died. It felt like he didn't know who I was—he didn't know all of me—and so I felt it was really important that I finally just told my family who I was. My friends, well, that was easy. Many of them were like, "Oh, finally." I have a twin sister, and that's important to me, being a twin. When I came out to her, she was like, "Oh, that's no big deal."

At school, my former teaching partner, she talks about her family a lot. Her husband, he was a hippie in the '60s, and there was a project where the kids interviewed him. Her son goes on trips with her class. To me, every teacher should be able to bring their family into the classroom like that. Being openly gay means that I'm saying, "This is my partner, this is my child, this is my life because that's part of who I am as a teacher."

So now, my way of coming out is just saying, "This is my partner,

Tina." There hasn't been much a reaction. I'd say other gay teachers are like, "Oh, we should hang out." That's been the main reaction. I also get, "Oh, I'd love for you to get to know my partner. Are you married? Are you guys going to get married?" Especially after the Supreme Court ruling. The reactions have mostly been about asking questions about my relationship in terms of marriage or do you have kids. It is mostly about who we are and there hasn't been any bad reaction; there hasn't been many negative reactions to being out.

I came out to one student who was doing a project on proms. An eighth grader wanted to know. She was interviewing people who didn't go to their proms in high school, and I volunteered to talk about it. I talked about how for someone who identified as gay, the prom didn't really seem something that I wanted to go to. She didn't really have a reaction to that.

Part of what I did over a year was to introduce myself to the kids, and so I wrote them a letter. My introduction of myself was introducing my family. It was just a very easy and natural thing to do. We also read the book *The Misfits*, I don't know if you're familiar with it. It's a pitch-perfect book for middle schoolers by James Howe, and one of the main characters is a 12-year-old who identifies as gay. There's a sequel called *Totally Joe*, and it's all about him and his relationship with his new boyfriend. We read *The Misfits* together, and so it was an inevitable conversation that happened. It was really easy to be out to my students.

I'm working with a cross-section of grades, and I'm with kids in their classroom for maybe a few weeks at a time, and then I don't see them for one time. I don't know how to be out to them. I know that I am not their expectation of what a female teacher looks like. There's this kindergartener who ask me every time she sees me, "Are you a boy or a girl?" Yeah, every time she sees me. I say, "I'm a girl." She says, "You have hair on your chin." I say, "Yes, but I'm a girl." She's very perplexed.

I think being here and having families at the school that are gay families helps. The other part of it is that it's a Quaker school, and I feel there's that real feeling like everyone has a light inside of them. The school really tries to affirm that and live that, so that's part of my light, and so it's part of who I am. It feels like the school is a place where it's okay to be who you are. I know there are a lot of schools like that, but I feel there's this spiritual or mission-driven basis for that. If, for instance, there were a family that had a problem with there being openly gay teacher, I feel the school would have pointed at the mission and said, "This is part of who we are."

I had to make a conscious choice to share my family with my students. I felt it was important that I do that because they need to see all kinds of different families and, as a teacher, I'm modeling for them different possibilities in the world or one of the possibilities in the world. I feel teachers play this great role in kids' lives. We're adults that care about them, and we show them ways of being adults. If I'm afraid to be out to my students, I don't know what kind of message I'm sending to them about what it means to be an adult in the world.

4

MIDDLE SCHOOL

William

I knew in first grade that I liked boys.

My identity: first, a priest because I wear a collar, so visually I stand out from everybody else in the entire community. Secondly, I am male in a school where most of the teachers are female. Third is my identity as a teacher, which has an authority component to it. And somewhere in there, I feel like part of my identity is as gay man. I do not know if you asked one of my students if that would come up. In fact, I would probably say, for most of my students, that would not be a part of their answer, but they may say priest, man, bald.

I knew in first grade that I liked boys, and I knew a word for it in sixth grade. I have a distinct memory, in fact, in first grade of tussling on the floor with Meg and Andrew. I remember exactly where we were in the first grade classroom. It was winter time because the heater was on and we were close to the heat source. I remember rolling on the floor, and I remember distinctly that I liked touching Andrew better than I like touching Meg, and it is as clear as day. There was nothing else that accompanied. There was no attraction. There was no shame. There was no identity. It's just that I knew that I wanted to touch Andrew more than I wanted to touch Meg.

I never really came out of the closet because I never was in one. I was out in high school. I grew up in a small rural Mississippi town, but I grew up in a widely known and well-respected family. So I was insulated from, not all, but a great deal of harassment because of my sexuality. You didn't mess with who I was. My family was known as a good family; my father was known as a good man. I was treated, therefore, the same way. I got teased, of course. All of my peers knew I was gay, because I never was not gay. That was the whole thing: I never pretended to be anybody else. I never dated women, but I didn't date guys in high school, but all of my friends did know that I was gay.

I've never had a coming out, so I don't know what that's like. I can imagine that would be a fabulous party, and maybe I should have one now! I remember, I guess it was in high school, praying one night saying, "You know what, God? This is it. So if this is not who you want me to be, then let me know, because otherwise I'm pretty sure this is who I am, and I know I haven't made a choice about it, and I know that you made me who I am. So if I'm wrong about this, do something about it." That was the only time ever that I've questioned it, and I didn't *really* question it. I just said, "Okay, this is it. You tell me."

I was lucky. I never got the messages that most Southern kids did. I never got the message that it was bad. I never heard it preached from my pulpit, and I grew up a Methodist. Methodists are happy people and they're joyful people. I never, ever heard that gays were bad. I never heard sexuality preached from the pulpit. All I knew was that God loved me, and that was a beautiful message for any Southern boy, any Southern gay boy: God loves you. That's the only message I heard.

God showed up with the affirmations of everyone else around me who said, "We love you and you are loved and you are beautiful and you are different and we love you because you are different." It's the South. We never said, "We love you because you like dick." We said, "We love you because you're different." We live in a society where we're forced to make a declaration about it because people assumed the contrary. If we lived in a society where no one assumed that I liked women and all the package that goes along with that, then there would be no need to come out. It means that we live in a society that privileges heterosexuality, because no one ever has to come out as a heterosexual, which means that we just assume; we privilege heterosexuality.

I used to say in my interviews, "You know, I just want to be up front. I'm a gay man." I was working with my therapist and she said, "Why are you having to say that? They're hiring you for who you are, and that's a part of who you are." And, so I stopped saying it. I mean, it's pretty obvious.

I actually preached a sermon as the guest preacher during my interview. The way this school works is, of course, the administration talked to the kids and said, "All right. What are your thoughts?" And the kids all wanted me over the other candidates. One of the kids said, "Because he reminds me of that guy in *Modern Family*." When I was being interviewed by the faculty, one of them said, "I just want to let you know, the kids already see you as the guy in *Modern Family*." And so I said, "It's fine." I mean, I am who I am. I'll speak about my partner, but I never made a point to say, "I am gay." I probably said something about my partner, so I didn't have to come out in my job interview. But I am completely out at school.

Moving to the South, again, I found to be far more conservative. There has been vocal parental opposition to me. Some parents have gone to the board. It's a minority. It's by far a minority, but they are vocal. They have spoken to other faculty members. They have had appointments with the head of school. In one of my early classes, I said, "My husband and I," and thought it didn't upset most kids, it was a shock to some of the kids because no one had ever said that. They went home, then the phone calls started coming in. I still have parents who will not shake my hand. I have parents who will not return my emails. On the whole, most people have been very welcoming—completely supportive. The administration has been completely supportive. But there are some parents who are very vocal about it, so that's been difficult.

They will speak at parties about me. They will come to meetings and speak about me. No rumors, but there's always Twitter, and there's always an undercurrent among certain parents of "What do we do to get rid of the gay chaplain?" Mind you, there is another openly gay art teacher, who is married to her partner. But it's different when it's the priest, and it's different when it's a man who is gay than it is for a woman. So the discrimination is actually been remarkable at this school, far greater than it was at my prior school.

Gay men are viewed more predatorily than gay women are. Then add on top that I'm the chaplain, that I wear a collar, that I have a religious component. That makes people nervous because it challenges their own misunderstanding of faith. So there is a whole lot of unpacking that needs to be done, but it's been a difficult year for me.

I am uber-sensitive to bullying, and I am uber-sensitive to even the slightest whiff of pejorative words, intonations, and teenage boy pranks that may feel dangerous, that would have felt dangerous to me as a seventh-grade boy. So I am always listening to that; I'm hypersensitive to that. Does it affect me as a teacher? My life, as someone who has been discriminated against and who endured a childhood as a gay kid, makes me sensitive to creating a safe environment for all kids. That's what I've tried to do for sixteen years, is to create a safe environment. It doesn't matter whether I'm teaching English or religion or music or whatever I've taught, but I must create a safe environment for a child to be who a child is, because it's a discovery time.

I talk in the very first days to children about safety in the classroom, and I establish classroom rules. We talk about mutual respect and honor and integrity. It adds weight that I chair the Honor Council at the school. "The Honor Council at the school is chaired by the priest who is also my teacher," and so there's a whole lot of weight in that conversation. I make sure, because I don't ever want it to be the secret, because secrets are dangerous and they have power. I always in the first couple of days of class make sure that I mention my husband or my partner. Not intentionally. I don't come out and say, "You know, shocker, I'm gay." But I make sure that they know, this is no secret. I am who I am, and I encourage you to be who you are and in this place, you may be who you are.

This one kid, of course, this year, said, "Ha. You said husband. You meant to say wife." I said, "No, Joshuah. I said husband for a reason." And the look on his face! Then another girl in the exact same class to my left said spontaneously, "Oh, cool." I'm the very first one this school's ever had, so there's got to be a little bit of nervousness. This next year, it will not be. They all know I'm gay. They all know it's not a secret. They all know they can't whisper about it, so it changes the dynamic. I'm actually going to be teaching the exact same kids next year in eighth grade. I'll take the same kids up, so there's nothing new there.

They see me because I'm more than just the teacher. They see me in chapels. Once a week they see me, I lead the prayers. I offer them communion. I offer them the Grace of God, from the hands of a gay man.

Mark and Paul

Did you know that Mr. Paul...has a husband?
He married a guy. His name was Mark.

Paul. My first year of teaching I really wanted to make sure I established that I was the good teacher, a well-liked teacher, and the good colleague before I was the gay teacher. I say it is important to me that I'm also a gay teacher at school. I've been out in both the schools, with the exception of giving it a little time when I first got to my first school.

I've been out the whole time. That's definitely an important part. I want to be like the good role model, but I just made sure that's one of many things—a second tier thing to being an effective teacher, a good colleague, those kinds of things.

Mark. My identity doesn't really center around my sexuality because I feel like I tend to do more activities and hang around with people that *happen* to be gay but have the same interests as I do. For example, I am in the Gay Men's Chorus because I love singing. I do musical theater, but that happens to have a lot of gay people. I play soccer, and that happened to be with a gay group. In all these activities, my sexuality isn't an issue. We're just people who share the same interests and hobbies and happen to be gay.

Teaching math, I find that most of the kids really appreciate when I can actually bring my personal life into conversation. Just talking about things that I did over the weekend with any of the groups I am in, I think that really makes kids feel like they're learning from a human being; we're not just these robots that don't have lives. I find that especially with this independent school, talking about the weekend really helps just anchor the learning. Kids understand that we have personal lives and that's part of who we are.

Paul. I came out in the middle of high school—end of sophomore year, beginning of junior year. I went to school in Northern Virginia. I went to magnet school for science and technology. I think in some respects I was actually in a school where the grade above me had gotten super keyed up on sexual orientation as like a civil rights issue on both sides.

I was the observer because it was the older kids who argued the school board over things. This was right when the issue of gays in military was coming around with Bill Clinton the first time. A lot of times I was like along for the ride because I was doing the simpler thing. It seemed like coming out was almost a little simpler than advocating or trying to change federal policy.

I had a relatively good coming-out experience. My parents were divorced, and I lived with my mom. I came out to her early on. I didn't actually come out to my dad for about ten years because he was much more conservative. It took me a while to be more comfortable with him.

I came out to my mom when I was 16. She was actually a part of a very conservative religion. She was very emotional and supportive, but it was tougher for her I think just because she was worried for me. Maybe it took her a couple of months to get her head screwed on straight about it. She wasn't negative, but there was just a lot of crying, a lot of worrying.

Then with my dad, ten years later when I was 26—that was much more uneventful. I don't know if he had more time to figure it out on his own. He doesn't show a lot of emotion anyway; very matter of fact. He's conservative but not religious, so that might make it easier for him.

Mark. I totally identified as gay in middle school, but I came out in high school when I think I was a junior or senior. I was in the middle of a musical, at a party or something. There were other people who were gay who joined the musical. That made it a little bit easier. But family wise, I didn't come out to them and totally identify as gay until college when I was living on campus away from my family, not going to church. That made it significantly easier just staying on campus. I think they're still grappling with the idea that their son is gay.

I had a really remarkably uneventful coming out, and then I went to college where it became a non-issue. I was raised in a pretty conservative family. My mom and my brother ended up choosing not to come to our wedding. They still haven't come to visit baby Samuel. He's three months. They were all invited. My mother didn't RSVP. My brother RSVP'd but changed his mind last minute. We were willing to actually buy his plane ticket. I don't think he understood that we actually bought a ticket or was going to buy it, and he was like, "Oh yeah I can't make it." It was hurtful, but I'm not actually that emotional. I'm not really that close with my family, so it really wasn't a big deal to not have them there. I've gotten over it.

Paul. Yeah, my family was there. Again, partly the fact that it was an East Coast wedding, and I got a lot of family around here, so that was part of it. Also, my parents were definitely more comfortable with it.

It's interesting his family. We've been out to Vegas before, and his mom and brother are totally sweet with me, and she almost can go on one breath like, "Oh my goodness, you two are so nice. Take care of Mark. Read Leviticus." It's all in one breath sometimes. It's interesting. I don't really know how to understand it completely.

In my first school, I was in this place in Maryland, somewhere outside of D.C. It was some sort of liberal democratic area, so it was fine being gay. I got a lot of non-response, and so I think that might have been people who thought it was great but weren't going to make a big deal about it, or people who thought it wasn't great but weren't going to make a big deal out of it, and then are people who are really excited about it.

I've never in my whole life had really any over-negative incident. The closest I remember was a mom complaining socially to some other mom because Mark was coming to the baseball games that I was coaching. I'm like, "Well, if that's the worst I get, that's not too bad.

Mark. Paul has a picture of me at his desk, and I don't think my first year I actually had a picture of Paul. I think it actually meant a lot for him to have a picture of us together. My first year, one of our kids said to me, "Did you know that Mr. Paul has a husband? He married a guy. His name was Mark." I was like, "You do know that's me? I'm Mr. Paul's husband." She was like, "Oh wow, okay." This year was the first year I actually made a photo album that had a picture of Paul. Had a picture of both of us. Paul has a pride flag and a bunch of gay paraphernalia around his desk. I don't know. Is it easier for me to say that, as a math teacher, I don't need that stuff? I don't need an HRC sticker, I don't need a pink flag or rainbow. I feel like I can justify not having that, and I also feel like some people are like, "Why are you hiding it?"

Paul. It's interesting, because when I got here, I was already living with Mark. A lot of students already knew him because of me. He would come to events at school. They knew we were a couple. They knew we were married. I would say, "We have math opening. You should come over." I called up and told him to come interview, and we offered him the job. It wasn't an accident that we ended up at the same school. Part of that was I think the school really wants to foster a family environment in general. I think that we were a cool family to have there as well.

I don't think that, deep down, my Head of School was really comfortable with it. I think the middle-level administrators were, but I was always like, "Is this going to be the time that some parent complains?" I didn't really feel like I was quite protected by the system. I thought I was protected by the fact I was a good teacher. It put more pressure on me to be good and be well-liked so that I didn't have to deal with a lot of other stuff.

The school has a stated social-justice curriculum. It's really an embedded part of the school, so I don't really feel like I have to worry so much about it. I am helping to create the community I want to live in. There's still a lot of good work that we do but I don't feel like I'm freelancing in it anymore. I'm at a school where everybody is theoretically doing it.

Mark. As a math teacher, my personal life doesn't really come into conversations or in whole class discussions or content—not in my classroom directly but in passing in the hallway or in morning meetings or during lunch. I feel like that's made me more of a human being and just a person, as opposed to a teacher like a role model.

As an Asian, I feel like I meet the stereotype of being an Asian who was a math major and became a math teacher. It's funny because during recess, we see a lot of the kids who get picked up by their nannies. Coincidentally, a lot of their nannies are Filipino, so it's nice being a Filipino male.

I am a Filipino male teacher. Filipinos don't only have to be nannies; they can be your teacher. They don't have to work in stereotypical jobs around the town. Even in my old public high school, I was the lone token Asian male. After Caucasian the next race minority was Asians. I think it was good seeing all of those kids seeing that you can be a male Asian and be a teacher. I think that helped build some confidence and just build some hope in future educators.

Paul. Essentially, as a white guy, I still have enjoyed an awful lot of privilege. And because you could put away the gay part, that makes it even more true. There are definitely times I feel like my voice is heard more at school. There are times in conversations or meetings when I'll notice someone is trying to speak, so I go out of my way to make sure that they're getting called on, or what they're saying is heard. At the same time, I try not to reiterate what people are saying, but sometimes I found that she says it, but when I say it again and it carries more weight.

It's all encouraging someone to repeat what they said earlier, or saying I thought their point was good. It isn't like I'm swooping in and picking and choosing and giving some white male privilege to what everybody else was saying. I'm definitely aware that, as a teacher, I co-teach in a room with someone else. We work together full-time. She's a woman, also white, and so I think we're conscious that we bring different skill sets to the class.

Mark. All of the math teachers are female besides me. In my old high school, public high school they pretty much had a good mix of male and females. I think boys respond well to male math teachers. I just feel like that. I had really successful experiences there, but having a co-teacher next year that will definitely help change my views on teaching in general because I've never done co-teaching. I think gender plays a role in learning. With our son, with having two dads, we actually consciously decided to have an au pair that was female because we want there to be some exposure to a female role model.

Paul. Being gay absolutely impacts my identity as a teacher. I've always felt like it does for me more than it does for Mark because when he was at his other school, I was always going, "Come on, talk about us. Be a good role model."

I taught at schools where it's been about the whole child, and not just about the content. I really feel that exposure to and an understanding of LGBT people and issues is really one of the things I've been able to contribute when thinking about the whole child beyond just content. That's my built-in extra.

Joshua

In general, if someone is out or openly gay, that is not a secret. It's something that is generally known. It's something that that person doesn't mind that other people know.

I started playing water polo in college. I didn't play before then, and I had only done very little swimming when I was younger. I really started swimming competitively in college as well. My degree was in engineering, but I didn't really take to engineering as a career. I got into teaching a little later.

Outside of class, outside of work, my identifiers are that I'm a gay, white male in New York City, in my 30s. I'm aware that many of my friends are close to that as well, so it does become this homogeneous group. Summertime especially is my personal time. It's catching up with friends and getting some time to also then explore interests outside of teaching—mostly travel this summer and spending time with friends. This last weekend, a bunch of us went up to Montreal. Earlier this week, several people went to a concert and things like that. It's taking the time to spend time with friends, which I feel I have less time to do during the school year.

Growing up, I learned to be very cautious about who I let know all the aspects of my identity. I certainly was not out in high school. I started coming out to friends in college, and then I'd say that after college I was pretty much always out. Even here, which describes itself as a very progressive school, the first year here, I was teaching math full time, and I really just stuck to teaching math. I would teach my four classes. I'd go back in my office. I'd plan lessons. I'd maybe chat a little bit with my office mate but nothing too in depth, typically very superficial. I didn't really get involved in clubs or anything else that first year here. Just while I was feeling out the school and getting a sense of if this was a safe place to be myself and have all my aspects of my identity.

The second year, I know that there was a gay-straight alliance. I knew that they had an assembly every year. I wanted to get a little more involved, so I participated in the assembly. I gave a speech to the entire high school—all of the students, most of the teachers—and talked a little bit about my experience with sports and being gay. I talked about how sometimes those two identities of being an athlete and being gay stereotypically are exclusive identities but there are ways to bring them together, whether it's playing on gay sports teams or seeing mainstream athletes coming out in the media. I gave this speech before Michael Sam and Jason Collins and all these people came out. It was a timely speech a few years ago.

That was my way of coming out to the whole school. Since then, it's been a glass closet, in that I don't have to keep coming out. People know but at the same time, it's nice that the awareness is still there. I'm still involved with the GSA, which now calls itself the queer-straight alliance, so the QSA. I try to play my role as the older-history adviser. The kids are very well-read on modern gender theory, queer theory. They have all their pop culture YouTube personalities that they follow. I try to say, "But let's learn about what happened at Stonewall. Let's learn about the AIDS crisis of the 1980s and remember the history that came before that"—and stuff like that. I have a lot of outlet there to bring my personal identity to that club. I think even as a dean, a lot of times it's just getting to know the kids. They're pretty relaxed around me. They'll talk about what's going on in their lives. If a group of girls are checking out some BuzzFeed article about some hot guy, they feel comfortable, I think, asking me, and I'll be like, "No, he's not that hot." I can comfortably say that stuff.

I don't know if there was a moment of realizing that I was attracted to other guys. I guess around puberty. I don't remember a moment. It seems like as soon as one realizes they're attracted to anyone, I realized I was attracted to guys. I don't even remember as far as identities and labels when that came in. It's always been there.

I think the first friend I told, I felt like I should share this with him in college. I was a freshman. He was a senior. He'd gotten to be a good friend. I think at that point, I was just really feeling conflicted about keeping it a secret. I started to come out to friends in college. Came out to my parents when I was a junior in college, and my sister.

There's the longer process of letting people know, but then there's the process of actually accepting it and being comfortable with it. I think that's a longer process. I think I've only truly gotten what I would call "comfortable and accepting" since I've moved to New York and been here and felt like I've had to wear it as my identity. When you find yourself in those situations where you might get pushed a little bit, you're saying, "I'm not going to hide this about me anymore. I'm proud and happy of who I am."

I think a lot of that's tied to teaching, my identity as a teacher and that responsibility. There's an integrity of, "I can't stand up in front of these kids and ask them to be authentic about themselves if I'm not being fully authentic about myself." I think that's a little different than just saying, "All my friends are gay, but I'm not going to talk about it at work," or something like that. I'd say it's really only been in the last several years that I've really hit being comfortable with it.

I was brought up by very conservative parents. That's all back in central California where I grew up. Physically moving away from California, I think helped. Again, it's not a coincidence that I've worked in education, I've learned more about the value of integrity and authenticity to my identity; whereas, in a lot of career fields, people can compartmentalize a lot more. They can say, "I'm going to work at the ad agency today, and then I'm going to go home and do this." They can have their separate facets of life, whereas I feel there's something about teaching where I bring my full personal self to the school, and I bring my full academic self to my personal life. My friends all know me as a teacher and a coach. To me, that makes sense. Everything is integrated. It's the same person, just in different buildings, in different environments.

Our head of school is gay and has a husband. That's why I say that I almost feel I got to be promoted to a dean partly because I'm out. If I hadn't been, I would have just been another white male math teacher. I think our school values that. There are a few teachers that are out but, what is surprising is it's not common knowledge unless it comes up in conversation and someone tells me about their involvement in a Pride parade or something like that. You can't always assume, and not everyone wears it on their sleeve.

I try to be more aware of how students interact with each other, how they group with each other, how I interact with students. I try to be aware of their identities. If anything, I might even call on under-represented groups more often, but if I see certain guys are real eager, then I work with them to an extent. I want everyone to feel like they contribute. Without that conscious effort, a math classroom could easily turn into the white boys always raising their hand and always getting called on and everyone else being silenced. I do try to be aware of all the identities, and I think that shows. I can allow myself to be more sensitive and not always have to dominate a conversation and things like that. I'm actually fairly introverted. I think in group settings, I tend to be the one that just listens first. One-on-one, I can ramble.

I've been self-examining more my role as a male in the community. The idea that gender is not just a binary but a continuity, an idea that affects a lot of modern gender theory. This is where I learn a lot from my students. Talking about feminism and women's roles and men's roles, there's another conversation about gender not really being a binary. You can exist somewhere in the middle. You can be a man. You can be a male sexed person who identifies as male but still have some feminine traits. That's cool. You can be a female sexed woman who identifies as a woman and have some more masculine traits. That's cool.

You can identify as someone completely genderless. You could cross the mid-point and say that you're more transgender, where you identify as an opposite of your body's sex assignment at birth. It all gets very confusing. People can exist along a spectrum. Being aware of that, and how you perceive other people as well, and realizing that respect for others is important. Just because they identify as male, they're not going to have all of the same male characteristics. There isn't this ideal male or this ideal female that people have to live up to.

We have a message at the school of acceptance. It's not just tolerance: we really accept diversity. Again, it's part of our mission statement to have a diverse culture. I think the implied messages come from having an administration that is openly gay. I was able to convince our principal to talk at our last GSA assembly. She talked about her experience coming to work here and how much that meant to her to be in an environment where she could be open about her wife, whereas when she had worked in boarding schools, that was something she had to keep closer and more secret.

We had a kid come out a couple years ago. He was a football player and a hockey player and everything like that. He was actually one of my students. I was his math teacher his junior year. It was halfway through that junior year that he started to come out. He came out to his family first, and he was really worried about coming out to friends because he felt that even at this school, his friends might not accept him. He did come out, and he was embraced by everyone, almost to the point where I think it rubbed some of the other openly gay students the wrong way because he was raised up on this pedestal of being like, "Here's this golden-boy athlete who's getting all this attention for coming out." Some of the other kids felt like, "We've been out for a while, so why is he getting all the attention?"

I think it's a safe space to come out when you're ready. I don't know if we always do the best job. I don't know if there's more that we could be doing. I do feel like there are still kids who don't feel they're ready to come out here. I don't know if that's because we're not doing something or if it's just a developmental thing. Some kids will be ready when they're ready.

Jessica

I feel like you can't separate your personal identity from your identity as an educator. If you try to separate that, then you're not bringing your full self to the classroom.

I originally thought I wanted to be a basketball coach, and then I thought teaching math would be a way for me to be a basketball coach. It turned out that when I started coaching and teaching that teaching was really the thing I enjoyed a lot more because, in coaching, I wanted to be on the court more than I wanted to be on the sidelines. With teaching, I had the amount of patience necessary, and I just enjoyed that so much more. My identity as a teacher didn't really form until after I had actually been teaching for a few years.

For me, it was always much more than the subject matter. Even though I was a math teacher, I considered my relationships with my students to be much more important than the topic that I was teaching. For me, I always felt, as a math teacher, my goal was to get them to have a positive experience, especially in middle school. I feel that if I can get them to want to continue math, then I did my job. I felt that was done much more on the personal level than on the subject matter being taught, if that makes sense.

My personal identity? I guess I would consider myself an athlete still. I played college basketball, and I've remained active and interested in athletic endeavors, so that would be a big one part of my identity. I have a twin sister, so I identify very strongly with being a twin. I have very strong relationships with my family in general, so that's a strong link to my identity.

I suppose the fact that I'm a lesbian also matter. It's interesting that's not one of the first things I say, but I guess that's because I it's just part of who I am. I would definitely say that's a big part of my identity. I think as a result of that, I think my passion for equity and inclusion is a big part of who I am as a person in general, even beyond my role as an educator in that area.

I feel like you can't separate your personal identity from your identity as an educator. If you try to separate that, then you're not bringing your full self to the classroom. I think a big part of impacting kids is them seeing you for who you are and sharing that.

I was fortunate enough that I was able to teach a class within the science curriculum called Issues and Choices, where I was able to actually devote time to talking about gender and sexual diversity. At that time, I would formally come out to the students. I would do it otherwise if it just came out naturally. I would always feel a little nervous about doing that, but I always felt if there's just one kid there who can see someone who is comfortable and confident in who they are, that that makes all the difference, right? I feel that to be an effective teacher you have to bring your full self. You can't compartmentalize because kids can see right through that anyway.

When I was in college, when I was a freshman, there was a player on my team who was a fifth-year senior. We just spent a whole bunch of time together. I remember one time asking her, "Is this normal? Is this how you always are with your friends?" Even though we actually were never intimate, the feelings just were clearly beyond what you would consider normal—I hate to use that term anyway. I just stopped using that term. She really didn't want to discuss it with me, and so instead of jeopardizing that relationship, I just stopped asking her about it.

I continued to date men, kind of, in college. Then, right out of college, I started developing what felt like a similar relationship with a woman, and then eventually we actually became girlfriends. I crossed the line to, "Okay, this is actually what this is," but still feeling like, "Oh, well, it's just this person; it's not who I am." Going through and struggling through that process was hard. There really wasn't a whole lot of role models for me in 1989 or 1990.

When I came back to California, I met another woman, and then I'm like, "Okay, well, maybe this isn't just a one-time thing." I would say it was a gradual process that started when I was about 17 years old. If I look back, I could finally say, "Oh yeah! I had a crush on that college counselor" or that teammate or whatever.

I think there are lots of different levels of outness, like coming out to yourself and what you choose to say to people you just meet or to your friends. And then there's also I think your behavior when you're out in public. When you're with someone you're dating, when you hold their hand, some of that I think is also related to being out or not or your comfort level.

I definitely came out to myself first. The first person I told outside of the relationship I was in was my sister. I can't remember exactly how long it took for me to actually tell her from when I was in a relationship with a woman. It didn't happen immediately, but eventually I did tell her. Then my family: I didn't actually come out to them. They asked me.

My mom, I remember her sitting me down and saying, "You know, Tina?" Tina was kind of rumored to be one of the town lesbians or whatever. She said, "You know, people say that she's a lesbian." My first reaction was, "That doesn't mean that I don't want to be friends with her." I put it off for a while. Then, finally I was like, "You're right, mom. Yes! We're in a relationship."

Of course I said, "Please don't tell my dad." I was nervous about my dad finding out, but it turns out that he was a little more open. His reaction was a little less strong than my mom's, which really wasn't that bad compared to other stories that I've heard about. It wasn't the life that she had envisioned for me. My dad's question was to ask if I went through some horrible experience when I was young. He was thinking about something happened to me that made me be this way. My mom thought it was a phase. A couple of times she said things like, "Well, aren't you ashamed about what you're doing?" Of course that sticks. Another thing was that I had a picture of me and my partner taken, and they put that picture up in their bedroom; whereas the picture of my sister with her husband gets displayed prominently on the mantel, right?

At my school, I feel super fortunate that sexual orientation is explicitly stated in our mission statement as one aspect of diversity that we celebrate or embrace or however way you want to put it. It's part of our school to be accepting along all levels of diversity, including gender and sexuality. At least to my knowledge, I've never had any bad experiences based on my sexuality.

I feel pretty proud of the fact that I'm an open lesbian on the administrative team now. There's only been one other instance where we've had an out gay person on the admin team, and he was in development, so we never had someone at the division level or head of school. I feel really proud of that for our school. I think it's important that I have that voice.

Being a lesbian makes me very aware of how, for kids who don't identify in the binary, heteronormative way, what kind of a learning environment we're creating so that they feel comfortable and included as well. That's one area that I feel it really impacts. I also think that it just makes me more sensitive to other areas of diversity more naturally by way of being part of an oppressed group in society. I feel thankful for that. I think that's important. I would say there tends to be more female educators than male educators. If there's an opportunity to hire a male teacher, I think it's good to have more of a balance or that voice to have someone of their own gender to look up to.

The one thing for me, though, is a little bit about gender expression. Along those lines, it's something that I think about more in my new role, is how I choose to express my gender. I think it's important for people to see a woman who will sometimes wear a tie or sometimes wear a dress. I think that's good. I think it's good for all the teachers. I think it's good for the whole community to see someone who's comfortable in playing a little bit with gender expression and gender roles. I think that's an area where my gender expression will affect my job. I think it's important for everyone to see an example of someone that can cross over from what you think a woman is supposed to look like in this role.

David

I never thought that "I'm gay" should be part of my presentation. Not because I want to hide it, but just because I don't hear other teachers say "I'm heterosexual, by the way." If they don't have to disclaim their sexual orientation, why do I as a gay person have to disclaim?

It's not easy to go from a conservative school into a liberal school, so I think that I'm still opening up to being who I really am and feeling comfortable with it. I feel like the years I worked as a teacher, first at the public school and then in the private school, I have always put a mask on. I was this teacher and had to act a certain way, speak a certain way. But right now, I feel like I am really the same David I am at home or with my friends when I'm teaching. But as I said in the beginning, it is not easy, because you are not used to being yourself for the most part, in the classroom. You are also confused about what's the limits are. How much of myself am I supposed to show? And how much of myself am I supposed to cover or keep to myself?

I grew up in a Catholic school with very demanding teachers, but my parents were not extremely demanding. I think that many of those standards grow within you, and when you are teaching, a lot of that is what you have inside of you. It is sometimes impossible to control because it is so natural to you, you feel like, "This is what I'm used to doing." So, yes, I feel like my personality impacts my teaching because of all of these things.

I think that I was probably in the seventh grade when I realized I had feelings for other boys. It was very early in my life. That was in a Catholic school, so it was very atypical in the '80s to experience this. I grew up in Argentina, we didn't have anything in my school for gay kids. It was a big struggle inside of me because, as a pre-teen and teenager, I knew already what I was feeling, I tried to masquerade it a little bit.

I was pushed by a friend who I was confident talking to and who knew that I was gay. He was the one that kind of grabbed my arm and said, "Let's go." I was already 23 years old. I grew up in a time in Argentina when police would go inside gay clubs and detain everyone who was in the club. Then they took you into the police station, and you had to call your parents, who had to come and bail you out. So I was always scared of that situation of calling my mom and saying, "Hey, I'm in jail." Why are you in jail? Because you are gay. It is incredible, because twenty years after, Buenos Aires is one of the most gay cities in the world, and they have so many clubs and bars, and it's talked about on TV and on radio. Being gay is nothing extraordinary. It is so common now, but when I was growing up, it was a different story.

We've never had that conversation officially where I say, "I'm gay." My two sisters know. My mom approached me once and said, "I don't care who you are with, I just want you to be happy. I want you to know that Mom and Dad will not always be physically here with you. We want to see you happy the day that we leave." I think that those words of my mom were clear in saying, "We know what's going on. We don't need to have the formal talk." So we've never had it. With my sisters, we did.

I have one sister who is five years older, and I have a sister who is five years younger, so I'm the ham in the sandwich there. They were fine. My younger sister was easier to deal with. She was more receptive. She's a younger generation than my eldest sister. Although my older sister is fine now; she knows what's going on, she's been here, met my friends and their partners, and she doesn't feel uncomfortable around those. It's not that she doesn't want to deal with gay people. I think that I may have been one of the first gay people she ever met or dealt with. Later in life, as she knew more people, she was a little bit more okay. For my youngest sister, it's easier. She has friends she sees regularly who are gay and neighbors, so she's more used to the cause.

I don't think that my parents are going to reject me by any means because they are the most supportive and wonderful, caring parents a person can ask for. We're a very close family, all five of us, although I'm here and they are in Argentina. I call them every day. We have a very strong connection. They know what's going on in our lives.

My parents met two of my partners. They never knew exactly that they were my partners. They met them as my friends. These were partners that lasted for a year, year and a half, so nothing was a very long-term relationship. I thought, "If I don't have a long-term relationship, why am I going to tell them, if this is not going to last?" The moment I break up with any of them, they are going to be suffering because I'm breaking up. That's how it felt.

I teach the grades when they start developing feelings. I teach the grades where they start trying to decide whether they like a boy or a girl. Because I didn't have any teacher who approached me when I was growing up, I thought it [being gay] was wrong. I thought it was bad. I don't want my students to grow that feeling inside of them that if you are in love with a boy, it's something wrong. Or if you're a girl and you're in love with a girl, it's something wrong. I think that we teachers many times go beyond teaching our core subjects. We go beyond and teach about life. I think that teaching about life would be just telling them, "It's okay. It might be a little bit harder, it might not, depending on you."

Being openly gay means I don't have to put on a mask and fake being a macho male. If you were talking about your family, you don't have to hide. We can call our partner "husband" now because we can get married. In the past, it was impossible, but now you can say husband. So I think that that's it: if you're dating someone, and you're in love and you put a picture of your loved one on your desk, no one is going to be like, "Oh, who's that? Your brother?" "No, it's my partner." I feel like that's a little bit more openly gay. It's just the opportunity to tell students, "This is me."

I think the other thing I had carried was the label "Latino," and I think that from the understanding of a lot of people, Latinos are very macho oriented. In a macho society, it is harder to be Latino and gay. It is not the case in Argentina anymore, at least, but it might be harder in other countries. It might be harder in Central America and other parts of South America. I think that through other teachers, I don't have a problem if they ask me to say, "Yes, I'm gay." But I don't feel like I need to announce it. If you realized or if you ask me, that's fine, no problem, but I don't feel the need to announce it. No one goes walking down the street saying, "I'm heterosexual," so why should I say, "I like men"?

In my school setting, being openly gay, I think I'm treated just as any other human being. It's just that kindness above all. No matter whether you're gay or straight, you're treated with respect, you're treated with kindness. You have that prerogative, that freedom of saying, "My partner's name is John." If you're going into a celebration, they say, "Bring your significant other." And your significant other might be someone of your own gender. Even little things like in the paperwork, where parents are signing up their child, it doesn't say "mother/father," but "parent one/parent two." Those type of little details make a big difference.

I think that I'm treated with respect. I'm treated with kindness. I don't think that anyone is talking behind my back because I'm gay, which is always a fear that you have in other places. I'm okay with them knowing, but I'm not okay with all the talking behind my back. Here, I don't have to worry about that and if they're trying to send me to a psychologist, psychiatrist, or wherever to heal me or cure me.

I think that even male teachers have a lot of characteristics that are probably not common in males. Like male teachers are caring, are understanding, we have to be listening, we have to be parenting. A lot of the time, it doesn't matter if you are gay or heterosexual; that's just your job. That's how you have to deal with students. I did not choose to be a teacher because I'm gay. I love being with students, and I teach adults also, so that idea of sharing, communicating is important. Other than that, how my being gay impacted my career, I don't know.

I don't think it is a priority to tell my students when I introduce myself that I'm gay. If they ask me, they can know that yes, I am. I tell them a lot of things about me. I tell them I'm from Argentina, I tell them I'm a vegetarian, I tell them I'm home alone here because my parents and everybody's in Argentina, but I never thought that "I'm gay" should be part of my presentation. Not because I want to hide it, but just because I don't hear other teachers say "I'm heterosexual, by the way." If they don't have to disclaim their sexual orientation, why do I as a gay person have to disclaim? I always feel that way. Others don't have to say, why do I have to say?

I like being gay. I like being Latino, and I like being a male. I mean, I'm confident and comfortable with all of that. I think that I have a huge responsibility on my shoulders, especially to show Latino kids that not all of us end up in construction or landscaping or as service or cooks in a restaurant. I have an enormous responsibility of showing them you can be professional, and you can be gay also if you want. It's not a bad thing. A lot of them will grow up thinking gay is a bad thing.

Although the newer generations are changing because of what they see on TV and what they are listening to on the radio and exposure to media. It's easier for them to see what's going on in the gay world. For me, it was hard. I remember going out for the first time being completely scared of running into one of my students. Am I going to tell if I run into one of my students at a gay club? So this friend that pushed me to the clubs would say, "You know, if you run into a student at a gay club, it means that your student is also gay, so most likely he'll be happy to see you here and it would not be a problem."

Barbara

Now, I understand there are a lot of complicated reasons why people do or do not come out. But, in high school, we needed [that teacher] to come out.

I had always been a theater kid, and I didn't know exactly what I wanted to pursue in terms of vocation. I went through phases. I wanted to be rabbi, I wanted to be...I don't even know. In college, I got really involved in a lot of social justice education communities, and leadership in those spaces, and then I also performed—I did improv.

For a very a long time I compartmentalized. I mean, it was like, "This is the indulgent thing I do, and this is the meaningful thing I do, and I'll figure out later what that means." It wasn't until I was leaving college that I was like, "Wait a second, I am a complete person. I don't have parts of myself; I'm not different and turning it on and off when I'm in different places. This is actually, to me, important, and maybe I can use the politics of embodiment, a voice of enactment, in my theater work, and use theater as a tool in these spaces as well." And maybe it's through teaching that I'm able to occupy multiple parts of myself and my identity.

I decided, "This is my dream, I want to teach theater is what I really want." I almost did Teach for America, but I had too many issues with the program. I knew there was a part of me that wanted to pursue performing myself, and I knew that was going to be impossible if I did Teach for America, and so I was like, "This is something I really want to do, so how am I going to make it work?" I fell into it through doing after-school and subbing, not just for the theater department here, but I was like their super-sub, and I was subbing everywhere and learning about teaching. Then a position opened up, and I was like, "This is a dream come true."

I am very non-hierarchical in my teaching. I really try to emphasize that I have some knowledge of experience, and my students do not have that. I can share, but this is a communal process and it's a conversation and dialog. For a long time I didn't even want to go by "Miss," but you can't go by your first name here—it's really, really, really, really, really frowned upon. But, I was like, "There are so many other ways to share respect."

In my classroom, I ask a lot of questions. I'm very aware of the dynamic in the space, so if students' minds are occupied with something else, I won't be like, "You need to push that aside and we need to keep talking." I will be like, "Okay, I'm noticing that this is more important, so we need to go in this direction." I feel like I get a lot of freedom, especially because it is the theater class, to do that in my classes a lot, or just like, "Okay, well, we all went to this assembly and we feel some sort of way about it, let's talk about it more." Or, "You all are not taking care of yourselves. Take a 15-minute nap right now, you have to. This is your homework."

I emphasize community so much in my classes, which is interesting because this year I had nine students in my tenth-grade acting class, and I felt like I had to teach nine different classes at times, because everybody's skills are so different. Some people want to be professional actors, and some people are like, "This is just the class I take because I have to take an art class." But everybody contributes according to their ability, and everybody gets out what they need. That's not equality, it's equity, you know what I mean? That is something that I try to model in my classes: it's about meeting people where they're at and trying to then push them to do the best that they can in those spaces.

I was a very out student here, so when I came back I was like, "Well, I fought so hard to come out then, so I'm going to be out now." Also, any student who picked up a yearbook from 2006 or 2007 would figure it out pretty easily.

I remember how frustrated I was as a student there. The only out women teachers were PE teachers; I got mad love for the PE department. I'm not a sporty girl, so I didn't have role models. I actually had this really weird thing with a teacher who was super, super, super, super closeted, but I only figured it out at the end of school. She would write me these really coded report cards about how much I reminded her of herself. I was so angry at her because I was like, "Just come out, then. Come on." Now, I understand there are a lot of complicated reasons why people do or do not come out. But, high school, we needed her to come out.

For a long time I was very, and I still am, clear about who I am, but what I do really isn't their business. For the most part, students know that I'm gay. Now, gay is one of my identities, but to add new ones to it, I would usually identify as queer. But, I'm not going to get into [my sexuality]: "Well, you know, I'm with a woman, and I've had the most satisfying relationships with women." I'm not going to say all of that.

Recently, I've gotten a little more open about just saying, "My girlfriend this," if it comes up with older students. If they ask me [if I'm gay], I don't say no, but I don't have a picture of her on my desk, because I think that's flashy no matter who you are. I still can't believe I have a desk. (As a performer, of course, one of my identities is being a comedian.)

It obviously isn't forming everything that I do. I feel like it comes out in different ways. My tenth graders, a class of predominantly boys—and not just boys but athletic boys—and I started talking about how I was excited when Michael Sam got drafted to the NFL. Then it became this joke in class of like, "Teach Miss Barbara about sports, because she doesn't know anything about sports, and explain football, and explain what Michael Sam is doing." That was this thing in class that they enjoyed—educating me. It was this little joke between us, so they understood the context for why I cared about Michael Sam in the first place.

There was an assembly once and they were like, "Miss Barbara, we know you feel something about this. What did you think? And don't give us a teacher answer—tell us what you really think." I'm very upfront about my positionality and my politics. I do that to say, "This is my opinion. This is how I'm filtering the class. But I want to hear your other opinion because I don't want you to think this is the only one."

My coming out has been a journey since seventh grade, well, maybe fourth, but in seventh grade, I was like, "Oh, I think I'm bisexual." Then, it was an evolution. By the time I left high school, I was like, "I need to figure out am I gay or am I bi?" Then I was like, "Okay, I'm gay, I'm gay." Then I started to realize that sexuality in general is more complicated, and my sexuality is more complicated, and it's more political and politicized, which is why I've also claimed "queer," which is usually how I describe myself. Lesbian is a word I've never liked, for some reason, so I've never used it to describe myself; I've always said that I was gay or queer or bi.

I don't believe in a gender binary, so I'm not bisexual. Yes, I find myself attracted to men, but I know that I don't want to engage in sex with them. I just find them hot. It's much more complicated, and I'm much more comfortable with it being complicated, because I was searching for a label for, I don't know, five years. I was like, "I must label myself and know what my true identity is." Now, I'm always surprised by what my own impulsive attraction. "Okay, well, that's a part of me now. Yes, yes, I am attracted to trans-women. Okay." Because I'm in a relationship that is not monogamous in politics but is monogamous in practice, does it matter whether that's something I act on? To me, it doesn't.

Yeah, so it's just become more complicated. But that started this whole journey of naming it, and very much just being like, "This is who I am,." Coming out to my parents, they were like, "You are 13, what are you talking about?" I was like, "No, I have a girlfriend. We talk on Instant Messenger," which is what all relationships at that age are now.

I've always been a really open person, and I've always had, to a fault, a no-boundaries relationship with my parents. What that means is when doors are closed, they don't care. I knew that I wanted to tell them; there wasn't a thought in my mind that I wouldn't. Similarly, being out at school, there wasn't a thought in my mind that I would conceal that information. Of course, when you're young, it spreads like wildfire. I was a precocious kid, and I talked a big mess. I talked a huge talk, more than I would walk the walk. I would say very sexually explicit things because I had just learned what they meant, so I was that kind of kid. I think high school people were mostly cool, they didn't really care. There was the, "Would you have a threesome with this person?" conversation a lot. Guys were like, "Do you think she's hot?" which was a conversation starter.

It was fine. I guess I realized it's fine because I was able to be out and never feared for my safety, and I've never really felt that judged even. I got pretty gutsy by the time I was leaving school, and I remember there was this ninth-grade girl who I thought was really cute, and I asked my friend to ask her what she thought of me. It happened, she was probably the most conservative girl in the entire school, and she was just like, "No, I'm not interested." She looked at me funny for the rest of school, but I think the hardest thing for me was just not having someone to date. I just was desperate to date people, and that was impossible because there was nobody that was out. There were one or two people, and they were all my friends. That was challenging.

My parents struggled to see me as a sexual person period, and they so quickly conflated identity with the sex part. Then, there was also this: "You don't know what you're talking about. It's just a phase. You haven't had that much experience." In ninth grade, I had a boyfriend for a long time, and I was very much still firm in my identity as bisexual at that point. The guy I dated was completely aware of that and supportive. But I think my parents thought, "Oh, great, this is over. Here's a dude." Then I had a girlfriend in eighth grade, which was a great two-week thing. Then, I dated a guy, and then in 11th grade, I had another girlfriend, so I came out to them again, and they were like, "Oh, yeah, like what you said before." I was like, "Yeah, that thing is still a thing."

Then, in college I started dating my girlfriend that I'm with now, and I was like, "I need you to actually be happy for me and supportive." It was a really long process. Now, of course, my sister, my younger sister has a girlfriend and identifies as queer; they don't even bat a damn eyelash. They don't care. I mean, they do care, but it's so not an issue, and I so would not have seen that coming. That always reminds me time is really amazing.

I still closet myself sometimes because I have to for a safety reason. I'm trying to think of an example. When my girlfriend and I went to Jamaica, we were at a resort and were just walking around the resort. It's mostly Jamaican tourists, Canadian tourists, US tourists. At one point I just grabbed her hand, and she was like, "Barbara, we are basically in Uganda right now. Stop." I was like, "Whoa, wait, what?" It also made me wonder, "What does it mean to be closeted?"

To me, being out means I talk about my relationship, I talk about my identity. If someone asks me a heteronormative question, I redirect it, or I clarify. I don't let them assume: I talk about my relationship, I talk about my friends that are gay, I talk about issues that are important to me. I mean, it's hard. In college, you literally could put a poster up in your room, and that was enough. That was coming out. It's funny, because on Facebook, for example, I don't say who I'm attracted to, yet I'm super-duper out in the content that I post.

I'm a faculty advisor for GLOW, our Gay, Lesbian, Or Whatever club. My co-advisor actually was my advisor in seventh grade, so he and I worked together with GLOW; he came out to my advisor group when I was in seventh grade. I'll never forget the impact that he had on me, and now we get to work together, which is so cool. He pushed back on the students, and was like, "In a perfect world we wouldn't have to come out." He's like, "I'm with you, but this is not a perfect world, and there is something powerful about stepping forward and being counted." When he said that, I was like, "Oh, you're so right."

I think it was interesting to see this because I can't tell sometimes if it's generational. Was I like that at that age? Or is there a difference between kids that are ten years younger than me, eight years younger than me? Is there that much of a difference? Which is something that I think about a lot, and I don't know. What does being out mean to them? To them it means not having to talk about it at all. That's what I see: they want it to be as much of a non-issue as possible. Personally, I think that's probably something internalized homophobia they're dealing with. I think that there needs to be some moment of just saying it. Now, should straight people have to come out? Yeah, of course, they should. We shouldn't assume anything about anyone. It's annoying that you have to come out if you're non-normative; but, I do think that being out is an important thing, and to me, it's something that I live every day.

I came out to my parents four times. I come out to every person I meet a new time. I come out to people that make assumptions when I say "girlfriend" the first 400 times, because they think, "She must mean, 'Hey girlfriend.'" It is a constant process being out and living out, and practicing outness, and it looks different at different times. Sometimes it means holding hands in public, and sometimes it means explaining to someone, "This how I feel."

I feel like there are cliques in the faculty. Definitely being married and having kids has so much cultural capital here, and being on a marriage track is good enough. People my age getting engaged and that kind of thing, and I'm like, "That's just not my thing." It doesn't mean that people aren't supportive, but it's just like the culture is not one that has space in it already for me, so I have to make that space. Sometimes I feel like I'm the one that everyone calls me when it's like, "Oh, we need to talk about something gay. Let's call in Barbara."

In some ways I really love that because I'm like, "I'd rather you talk to me than someone else." But, in other ways, I'm like, "Jeez, this is exhausting." Sometimes, I can't tell if my colleagues that are out to me or out to their students and what that means, but there are more out teachers, period. That is a fact, and they are teaching in a wide variety of places, and they are holding positions of power, and that is great.

I think being out is something I couldn't *not* do, and maybe I could do it in a different way. Sometimes I think, "I wish people didn't know my business. Get away from my business!" But I share my business, so that's me, but if I went somewhere new, maybe I would just be more private in general. Here it just didn't feel right given the fact that I became who I am in this space, basically, and that's obviously a real specific context.

For me queer is not just who I am interested in, or whoever I sleep with. At the most basic level to me, it's not just who I fuck, but how I fuck, and how I live, and obviously I don't share this with my students, but it is a lens through which I understand people and power. I think that's it, really: I'm interested in "queering" teacher. To me, queer is a verb, and queering teaching is about power, knowledge, and how we share, and respect, and create community. Those are things that I'm interested in fucking with, and for the better and stretching them to their full potential, and really seeing what happens when we do that as a community. What are the possibilities? What are our creative options?

Matthew

*I think, in our fight for equality, we should not be labeling
ourselves. If we're truly to be equal, then I can't be
the gay band director. I've got to be the band director.
My identity is not in my sexual orientation.*

I did not intend to be a teacher. My degrees are in music performance, not in education. I was teaching in Tennessee, just a one-year entering teacher there, and it was a stopgap to help the school rebuild a music program, almost the same situation at D.C. I was brought in to rebuild a program. That's my specialty in church work is repairing broken or declining programs, breathing new life into declining programs. That is what I was brought in to do in both cases.

I'm not a traditional music teacher who is after perfection from the get-go. My identity as a teacher is more inspirational. I want to instill a love of music in the students first, so instilling a love of the content matter is my first goal. Because I believe that if I can instill that joy and that passion in the students, they will strive for the perfection on their own. If I start demanding perfection from day one, then it's off-putting for the students; instead of a collaborative effort, it's more of a dictatorship.

I don't want to be known as the gay teacher or that gay organist. I want to be known as an educator and as a performer. I feel that part of what we strive for in equality should not come with that label. I'm in a legal battle right now, which you can look up online. I'm being labeled as the gay band director. I think, in our fight for equality, we should not be labeling ourselves. If we're truly to be equal, then I can't be the gay band director. I've got to be the band director. My identity is not in my sexual orientation.

My first realization was probably when I was seven, when I did not conform to the stereotypes. But I didn't really even come out to myself until I was in my 20s. That process was difficult, because I was raised in a very conservative, Christian home with those "traditions." For lack of better terminology, I tried to fix myself. I went through reparative therapy. I was involved in what a lot of people would label as a cult. I was involved in a group that was supposed to fix me during my first three, four years of college. It wasn't until I realized there was nothing to fix that I was able to come to grips with who I was personally. I was 25 before I came out to my family.

There were mixed feelings on that with my family. I don't know a parent who wants their child to be gay, not because of sexual orientation but because of the experiences that coming out comes with, the experiences that can be hurtful and harmful to us as people. I don't know a parent that wants their child to go through that. My parents did not want this because of that. It hurt them that I didn't tell them sooner, so there was some pain there on their side. Since then, we've cleared that up. They very much support me and my relationship and what I do and who I am.

For me, it's not that I just proclaim that from a soapbox. It's just not changing who I am or how I'm perceived. If someone asks me, then I'll answer truthfully. For me in the workplace, because I am a church musician first, it can be a very hostile environment whether you're gay or not. Church work is not easy. I was run out of a church in Texas when they found out that I was gay. That was in 2004. Since then, every job interview I've had has started out with, "I'm gay. If you have a problem with that, I don't need to work here." I've been very upfront and honest with that, because I don't want that same experience. I don't want to involve my life for two or three or four years and then have that be the reason I'm pulled out of a situation. I've been very upfront with hiring entities about that.

Students knew I was gay because they went to my Facebook page, and they found pictures on Facebook. The administration knew because I told them in my first interview who I am. One of the administrators is actually a member of the church where I was serving at the time. She is still very close with my partner and I, so that's not something that I hide. It's not something that I speak about in the classroom, because I don't believe that's the place, but I'm not going to hide if I am asked.

I don't conform to a lot of stereotypes. As a musician, a lot of musicians are seen as scattered and unorganized. That part of the brain that is the creative part is not the logical part, and I don't conform to that stereotype. I am highly organized. I am ambitious. I am driven, and I know how to get what I want. I've been in church work for 20 years, so I know how to work the politics side of things to get what I want and get what I need for my program. Part of the reason I was not treated differently is because I don't conform to that stereotype, and I don't conform to the huge world stereotype of what a gay person looks like or how they behave. I don't wear that on my sleeve. Unless somebody knows me, they don't really know that about me. I don't choose to make it my identity.

Because it was a Catholic school, there's a mixed message in the teaching of homosexuality. The Catholic church sees homosexuality as a disorder. It's disordered in nature, despite the fact that there are scientific studies of other species of animals with same-sex proclivities, it is seen as a disorder in the human race by the Catholic church. Basically, what the students are told is, "It's okay to be gay; it's just not okay to act on it." I think there's a disconnect there, and it comes from that teaching in the Catholic church. It's okay as long as you are in the closet and don't do anything about it.

The school has made it very clear that they did not fire me because I was gay. That's been a statement from day one. "We did not fire Mr. Matthew because he was gay. We fired him because he's getting married, and that goes against the Catholic teachings of the sanctity of marriage between one man and one woman." I don't think that it was homophobia so much as just flat out discrimination, which was painful to be on the receiving end when I had been so welcomed at the school.

Donald

Any other straight person could have a picture of their family up there, have their wedding ring on, talk about their weekend with their family, but for me, I feel living and being out isn't necessarily waving a rainbow flag every day. It's me being comfortable, being able to talk about my life and my husband and my brother and his husband, and to talk about my life in a way that is honest and just normal.

I'm totally gay. I am a really gay guy. I need to talk about that a lot. Everybody knows that. The kids know that, and when I started at here, I was very much thinking that's just a part of me and compartmentalizing my life in different places. I'm funny and I'm sarcastic, and the kids know that I love them and they know that my sarcasm comes from a place of actually liking them. They know that I'm sincere and that I'm sweet, but they know that I'm sincere and a nice guy but have a really good sense of humor and never say anything really serious.

When I do get upset with kids, they can immediately tell. It's like when your parent yells at you or when your teacher gets mad at you that's my personality, but I generally operate with a smile and good motivation. I think I am actually a little bit more reserved at times, like at a conference or something, just a little bit more quiet and reserved. But I think that I'm still sincere, I'm still sarcastic. My child is totally sarcastic. He gets it from me, but I feel I'm pretty much the same person just maybe a little bit less "on" when I'm not on a stage teaching.

I'm a twin. I think the kids think it is cool that I am a twin, so we talk about that sometimes, but I also talk a lot. I talk about my family. My kids know I have a kid at school, and sometimes they'll say, "Hey, Mr. Donald your husband is upstairs waiting for you." I think it's just part of who I am outside of the classroom—not everything but a big part of my life and they definitely know. I have had incidences where it makes some families uncomfortable, so it's been interesting to navigate that too.

I'm in charge of social media, and I do a lot of advertising stuff. There's an awful website here, and it's a place for parents to post anonymous stuff, for people to ask questions generally. It's totally snaky and messy. Somebody started posting an LGBT event for LGBT parents. This person kept posting they didn't like the gay agenda. "What was this agenda?" people kept trying to say. "We do all kinds of events. Black student fun fair, Latino fan fair, we go to Arlington, we go to PG County." But they just couldn't get the gay agenda thing out of their head. It ended up being one of advisees parents that kept talking about it because I could tell through her comments who she was. She ended up having to talk to head of school who set her straight. I got over it. If they are uncomfortable with it, that's their problem. They can deal with it because that's who we are as a school. It's not all the time, but it's every once in a while. There's going to be little blips along the way.

I didn't come out until I was 22. I have an identical twin gay brother, and we both came out together. I came out to my dad when I was 22. I came out to my college professor when I was a freshman, and I came out to my brother and he came out to me. It's the same time because we never talked about it before. We both came out to my dad when we were 22; we wrote him a letter.

It was weird because we grew in the Midwest. We didn't talk about anything. We never dated anybody growing up. We were fat, band kids. We were in the band and then the speech and debate team. We just had a big group of friends we hung out with. Sexuality, dating was something we never talked about.

I remember it was in college because he went to the same college as I did, and we were just walking along with my friend, Meg, and my brother on a nice sunny day. I just told him I was gay, and then he wrote me an email to tell me that he was gay. We were roommates, but he couldn't tell me—he had to email me! In our heads, we thought were going to be alone for the rest of our lives...plus, there was nobody else out there like us. Then we went to college, and we watched *The Real World: New York* and saw that there are people like us out there.

Coming out to my dad, I was worried. We wrote him a letter. When he got the letter, he called us and said, "No matter what, I love you; you are still my sons." Then, we were just out. He just left this morning. He was out here for a week, and we were over at game night with friends. A bunch of gay guys playing Cards Against Humanity, and my dad was there. And they love my dad and my dad had a really good time. He's a Navy vet, and he's been really awesome support.

Being openly gay means being who you are. For me, it is just being honest with who I am and not feeling like I have to hide it and not tip toe around people to talk about my life when I feel like any other straight person could have a picture of their family up there, have their wedding ring on, talk about their weekend with their family, but for me, I feel being out isn't necessarily waving a rainbow flag every day. It is me being comfortable, being able to talk about my life and my husband and my brother and his husband—and my husband's brother and his brother (because we are all gay twins) in a way that is honest and just normal. My partner, my husband's brother is also gay, and we are both twins. My husband is a twin and both of our twin brothers are gay.

All teachers at my school know I am gay. They don't care, but kids didn't know. I mean kids don't think about it really. There were some kids that were doing something I thought was homophobic in my class. This had to be maybe 10 or 12 years ago. I said, "Stop. What you are doing can be considered homophobic." They were my middle school band class. They said, "It's not homophobic." And I said, "It is homophobic because I think it's homophobic because I'm gay." I was convinced I would lose my job.

I had to tell the head of school and they were all right. I think that generally it's okay at my school to be out. Like I said, I think there are still people that maybe disagree with that. I think the biggest piece is religion and African-American families and feeling that there is going to be a natural conflict there. We have to be respectful. At the same time I'm looking at it as a civil rights issue and not a religious issue.

It drives me nuts sometimes that I am the go-to gay for middle school stuff. Teachers will be like, "Hey, I want to ask you if this is offensive or if this will work for coming-out day for my classroom?" I was like, "How about you figure it out? How about you get up on the issues and figure it out as a straight person so that it's not just the gay guy doing it!" But I guess I'm happy to do it. I guess there are moods when I'm tired of being the one who talks about it.

It's me feeling comfortable with taking my husband to school events. Whether it's a teacher event or whether it's a parent event (because we are parents at the school too) and just feeling welcomed and comfortable and not feeling you have to leave him at home or somewhere or pretend that he doesn't exist.

I feel like I'm attuned to different things because I'm gay. When I'm talking to kids and human development class, I just don't assume. I'm sure there are kids in that group that are gay, so I need to make sure that you broaden the language that you are using. My life experiences as being a gay person totally influence how I look, how I react to kids, look at kids, think about kids, especially when there's a kid I think they might be gay. Is that kid depressed? Does that kid have friends? Is that kid being teased? Are there other things that are impacting that kid? Could it be their sexual orientation? I feel that part of me has an external flag that comes up and just pays attention to kids that might need a little extra help or might need figuring out if they are gay.

I've been to so many diversity conferences that I always recognize I'm a white male that has privilege and that sometimes means shut up and listen to people. I love to talk, and I love to be funny, and I love to be sarcastic, but I think that, for me, the diversity training that I've gone through has allowed me to recognize it.

I grew up poor and gay, whatever. I'm still a white guy, and I have a lot of privilege because of that and sometimes I recognize that. I think I have to step back and realize the privilege. I never really felt super comfortable in all male groups, does that make sense? That I'm always assuming that straight guys are thugs and are going to judge me. They are going to be mean, and I don't have time for that. I think that I naturally pull away from that.

I feel we do a good job in the high school, in the middle school. But sometimes we still fall into the trap kids are too young to hear about that. A lot of times people conflate homosexuality and they immediately have to think about sex. We do the "Day of Silence" and "National Coming-Out Day" in the middle school and the high school.

I don't know what qualifies as homophobia. We had a Facebook incident a few years ago, several years ago, where a kid started a Facebook group called "I Hate Gay People." I was at a meeting for Gay Student Alliance, and I said, "That makes me feel unsafe." I was whisked up to the head of school's office and told I wasn't allowed to say that because I was an administrator, which I thought was a bunch of bullshit, but I am sure she wouldn't say that anymore. I think the head of school has grown in a lot of ways. There was a girl who was threatened on Tumblr. If she brought a girl to prom, she was going to be killed. I think that the school reacted effectively and efficiently. Nothing has been directed towards me directly, but indirectly with those incidences. And who knows if it was even a kid from the school who said it? Those moments remind and make me pause a little bit.

There's a woman she hates me. I know she hates me. She's a lesbian, and finally she got married to her partner and actually talked about it in public, but she never said anything about it before, ever. I just saw that as a model of shame for kids who were gay. The message was they should never talk about it, they should never be who they are. How do you combat that respectfully and give her space but at the time try to help her and others in the community realize that that model is one of potential harm for kids that want to live their lives out loud? I am not going to be a model of shame.

Patricia

> *I still don't know if I can check that box, but I think like it would seem a lot easier, a smoother transition, so to speak, for a woman who is open about her sexuality, her sexual orientation, than it would be for a male teacher in a school environment.*

You know I tried to stay away from education as much as possible because I come from a family of educators. My grandparents were both educators for a while, both in middle school and high school and the collegiate level.

I was trying to go to med school. That was working. I was on my way. I went into this English class, loved it, and said, "Oh, I can major in English and still go to med school," and it didn't happen that way. I said, "Okay, well I'll teach college," and I did.

For five years, I taught at a university while I was working on my doctorate, while I was working on my master's. This will probably be a little confusing to you. I was married at the time, and my husband and I lived between where he worked and I worked, so it was about 45-minute commute. I said, "I think I should find a job closer to home." I just applied to the first independent school that I found, and I just fell in love with middle schoolers and independent schools.

Linda is the first woman I've ever been attracted to. She is the first and only woman I've ever been in a relationship with. Just talking about my personal identity, I don't even know if I can categorize myself as bisexual. I fell in love with a woman. I fell in love with her as a human being. I think that's just her personality. I was physically attracted to her, but her spirit is what is really attractive too. We were friends for a while before, and I knew she was gay. We've known each other for eight years now, so I've known. I've known her in other relationships.

We didn't hang out so much outside of school, but she said she developed feelings for me a while ago. She didn't want to because I was married. She was like, "That would have just been complicated." We've been together for two years now.

I think I started telling people who I was comfortable with first. You know, like my really close friends. They were kind of like, "What?" But then saying, "We just want you to be happy." I was like, "This is easy. Why do people make this sound so difficult?" Everybody I talk to is okay.

Linda really fought us being in a relationship because she said, "I don't want you to get hurt." I was like, "Hurt? Who's going to hurt me? Are you going to hurt me?" She was like, "No, your family. I've been through this." I was like, "My family's going to be fine."

My family is fine with other people, not someone in their family, so my cousin, who like me has kind of branched out, lived in Connecticut for a while, lived in New York for a while. He's in L.A. Now, he's like, "Oh, I love Linda."

But my mom she says, "I like Linda. But why can't she just be your best friend?" I was like, "Well she is, but we're also in a relationship. She's good, my daughters love her." She's making it about her. It's kind of hard. Having that wall put up with my mom is making it difficult to kind of share with my other family members. I have two aunts who know, and they've met Linda and welcomed her with open arms.

I haven't shared her with my grandparents. I don't want my heart broken again by people who have one perception of them, and I even told my mom, "How did I not realize that I had all of these biased family members?" One of my brothers knows and the other doesn't. It's becoming strenuous on our relationship because I feel like I'm hiding her now. I was for awhile just open and just happy with us being together. Now it's kind like, well this one person has denied our existence or can't acknowledge it or accept it, so now I feel like if I tell someone else will they say the same thing. It's hard.

We just had Pride Week here. Sometimes I feel like I don't fit in. I've never been the type of person to want to put myself in a box or categorize, but other people do it. I'm in a relationship with a woman, so does that mean you're a lesbian? I've gotten this from my ex-husband. It's having me question my identity a lot. Was I hiding it? Was I repressing these feelings? I don't feel like I was. I was in a sorority, I had 37-line sisters. It was like nothing. I don't know. Right now, I think it's having me question where do I fit in. Like is there another, a box that we haven't created yet?

Pretty much everyone knows that we are in a relationship. If they don't know, they assume it. I have not disclosed with our new head of school. He just finished his first year. I'm sure he's gotten wind. My middle school director, my colleagues, the middle school team leader—everyone in middle school knows. They've been to our house for retreats and things of that nature.

Linda is a very private person, but once we were in a relationship she became a lot more open and willing to share. A colleague of mine in her 60s, who I team teach with, is the mother figure at the school. She was just saying, "You know I just want you to be happy. I know Linda's a good person, but I'm just concerned about you." She wanted to make sure I was making the right decision. Others were shocked, but they were happy for the both of us.

You know, the Bible belt is really like two feet away. I would say that even though we're a progressive school, it's not as progressive as a school would be in the D.C. area, which is where our middle school director came from. He was used to having a Pride Week at his school, and we don't have that. I think that's a direction he's trying to lead us to. Also, this is our first year that we've had a gay straight student alliance. This is the first year and something that is new for us. But we can do more work on parent education, although I haven't heard any negative noise from the parents. I think we have a pretty safe environment.

We had a student who I was introduced to as Amy, and he came to school last year as Andy. My assumption is this is our first transgender student that we've had. A few parents were kind of like, "What's going on?" The students and the faculty members embraced him and gave him his space at the same time, and let that identity evolve as he wanted it to.

I think some teachers, especially the older teachers, are struggling. I have a five-year-old daughter who is a super hero fanatic, so Linda and I put Spider Man all over her locker, her cubby. She had some of her peers saying, "Those are for boys."

The teachers are quick—some of them, not all of them—are quick to have that teachable moment, and ask why can't girls? Can't boys play with? I'm constantly having those conversations. It's inconsistent, but they're trying I think. We just need to continue. We just hired a Director of Diversity. In the past we had Diversity Council. Just that continued education is necessary for the kids and for the adults in the building.

That same teacher I was talking about who is kind of like a mother figure to me, she'll say something like, "I need some strong boys to help me move a table." She's kind of gotten out of that habit because we said, "Well, I'm sure there are some strong girls who can help you too." That is the culture she was raised in, so getting her out of those habits is going to take a while.

You'll still hear teachers say, "Boys,'" thinking they have to be strong or they can't cry. We have a lot of criers. Boys and girls even in eighth grade. They're kind of in tune and sensitive in that way and know it's okay. Some of them, but not all.

I would say that the messages that are being sent about being male or being female are a little inconsistent at our school. The message on our website is that we're accepting of everyone. I am on the admissions committee, and looking at the files and having conversations with our admissions staff, they are always looking to diversify our families and our student body. I would say in admissions they are open, and they are accepting. Not all teachers are. Not all students are either. It's just part of the parent education. We talk about diversity education and character education just being one in the same. We're a work in progress, I think.

John

I've had students before who've basically come out to me. So, I think that would have never happened if I had never been completely open to them, because they did understand that I was someone that they could trust.

My mother and father did everything to discourage me from becoming a teacher. Not that they didn't admire the profession; in fact, my dad was a politician and local government official, and he was very supportive of teachers and education. But I think that like so many parents, they always thought I could do something better, you know? And yet, my dad comes from a family of teachers. His brother retired after 30 years. His sister retired after 30 years.

I came out very late, in the sense that I was married to a woman for ten years. I lost both my parents when I was in my early twenties. I think in some ways that definitely affected my coming out, in interesting ways. A lot of people would think, "Oh, you didn't come out because you were afraid to come out to your parents." That wasn't an issue for me because my mom and dad both died when I was 22. But I did sort of continued with the role that I guess I had always been expected to assume, which was to have a wife and children.

Fortunately, I reached a point, ten years in, when I realized that this isn't me and it's not going to bring me long-term happiness. My wife at the time was very supportive. She was very hurt initially, as you would expect, but getting over that, she's been my biggest fan and one of my biggest supporters. We're still very close friends.

I wasn't out to students or even faculty when I first came out because when I divorced, I moved back to the States and found myself at a very conservative, formal military school, in the middle of South. There were, certainly, a handful of openly gay faculty; well, I would say, there were certainly a handful of gay faculty, none of whom were really open. I think they very much led the two lives. You know, the mix-of-pronouns game that everyone seems to play. I never, at all, felt comfortable in that environment.

It really wasn't till I came here that I came out in a professional setting. Then it was slow to happen. It's again, navigating the waters very cautiously. I understood the school's reputation, and there's still, in my opinion, a great risk in coming out. It took me a while to figure out the students here as well as the parents.

I really decided about three years into my tenure here that—I don't know if "duty" is the right word—but I had a sense of obligation to the students that I taught, mostly based on my own personal experience. I didn't have openly gay role models when I was growing up. Of course, I'm 49 now; times have certainly changed. But even so, I'm subtle. I never stand before my class and announce it. I often share with them the essay that I shared with you, a very personal essay, about self-discovery.

I do choose at least one book a year that has an openly gay subtext so that book can serve as a springboard for discussion. I try to make the environment comfortable enough that they feel like they can ask questions. I'm usually successful in doing that.

Seventh graders, which is primarily who I teach, it's still a slippery slope with them. Some of them just don't understand. The whole idea of sexuality is a new experience. A lot of them haven't had open conversations about it. They don't have the maturity of, say, the eighth graders. I don't think any of them were surprised to learn I was gay. I think that gossip always does my preliminary work for me. Kids, when they land here, probably know, because it's not something I hide.

We do serve some students and families who are very conservative. I think that, with them, there's this struggle because they know me as a person, and they know me as a teacher. I'd like to think they respect me in that role. They come from very conservative homes where homosexuality is still a sin and homosexuals are going to burn in hell. I think they're really caught in this dilemma between what they've always heard at home and heard at church, versus here's a real, live gay man who seems to have the respect of his colleagues and the people he works with.

I had a student a few years ago. We were at the end of our unit of this particular book that I used. It's called *Geography Club*. The kids love it. This student was sitting in the classroom, and she said, "John, I just don't understand. I've never met a gay person." I just wanted to put out my hand and say, "How do you do?" Even though you can talk about the subject, and you can answer questions, they never make the connection. It's sort of that seventh-grade maturity thing. I do know that there are certain students who come from backgrounds that, no matter what I do, they're going have this idea or opinion. So, I said, "Well, I happened to be gay." She gets this puzzled look, and of course, nine or ten of the other kids are just snickering. They had figured it out long before her. They're just at different stages of development.

I was asked to talk about why I teach. I can't say that I formally came out until I delivered that speech. That was probably the most public moment, but there were certainly other faculty members prior to that time, some gay, some not, who had been to my home, who had met my partner. For the most part, I don't think it came as a surprise.

I've never not felt the support of the administration here, which I think is very unique, from the head of the school all the way down to the junior high coordinator. I think some of the straight male faculty (regardless of the fact that they know what type of school this is, and they know what the culture of this school is) are still uncomfortable at times, particularly if there's a group of women at the faculty meeting, for example, talking about how "hot" Mr. Smith is. I would not have the same reaction if I made the same statement, because there are a handful of faculty members that, to be honest, are somewhat homophobic, despite the fact that they teach here.

I had been here for six years and took the sabbatical and went to London. It was a high-powered international, fantastic school, but I feel like I had to step back into the closet for my year there, because of the nature of the parent population, more than anything. I was also understanding and respectful of the fact that I stepped down to teach sixth grade. Sixth graders are also at a whole different level. But there were certainly situations that arose that probably warranted my stepping up and being more of an advocate; I just didn't feel like I had the freedom to do that. Now I think, "What the hell," because I was there on a one-year contract. What are they going to do, fire me? You know what I mean?

I was an inexperienced teacher, but I do remember having a very difficult conversation with a parent during a parent conference, and her son was clearly struggling; he was stereotypically the kid that if you walked into the classroom of 20, you'd say, "Oh, there's the boy who's struggling." And the mother and father were not excepting that at all. I was trying to hint that he had some problems socially, but I wasn't going to go so far as to say, "I think he is gay." The mother said, "We just accepted the fact that he's a fruit." I remember just feeling so angry with her. That would have been the perfect opportunity for me to step up to the plate, and I didn't do that. I'm dwelling on 23 years of experience, some of which were in a public school, in a very conservative county in the South—and such a confrontation with parent would have cost me my job.

I've had students before who've basically come out to me. So, I think that would have never happened if I had never been completely open to them, because they did understand that I was someone that they could trust, and I think they saw me as someone who could provide advice. I always advise them to be somewhat cautious. Not a kid who absolutely knows, but the kid who's not 100 percent sure. Because I've seen kids go through the high school here with a particular label, and all of a sudden, they make a different choice or understand their sexuality differently. It's very hard for them to escape that label that they attached themselves as a seventh grader. I think particularly during the adolescent years, sexuality's so fluid that they may not understand. I'm not saying that some don't have a complete understanding, but there are some that I don't think do.

My being gay and my being a teacher are very much melded together. It's hard to separate the two, in a sense because I do feel that providing a positive role model, especially for students who are in seventh and eighth grade is really important to me. As I look back at my own history, there were certainly gay teachers, none of whom were open. I wish I'd had even one that I could have had those discussions with.

Students are a lot more comfortable, today. Honestly, I don't think there's any student this year in my class who is uncomfortable with the issue. There have been years where there might be a couple who are less comfortable, but sometimes kids will just put it out there for a laugh because kids here, they're funny. It's never done in a disrespectful way.

I do this weekly Geography quiz thing about countries and capitals. I'm pointing on the map and said this country, and they're recording the name of the country and capital. I said, "This salmon colored country." The hand goes up and the student says, "John," she says, "That's what I appreciate about you. A straight man would say it's pink, but you know that it's salmon."

5

UPPER SCHOOL

Kenneth

I've had a really hard time creating an identity.

I didn't know how to define it when I was six or seven, but I knew something was up. I would say that I don't think I really fully admitted it to myself until I was in my early 20s. But I knew. I never dated girls. I've been gay since I've been aware of liking boys, since I was six or seven.

I'm 46 and single. My coming out was very measured. I was probably 29 to 30 at the time. Again, I think I waited until my career, all those things, could not be harmed. Then, I was changing schools; it was a logical choice. It was a logical decision for me to make. I started telling professional colleagues. I shouldn't say work colleagues at my school necessarily, but professional colleagues, who were also college admission people. That's a very gay friendly profession. They were the first people I told, and then it spread from there. I think in my mind it was euphoric in the sense I was finally free of it, but it really was a non-event. I have a few friends in Africa that know, and as far as I can tell, they've been very respectful of my not wanting to shout it off the mountaintops.

I think my being gay affects my being an educator in the sense that I'm constantly aware of how other people are feeling, who might be feeling disenfranchised in one way or another because I lived in the closet for years, even as I had my first teaching job. But again, I think I was a product of my environment, which shoved me way to the back of the closet. I think that my sense of empathy would not have developed in as acute a way if I weren't gay and constantly aware of what I was saying, walking on eggshells, and making sure I wasn't going to out myself or put myself in harm's way. I didn't come out because I feared I wasn't going to get a job, or get my green card, or because I wasn't going to get all these things that were in my mind. Until all of those things were resolved, in some manner or form, I was going to take it easy. But I was constantly aware of what other people were seeing, thinking, and feeling.

My parents died about ten years ago. They were in Africa, and I was living here, so I never really told them. They were older parents. I have sisters, and I don't necessarily have a relationship with them enough to tell them anything about my personal life in that way. They live in Africa as well, and I go see them once a year. I have aunts and cousins who live in other places. I'm out to them. I've taken an ex-boyfriend home to my mom's sister's house, and they're very supportive.

Because I'm not fully out when I am in Africa, chilling here and chilling there are two very different things. Whereas here, I don't give a shit—I'm not going to get jailed for being gay. But in Africa, anything can happen, and there's no one to protect you. So, if I'm just chilling, I would say I like to listen to people, to listen to their stories. That is an extension of what I do at work, but it's what I love to do in life. I love to listen. I love to figure out how people have encountered the world, and the challenges that they've had, and really admire and respect what people have gone through. I just love doing that.

I'm certainly a gay man. I would say that at least half, if not more than half of my friends here are gay. Mind you, I don't know that many people here. New York is one of those places where you are acquaintances with hundreds of people and you're friends with ten. Outside of school, I would certainly say I would be a good friend, a gay man, and someone who cares about social justice.

Out and openly gay mean the same thing to me. They mean being able, certainly in the work world, to talk about my life as other people talk about their lives, without feeling encumbered about the fact that I might be in love with someone from the same gender. Or, when they're talking about going to bars, I name a gay bar. The ability to do that with my colleagues, that has been very easy. That is, essentially, to me, being able to be "out."

As far as kids are concerned, being out means being able to put up a safe-space sticker. It means being able, in private conversations or in one-on-one conversations, to talk about being gay, especially if a kid comes out or mentions being gay himself. If the occasion arises to give empathy or some kind of message so that a kid can talk about being gay, then I will do that.

Our school is not a very gathered place, in the sense that there are not many forums in which to talk about any kind of identity Yes, there's a gay/straight alliance; yes, there's an Indian students' club; yes, there's an Asian student society; yes, there are general affinity groups for multiple affinities. As a member of the faculty, I think people who want to go to any of these clubs can go. If I had the time to go, I would go. I may go this year, because I actually have a colleague who is going to be helping me in the college counseling office.

It can get a bit political, in that there is a head of this group who's a teacher, who's been there for many years, and he takes great pride in running the GSA. I sort of say, that's your baby. Whenever there are conferences or meetings or things, then I'll go. There is, in fact, an affinity group of independent schools in the New York City area, and those professionals get together every so often, and I'll go to some of those meetings. That's basically what it means to be out.

I'm out to anyone with whom the conversation arises. It could be faculty members, it could be students, it could be administrators. I asked my headmaster when I joined the school, during my interview, about being gay at the school and what his impressions were. I laid it all out before I even started. It's New York City. I think it's a much easier place to be out. That being said, it's also a boys' school. Boys' schools have their own challenges with addressing homosexuality. I think in general they're very supportive, but there is definitely a locker room culture that is a little bit less so.

I actually don't think about it at school very much at all. I would actually say it's this mix of really interesting factors. I could walk down a hallway and you've got boys running around, crashing into each other, and backpacks all over the place. There are very few spaces in which they can congregate or even sit on a bench. I've got to say, the guys are fairly affectionate with one another, in the sense that they will actually sit on each other's laps, and they can be physically close and not feel threatened. There's very much that element of the school culture, which is not what I would consider locker-room culture.

The locker room culture is where some boys have this macho thing going, and you have to be cool. I think, to them, being straight is being cool. It depends on the guy. I think for the boy who is perceived as the straight athlete and the popular guy, it's much harder for that guy to come out in a school like ours. Whereas if someone's a bit nerdy, maybe a bit shy, and comes out, people have actually celebrated that. They're very happy—"Okay, so now we figured you out."

I think that we are a male place, and the guys are very proud of that. They take pride in their maleness, which is fine, particularly in a classroom setting without restriction and without feeling like they need to impress someone of the opposite sex. They do not worry about blurting out an answer, which they might otherwise be holding in, because they don't want to appear to be stupid.

I think for the very stereotypically straight white male athlete, even a black male athlete, I think to come out is hard. If too many people have ascribed an identity to that person, then I think they need to have a fresh start in a new place before they can come out. For 12 years, for some of them, they've been in this environment and been known as a certain thing. They aren't going to turn that upside down, because they don't want to lose their friends. They don't want to lose their stature. They don't want to lose their popularity. So then they defend it in the locker rooms.

It's complicated with a few boys because they don't want their parents to know. And they don't want other people to know at the school. Sometimes they actually are only out to their parents, but they want anybody else to know at school. There are varying flavors of how and when these boys choose to come out. I would say a number of them don't come out until they're in college. Again, I think some of it is living under their parents' roofs and not having that sense of security.

I really do enjoy talking to the kids. I can just sit there for half an hour, having asked a question, just listen to them talk and talk. If they're not talking, then then it's my job to try and figure out a way to get them to talk. I think the best part of my job is really figuring out who they are, helping them put their best foot forward, and then seeing at the other end what colleges they actually like and fall in love with, as opposed to which ones they feel the need to go to in order to impress everybody else.

I think the empathy part is key. If there are kids struggling with their identities—call it a sixth sense when you're correct about what you believe kids are struggling with—I want to make sure that they choose gay-friendly schools. Even if they don't talk about it. Again, the kid may say nothing about being gay, but I'm going to say, "Look, you need to look at Wesleyan, you need to look at Oberlin, you need to look at Vassar. If you don't like them, that's fine. But if I don't show them to you because all you're doing is focusing on Dartmouth, let me show you what else exists, in a place where my guess is you'll be happier." It certainly does have an impact.

Jennifer

> *The way I sort of frame it is "I'm going to tell you something that is perhaps a challenge for you, but it gives you permission to be whoever you are as well. So, you accept me and I accept you and whatever comes with you."*

I think that one of the things I really strive to do is to create a sense of community in my classroom. And so, I hope that my students will come to trust me. I guess in terms of an identity, I would say that I hope I model for them the behavior I expect from them, and it usually is related to respect and treating everybody with complete equality. I would say that I try to model the virtues of inclusivity. I mean they get that from the very beginning. Like this is going to be a family, and we're all in this together.

I don't put an honor code on any of my papers because it's what's in their hearts that matters to me, not what's in their signature. We talk about that. In fact, the first two days of my class are spent talking about how to create community before any learning takes place.

My whole view is colored by the identity I have as a gay woman, especially in today's society where every day you can hear something that's negative. There's not anybody in my life who doesn't know that I'm gay, so if you ask me what's one thing about me, what would jump to my mind would be the word gay. This is such a strong part of my identity...before woman, before teacher, before everything else. From a list of twenty identifiers, that would be at the top of the list.

When I was five, I had a dream that I kissed my teacher in the closet. I was in kindergarten, and so I think that was pretty precocious of me, actually. And sort of symbolic that it was in the closet. But I didn't talk about it, and I didn't really understand it until I was about eleven. Then I understood it and then decided that it had to be kept a secret. I didn't actually come out until I was 27, which was when I had the battle.

The way I coped with it was as sort of an addiction. I went into treatment when I came out. It was very easy because I was in a very protected environment, and I left the life that I had and went for treatment. I met someone in treatment, and the experience of meeting someone and of actually being able to meet someone, well, I think I was just so relieved to unburden myself of all of the whys and disguises. After that, it was like, even telling my family—it was like I couldn't wait to tell people. In that respect it was easy.

I taught at a school right after I got out of treatment. Those 12 years there were very difficult because I couldn't tell people, and that's eventually what propelled me to leave and to come here. Because when I interviewed here, it was very clear that I'm coming here because I can't be out at my school. "Can I be out here?" The answer was yes. So that was the reason I transferred.

The administration knows I am gay. It's not like I advertise it, but I'm not going to hide it either. Actually, with my advisees, my ninth-grade group, I tell them pretty early on because they're going to be with me for four years and they need to know. But the way I sort of frame it is, "I'm going to tell you something that is perhaps a challenge for you, but it gives you permission to be whoever you are as well. So, you accept me, and I accept you and whatever comes with you."

I don't ever feel any problems with parents or being accepted by students. I think that just this past year has been more difficult because they have tried to start a GSA. It's gone through waves where things are better, but when you bump up against something and you hit a new barrier is when you realize that they're not growing as fast as you would like for them to grow. And this year it was starting a GSA. It was actually a student organized group that wanted it, and they took it all the way to the board of trustees and met with them. They were granted permission to have one, but they didn't want to call it a GSA, and I actually realized that there was still this sort of homophobia in terms of naming it and claiming it, which upset me. I've been very open about the fact that it upsets me that they won't call it that and that they are treading so carefully. I've said, "You are afraid to deal with it, and it makes me realize that there's still some part of you that doesn't accept me completely."

They have been willing to listen, but it hasn't impacted their decision to call it that. Their justification is that they want the group to work and they don't want a lot of backlash. But I don't think the group will work unless they're prepared to take that backlash.

It's been an emotional thing for me. In both situations when I talked to them, I got sort of teary because when you really think about the lack of acceptance that comes with not wanting to hear the word gay or lesbian used, it just is very powerful. I mean, all I can do is continue to voice my objection, and I think they've listened, but their lack of willingness to change says a lot.

The reality of it is that I get angry at the other gay teachers who don't want to battle. I battle like I am supposed to be here. I realize that I need to be here because I need to fight that battle because otherwise no one is going to fight it. And I think the fact that there are students who want to have that club is because of the organization that we started a few years ago, which was TAP, Teens Against Prejudice, which was the first way we got around having a GSA. You can't be against that name. Then we sort of broadened that umbrella so that it would attract anybody that needed a safe place to be.

We've never had any openly out kids here. It's not that we don't have them, but they just don't come out until after they leave. And that was what propelled these kids to start the group is that they have friends who have graduated who have come out, and they want to give that to students who are still here. And part of it is because they have been to these TAP meetings and they know that there's a place where they could have that. But I didn't want it under Teens Against Prejudice. I didn't want it under the umbrella group. It's its own group. We can have them come to our meetings, but it's its own group. It's just like the Young Libertarians. We're not going to have the Young Libertarians come to a TAP meeting, they can have their own meeting, you know?

The school is just getting ready to start affinity groups because we haven't had them. But in fact, they do have affinity groups. You have the FCA, which is Fellowship of Christian Athletes, which has met for ever and ever and ever, and the Young Libertarians, the Young Republicans...those are affinity groups. But when it comes to having gay-straight alliance as an affinity group, then it's "We're not going to have affinity groups." Now they've decided they are going to have affinity groups, they're not going to call them affinity groups. Anyway, I think they're trying to move in the right direction, they are just going at a snail's pace. And they're saying that they're trying to protect the students. But I think that students pick up very quickly on the inherent homophobia.

I think it's changing. Our new principal is very much pro-diversity. I think it's a very kind place for faculty. I don't think it's that for students. I think there are a lot of mean girls, and I think there is a very white conservative population among the parents and the kids mimic what they hear their parents say. There are very few overweight girls, so image is very important. It's a privileged, sheltered school for the most part. Not everybody, but it's very privileged environment. That is the norm.

I mean everything from the way prom invitations are handed out. They do this heart-to-heart thing for Valentine's Day. Finally, I've got the message across that it's very privileged for heterosexuals, and there's nowhere on the form that says anything about if you were gay. It's a questionnaire you fill out to see who you're most compatible with at school. But it's always boy-girl. They've always asked me to fill one out for myself. But this year the tenth-grade advisor put up teacher's pictures with who they might be compatible with. And she put Dorothy Hamill up with me because she knows I've always had a crush on Dorothy Hamill. I mean I've made strides, you know?

I think student to student, they're more accepting. I think boys are harder on other boys. I don't think the girls have a problem with a girl being gay, but it's just like society, and there are a lot of guys who have issues with other guys being gay. And then I just think they don't think about it unless it's brought up; it's like most white people don't think about being white. It's just not a part of their consciousness.

With this GSA thing, there was a situation with one of the teachers when I first came here, where he was using the word "fag." I reported it, and he was dealt with. I've not dealt with anybody who has had an issue with me, specifically, but I think there have definitely been issues, yeah.

I really do hope that I can make a difference. I just taught at a summer class called Urban Experience, and I had a student in there I had met two years ago when I went on a field trip with his class. As I got on the bus, the very first thing I heard coming out of his mouth was some joke that he was telling someone, "Well that's so gay," or "You're so gay," or something like that. So I put him on the spot and had him come over to me, and I say, "You know, I'm gay, so are you saying there's something wrong with me?" When he heard that I was his Urban Experience teacher, he said, "I really feel like we got off on the wrong foot when I met you two years ago." And he said, "When I saw your name as my teacher for Urban Experience, I was a little bit afraid because I thought you were going to think that I was still that guy. But I really want you to know that I'm so glad that I had a chance to spend these two weeks with you, and I really feel lucky to be in your class. And I hope you know that I'm not that person anymore." And that, to me, is the kind of conversation that I hope for, you know.

I had a really, really conservative family whose child was my advisee, and he says I'm one of the most important influences in his life. And this is a kid, if he had not had me as an advisor, probably would not have grown to know someone who was gay. That was important to him.

Those are the kinds of things that I think make a difference, you know?

The hard part for independent schools is that they're different from public schools in that they are selling a product, so they are very con-science of selling a product that fits the demand. And if the demand is still homophobic, then they have to cater to the demands of their clientele. So, they want to be authentic, but they've got to be careful about not rocking the boat, and it's a precarious balance for them between living their values and pleasing their customer base.

George

Their understanding of gay men was simply from TV.
The issue was trying to convince them, "No, I'm not going
to die by just walking down the street."

I would describe myself as a teacher who's really passionate about their subject area, about the success of their students. I'm someone who's really committed to teaching my students how to be more than just a really good musician but how to be really good people who understand the complex world in which they live and will live, through my subject area. I think that music in particular is a great way to show them the world and have them learn about themselves through what we do. I would say that I am teacher who's really energetic, passionate, deeply invested in my students' success.

I feel like, as a teacher, I am the same person I am privately, but just on steroids. There's this intensity that comes because you're "on." I feel a little bit more of an energy through me. I feel like in terms of identity, they're more or less the same. I'm very open with my students about my personal experiences or about places I visited or people I know, because I think my goal is to try to relate, to help them understand where I'm coming from by sharing my background. I would say I'm not afraid to share my personal identity in the classroom, because I feel like so much of what I teach and what I do is also a part of who I am.

My coming-out process at age 12 was pretty straightforward and pretty easy. I didn't really encounter any physical violence, nothing like that. The older boys were definitely hard on me, but I had experienced that always, before I even came out. I'd been called all that kind of stuff, and I didn't even know why. I'm like, "I don't understand. Yeah, I have lots of friends who are girls. Why aren't you jealous of that? Instead of

calling me a girl, you should be like, 'Oh, I should do what he's doing.'"
I came out to friends and other people, and some adults in my life, like an aunt and a cousin. The parent thing didn't happen until I was 16.

My parents were like, "Okay. Pass the potatoes. Great. We've known since you were two. Lovely. We really don't care." My dad had the whole attitude of, "Well, I'm just thankful that you don't act... how do I say... real feminine." I'm like, "Oh, my God. But great, I'm glad that you're comfortable, I guess." Of course, he's evolved over time. I had to come to the realization that their understanding of gay men was simply from TV, which is of course very stereotypical, like *Law & Order* where gay men are being murdered in the streets of New York. The issue wasn't that I was gay. The issue was trying to convince them, "No, I'm not going to die by just walking down the street."

Being out and openly gay means that I just really behave in the world the way that feels most comfortable and natural. I don't edit myself. I don't withhold information when asked, or even when not asked. Not that I'm like, "Hey, I'm George. Nice to meet you. I'm gay," but I'm not going to shy away from it if it comes up. I try to find a balance between celebrating that part of my identity and also not making it the only identity that I have in my life.

I like to think that I'm out to everyone in the community. It's widely known and understood. I didn't have to come out. My colleague here jokes with me that as soon as she saw me in the hallway the day of my interview, she was like, "Oh, thank God, we have someone who's gay." That's because my predecessor was a straight young male, and it caused some issues in the performing arts department at an all-girls school, with them just being very enamored with him in ways that they didn't quite understand. Of course, she was assuming I was gay. She happened to be right.

I think from that interaction, I knew that it was an okay and safe place. Yeah, I'm out to everyone. It's been fine. I don't personally feel any sort of negativity in any way, shape, or form. We're quite an inclusive and open-minded educational institution.

Because it's an all-girls school, and because most of the faculty and staff are women—I'd say 75 percent—I tend to then be more comfortable around straight females. I always say if I had to work at an all-boys independent school, I don't know how I would do. I'm sure eventually I'd be okay, but I guess it's easy for me to be out here because I get the sense that everyone's okay. If they're not, it's because it's a religious issue, not a moral one or something like that. At that point, would I love to have a conversation with them? Yes, but I'm not going to judge them because that happens to be their religious belief, and they certainly aren't treating me any differently because of their religious belief.

Being out and gay has only served me positively in my time here, so I have no reason to act any differently. In fact, some ways I would say it's actually an advantage, particularly in an all-female environment. There's this idea like I'm "the" gay male in the building. A lot of people's experience is like, "Straight females love that, and they celebrate that." It's like, "Oh, my God. It's so cool, because you're gay, and I'm straight, and we can talk about these things." They feel so safe around me.

Sometimes I wonder, "Okay, are you treating me this way just because it's exciting and fun and exotic, or is it because you actually like me and want to know me and know other things about me?" I know the people who like me, and I know the people who like me because I'm gay.

I think if I were at an all-boys school, it could have a greater impact, but I often find when I go to use my sexual identity and orientation as a means of teaching with mostly straight females, it's hard. There's this disconnect where they get it, but it's not relatable to them. They're like, "Yeah. We love gay people. We accept gay people. If you're bringing that perspective into your teaching, it doesn't really affect us, because I just can't feel that." It doesn't stop me from doing that, but what it does is informs the conversations we have.

I live in these two worlds. On the outside, I'm the epitome of privilege, white male, whatever, but then I do have the gay side where I do relate with being a minority and having the world against me in many ways. In school, yeah, being a white male in this environment in particular and as a teacher, I'm sometimes treated the same as other white males in the building. Sometimes it's frustrating, because I don't get it. I'm like, "Wow, you really are just seeing me as that." Sometimes I try to push through that. I'll find I'll say things or do things to try to show that I'm more than just a white male.

It's very interesting how some people, especially my younger students and my middle school students in particular, who can't always pick up on that I'm gay. They just think I'm eccentric and happy. You can tell they act so differently around me than they do their female teachers. For example, a lot of them will say, "Oh, you look just like my dad," and their dad is literally 50 years old, and I'm 27. I meet their dad, and I'm like, "We look nothing alike other than we're both white males." That has really eye-opening, because I don't first identify as a white male. It's very interesting that you say that, because yeah, being a teacher, I think it has really opened my eyes to the fact that people view me that way, especially my younger students.

With the gay thing, girls are very open with me. They'll come to my office and ask for advice, or they need some counseling. It's really surprising to me how willing they are to talk about their romantic relationships or their feelings for a boy, or something like that, whereas I feel like if I were a straight male, that wouldn't be happening.

I would say most things are heteronormative. I would say that's the norm. I think because we are an all-girls school, it's less heteronormative than a co-ed school or an all-boys school, but it's still pretty much always through a straight female perspective. We pat ourselves on the back a lot because it's like we're empowering women, we're giving them so many female perspectives, but the elephant in the room is that it's a straight female's perspective. Yeah. I think almost all of their messages are pretty heterosexually oriented. In my mind, I always thought independent schools would just be naturally more open-minded and be okay, but it's so interesting.

I am happy to share my story, because when you're in your community, you feel how you feel in your community. Then when you find out what's going on, you can see, "Okay, I'm not alone," or, "Wow, that's really shocking. I didn't think that that was the case." Because just going into it, I imagine that it would be quite easy to be out at an independent school, but maybe that's not the case. It will be interesting to know, "Okay, I shouldn't take my experience for granted," or, "How great that now people can be out."

I feel really lucky and fortunate that I'm in a community where I feel valued and respected. I always wonder, if I ever leave here, do I have to do that process again where I'm like, "Can I be out? Can I talk about it? Can I bring my boyfriend with me to the potluck?" That whole thing.

Christopher

I always felt a little guilty not being out because I knew there were queer students who probably were getting almost no support at home, and I really wanted to be there for them. But at the same time, I had to make some pretty careful decisions about my own personal job security and safety there.

I don't know if there was any single moment. I guess I just realized [I was gay] in the context of people having seventh and eighth grade relationships, what I was doing. I had girlfriends through junior year in high school, but I started to realize what I was doing just didn't feel the same as what other people were getting out of it.

I came out slowly to friends and family. I came out to one of my best friends in high school my sophomore year. It was a pretty scary thing, but I felt very vulnerable. Then I came out slowly to a handful of friends and family, and then came out my senior year to the whole school as a final coming out. I came out in a speech. I went to a boarding school, and we have chapel four days a week. In chapel, a senior would speak once a week, so I used my senior speech to come out.

I've never been afraid of being different before. I've never been afraid of going to the beat of my own drum, but with this I've always been terrified, and I'm finally ready to live the life that I have always deserved.

It took me a couple of years to come out at work. I was out in high school, out in college, and I just didn't feel comfortable in my work environment because, I guess, I felt my job rested on being in the closet. I know there would have been a lot of families who would have not been supportive because I lived in an apartment attached to the dorm. I know a lot of families probably would not have been comfortable with that. I just didn't feel comfortable coming out fully to everyone. It took me a couple of years to release it a little bit. Then

I ended up coming out to all of my close friends there.

I always felt a little guilty not being out because I knew there were queer students who probably were getting almost no support at home, and I really wanted to be there for them. But at the same time, I had to make some pretty careful decisions about my own personal job security and safety there. It was a tough thing to balance. I think I still talk about queer issues the way I would have anyway. If I've been out, I would have conversations with students all the time, especially because a lot of our students go on to college.

A couple of times it came out very randomly, student will be like, I don't know what I would do if I had a gay roommate. I had really good conversations with them about that and talked the way I think I would have talked if I've been an out teacher—I don't think they would have asked me that. It was interesting. Fear was not the biggest thing. Rather, I thought it was maybe the guilt of not being out to everyone and only being out to some of my colleagues. If I wasn't gay, I would be a straight white male Christian from an upper-middle class background. I think I would have a really hard time understanding students from any sort of minority perspective. Not that being gay helps me understand the Latino students, but it helps me understand that I can't really understand their experience since it gives me some touch points, some questions I can ask and just some thoughts from my own experiences. I think that's the only way that it's really affected my identity as a teacher.

I'm ready to be the out teacher of the school. I really want that role. It's important to me. I had a tough time at the beginning of high school. There were two lesbian teachers and one male gay teacher at my school, but I didn't really connect with any of them. I just really wanted to provide some students with what I didn't get myself in high school. I think this is tricky because of the context: I was a white male in another country. In some ways, I was a minority, but in some ways, in many ways, it was still the dominant culture at our school is definitely the Americans. In many ways, I was wrapped up in that culture too.

I think the way for me that race affects how I am as a teacher is a constant struggle for awareness. I have been making more and more efforts just to try to be aware of my own race because I think if you had asked five years ago, I would have said being gay had no impact on my teaching at all. I know now it does have a huge impact, and it is something I'm trying to be much more aware of being a white gay male that teaches. I don't know. I'm struggling to put words to this because I'm having trouble putting those all together. For example, teaching has made me a more compassionate person. It's made me a more patient person. It's made me able to be quiet and listen to what other people are saying, as opposed to just always saying what I need to say, for example. I think some of my journeys with other aspects of my identity sit along with that and are complemented by that, but it's hard for me to stick those all together.

In my school there was no possibility of not being heterosexual, which I think says everything it needs to say. Students would write things on the walls—not about me but about each other—that would include homophobic remarks. There were verbal things that I would hear between students every now and then. That was really about the extent of it, but at the same time, I do know that the school, for example, tried to do the Laramie project. An American teacher wanted to do the Laramie project, and it just got shut down almost immediately. A lot of the students were really upset about it but there were bigger horses at play: people on our board and parents who felt, "We just can't talk about this. This is not a thing."

I'm very excited about my new school. It's a 300-person school, and it's all boarding. It's this very cozy community, and they seem to be very tight. Actually I got to meet the students in a confidential queer and questioning support group, which was a really, really cool thing. I was working with the teacher who runs it, and she's like, "Would you like to meet them? I said, "Yeah, absolutely; that would be wonderful." I got to meet them, hang out with them, tell them my story and that I am gay. They all talked about their stories. It was the night before prom, which is interesting because they were all trying to figuring that out.

I see the diversity in the queer community. I see how restricting things like labels can be. More and more I'm embracing the word queer. I just feel like it includes so many more people. I also used to struggle with seeing how trans people relate to gay people. I didn't really have a connection, and, for me, it was like, "Why are these people part of our movement? I don't understand." Now that I've figured that out, or come up with an answer for myself, I prefer the word queer because then I feel it includes them too.

Thomas

My dad grew up in a small town. I don't think it ever occurred to him that he even knew anybody who was gay.

I'm 6 feet 6 inches. That adds a lot of drama when I stand at the classroom door and step inside and outside to use it to show about we can think about things in this way or we can think about them in that way. At first, they see this as kind of funny, and then they come to realize the kind of seriousness of it. It adds that flavor of giving them a moment to stop and laugh and relax a little. I tend to take myself too seriously.

I think being gay impacts my identity because it causes me to look at how I want to present myself, and so sometime it makes me stop and think, "Okay is this how I want to go into the classroom? Is this how I want to present myself while I'm here?" Sometimes it's hard for me to sit back and not do that; sometimes it's hard to step back and not present myself as I want to. I also just try to present myself as human as I possibly can. There is a lot of ego at the school, and I try not to introduce that. Occasionally it's hard to back away. Again it's part of the taking ourselves too seriously.

I remember noticing there was something different when I was about seven. I was 34 when I came out. I was married to a woman, and I was happy in that relationship. It was not too long after my then wife and I had separated. We didn't divorce because of me being gay. One evening I just started to think, "Okay, I think there is something here that's unexplored. I see that's something here that I need to look at and do something about." I started to call around and found a good therapist who had been through the same experience, who had been married and discovered that she was gay, and so that was essentially it. The self-acceptance was very quick and very easy.

I just felt like this is who I am and this is what I'm about. I think a lot of what kept me in the closet before was that I was just scared. I didn't just like who I thought I might be. I was just afraid for how the people were going to respond, my dad specifically. He grew up in the South during the Depression, and he was pretty conservative when it came to social issues. I grew up in a house hearing racist jokes and homophobic jokes and all that. In fact, I was a bit concerned when I decided to tell my family. One of my brothers' immediate response was, "So, are you going to tell Dad?" That was the first thing that came out of his mouth. And it all went okay.

My dad only lived for eight months after I came out. He died very suddenly, so he never really came to get it, but it didn't change our relationship. He and I were very, very close, so fortunately it didn't change that. His immediate reaction was, "Okay, fine," and then he just had an increasingly harder time wrapping his head around it. He would talk to my brother about it, but he wouldn't talk to me about it. They even called me a few times and said, "Hey you know, I think you need to call Dad." I would have, if he would want to talk about it. I think he just didn't know how. He grew up in a small town, and I don't think it ever occurred to him that he even knew anybody who was gay.

I feel like I was hard on myself for long time after I first came out. I loved to teach Thoreau and Emerson and Whitman, and I felt like kind of a sham, because here I was teaching about being who you are and living the life that you want. Thoreau wrote about people who lead lives of quiet desperation. I was kind of hard on myself about how I had been a sham to my students, but a good conversation with a really great friend helped to clear that out. He just said, "Know who you are. You were married and you were wondering and you had to explore the fact that you didn't know who you were. Now that you're out, you're not doing that [hiding]. If you were doing that now, then yeah, it would be problem, but you're not." I was in a different school when I came out.

I never thought of myself as somebody about whom kids would say, "Oh, there is Mr. Thomas. He is gay, and he is cool with himself, and he is a good teacher who is successful in what he does, and he is kind."

This is one of my favorite stories. It was at the school where I taught six blocks in a day, and it was the fifth block and I was cramming for my sixth block. I'm sitting there working on my laptop, and I'm cramming, just lesson planning. It's a Friday afternoon, and she just pops her head into my room and says, "Are you busy?" And without even looking over, I just went, "Yeah, but what's going on?" She said, "Was it difficult when you came out to your parents?" I just thought, "Oh, okay." I just hit save and closed my laptop. I said, "Come in and sit down and let's talk about this." I mean, she was asking me on a Friday afternoon, and there was no way that I could let her leave for the weekend without the potential of somebody to talk to and that she was going to have this conversation with her parents without any kind of help. She is going to be a senior next year in college, and we're close friends. We're in contact with each other all the time, and we went out to see a play couple of months ago, and it all came from that moment she came to see me and I just thought, "Okay, here we go. Let's sit down; let's have the conversation."

I think that there are times when being gay impacts my identity. I think it would be wrong to say that it doesn't. There were times when I teach Whitman and there is that connection. There were times when I'm able to talk about James Baldwin, when I'm able to talk about the kind of perspectives that he is speaking from. I just feel like I can bring some of myself into that and I can deepen the experience by being able to connect to an author on that level, or more specifically to their writing on that level.

I teach a lot of Langston Hughes. When I first talk about him, I talk about how he is Black and gay—a kind of outsider on two different levels. Because we live in a time when our students are so much more sophisticated about sexuality and just more aware of more gay people through television and media, I feel like I can lean on my own past and my fear of being out or just being closeted or just feeling like an outsider. I don't tend to talk about myself all the time though; I just talk about him.

There was a time in Whitman's life when he created a fictional wife and six kids just to get out of the fear that he was going to found out. We talked about how scary that was, how scary of a time in his life that was, and how difficult that it was. That comes from being able to connect to that and being able to understand that fear of, "Oh my God. What if somebody finds out I was staring at some boy in the locker room?" That's kind of how it informs my teaching.

I don't talk about my sexuality very much in the classroom at all, but the students all know. During the end of the year, I was on a date, and I ran into student of mine, and it was just really funny, actually. She is the most uncomfortable kid that you could imagine, and she is also an awesome kid. I was walking into the restaurant, and she was walking out, and she wasn't paying attention, and she physically ran into my chest. I said, "Oh, hey." The next day she was like, "Mr. Thomas, I'm really sorry that I ran into you and created that uncomfortable scene when were in the restaurant." And I said it was fun and funny, and I told her I was on this date, and she went, "Oh my God! Right!" and then she was just even more horrified. I knew that she would have that response, but I knew that we could have fun with this as well. I know the other students were laughing. Yeah, I don't tend to do it much, but I just try to do it when you see there is something that's funny or if I can say, "Let me explain to you what this is like and let me help you frame this a little bit."

We had a couple of kids who had come out, and then we had like six who came out all in the same year, and it made the head of school a little bit nervous and uncomfortable. He pulled me into his office to have this conversation, and he said, "I've concerns that you're becoming known as a one-issue teacher." I wanted to say, "You would never say that to a female faculty member. You wouldn't say that to your black faculty member. You wouldn't say that your Jewish faculty member." But I didn't because I didn't want to make it anymore antagonistic than it already was. We've since moved past that. He said being gay was the one thing that I was becoming known for and for bringing that to the classroom. I invited him to come to my classroom and hang out anytime he wanted.

We actually had a really good follow-up conversation the next day, and he said, "I don't understand how a kid comes to realize that they're gay." He said, "So maybe sometime we can go out and have a beer and you can fill me in, and we can talk about how kids come to be aware." I said, "I'll happily do that."

Nancy

Coming out is just never over. It's never over. Unless you want to wear a sign or something, it's always that moment when you're with someone new or with someone you don't know well and you realize they don't know and you've got to tell them.

I was married to a man, and I had my child with him, and I separated from him. During that separation, I came to terms with the fact that I really was a lesbian. I think I was probably around 28. Now, when did I first actually come in contact with that fact? I was probably 11, but I just would not accept it. I had spent so long denying it, that once I accepted it, it was actually a kind of a relief because I had been fighting it for such a long time. But then the big thing that was holding me back was my son and knowing that it would affect him and knowing that there were not a lot of protections.

Coming out to my family went well, but certainly I had a lot of anxiety about that because they were very religious. I was raised very religious. That was a big thing holding me back all those years. I have a sister, and she was very helpful in coming out. In fact, she said to me at one point, right when I was kind of in that process of accepting myself, she even said to me, "Have you ever thought about this?" She made it okay for me to think about it because she was more, at that point, she was more liberal than me. She wasn't as steeped in the religion, so that made it easier for her to kind of break out of it faster than I did.

At that time, when I was coming out, my parents had been divorced for a while. Almost every single person I came out to said, "Well no kidding. We've known this." Except my mother. My mother acted like she had no idea, and she was so surprised, which was ridiculous. My father, he said something mean to me, which I'll tell you, but then once he said it, he was fine. He said something like, "Well, I guess it could be worse. You could be a child molester or something." He said something nasty, but then after that it was almost like he was just over it. He was fine after that.

My father passed away few years ago, but right before he passed he had a lot of trouble accepting my partner, but that was true when I dated men too. It wasn't really a gay thing. Right before he passed, he told us this is a crazy compliment but he was like, "You guys have more conservative family values than straight families that I know." He's like, "You're all about your kids and providing a loving environment for them." I'm like, "Great. Thanks for calling me conservative, Dad." But what he meant was good sentiment.

Coming out is just never over. It's never over. Unless you want to wear a sign or something, it's always that moment when you're with someone new or with someone you don't know well, and you realize they don't know and you've got to tell them.

One of the reasons I came to work here was for my children to go to school here. We have very generous faculty financial aid. But I also realize, I couldn't have my children go to school here and me being in the closet. That's not going to work because I'm not going to have my children lie.

Once I got the job, I read the employee manual and it said, "We don't discriminate based on sexual orientation." At that time my youngest was three. I said to my partner, "This is what they say. I'm going to test it. If it's not true, then I'll find another job because I don't want my kids going to school here if I can't be who I am." Before I even started work we had a math department get-together. I took my partner. It was just so awkward, but it was fine. There was never a problem with it. That's kind of how I outed myself to the math department.

I remember my boss at the time, second week of school, comes in my room, shuts the door, I'm like, "Oh shit." He's like, "I just want you to know that this is just never going to be allowed to be a problem for you." Then my heart is like...I'm having a heart attack. Basically what he was trying to say is he had my back if a parent complains about my being gay or tries to say there's some sort of issue with that. He's like, "I'm just not even going there. It's not going to be allowed." As far as I know, it's never happened. It could have happened and nobody told me, I suppose. That was kind of the beginning of the coming-out process. Then about five years ago, I was asked to serve on a new group that was forming called the Upper School Community Council. I think the reason I was asked to serve on it was I am a lesbian.

I had to have a fun meeting with my principal when my son started school here, which was a couple years after I had started here because my partner and I went to the parent orientation and we went to things together. I was running into parents of my students and I was like, "I need to just tell the principal."

That's the first time that I really had to deal with this thing that minorities deal with feeling like you're being asked to speak for your group. At that time, I didn't even know any other gay teachers. I didn't know anybody. I knew one, and she was in the closet. She was on the council too, for different reasons, so that was very uncomfortable because I was afraid I was going to somehow inadvertently out-her, which didn't happen thank goodness. I was very nervous and uncomfortable.

The gender thing is very, very new also to me. To even have a name for it and to realize that even if I'm around other lesbians, I'm different from them. I've even had experiences where people who were good friends. One time I dressed in a flapper dress for Halloween, which for me was going in drag, but I had a lot of friends who were lesbians that were like, "Oh that's so cute. Why don't you dress like that all the time?" I'm like, "What do you mean, why don't I dress like this all the time? This is not who I am." That was very frustrating to me, to not be even accepted in my own community. As far as intersection, I don't know. I guess I just talked to you about them as separate things. I don't think that I've integrated them necessarily into one whole thing.

As far as homosexuality in the student body, there are many students that are super supportive. A few years ago, our homecoming king was a gay male, and everybody knew that he was gay. It's like a popularity contest. He was popular even though he is gay. But then you have the subset of especially male students who are very uncomfortable about other boys in the class that are gay. We have a student that's really pushing the envelope, he's wearing scarves and he has his fingernails painted. I've never taught him, but even in my classes I've heard kids talking about him in a way that I don't really like. He's very polarizing, kids either love him and he's their best friend, or they're very uncomfortable with him. He's of course pushing every boundary that he can push. That's how he's establishing his identity.

He tells me, "The two of us are best friends and this is how we tease each other. We tease each other by calling each other fag, and even my mom calls me fag." He's like, "I don't mean anything bad by it." I just had to tell him, "It's not intent, it's impact. Your teacher saw that on your paper and was distressed because she thought that you were being harassed." I was like, "You know, that's a loaded word and you shouldn't use it."

Anyway, he was just irate but apparently, he's friends with the student who's openly flamboyantly gay and that student has reclaimed the word "fag" and uses it to describe himself. That word is actually getting more use, not less use, among that grade. I think they're in 11th grade now. It's just interesting.

I enjoy the individual relationships with the students. The students that you really connect with, then you touch their lives and they touch your life. Being inspired to try to reach more and have that connection with more students, "Why didn't I connect with this student the way I did with that one?"

It's ironic. Sometimes the students that I have the strongest connection with are actually students that are not good math students. Sometimes the best students, they really don't need me. I'm irrelevant to them. Like, "Okay." But the students that really need you, I think they really come to appreciate what you're doing. That's one side.

In fact, students when they graduate have an opportunity to make a gift in a teacher's name. I think I've had three of those over my eight years—that's a long time of teaching. I had three. Two of those three were some of the weakest math students I have ever taught. They really appreciated that, I would say how I helped them get through.

To me, that means a lot to me. Like you don't even like math. The one girl, in fact, will tell you, she flat out hates math, but she's going to make a donation honoring me, her math teacher. I honestly think that's pretty cool.

Edward and Andrew

The kids embraced the fact that we're gay and the fact that we got married so positively. We had three classes that threw parties for us. The faculty threw a party for us. The vice president, principal, the assistant principal, all came to the party. We got a "congratulations" from the president of the school. So many parents have sent us their well wishes, and they have even given us nice gifts, and it has been so good. I am very much devoted to the community and the kids, especially. It's all about the kids.

Andrew. For the longest time, I thought I might like to go into medicine, and then had a relationship, a teacher/student relationship, with my teacher in high school. He was such an amazing person, kind. My family didn't have enough money to purchase a suit for the state Spanish competition, and it was Mr. Ferguson who bought that for me. It was great. I realized along the way that I could help people even more, almost more than, say, someone in the medical profession could by being a teacher. Then I also realized that every great surgeon or doctor in the world has had one or more teachers that touched them in such a way that allowed them to be who they were, so I thought why not? I had a love of the Spanish language, the Spanish culture, and that is where I was.

Edward. For me, it came late in my education, the desire to be a teacher. I wanted to be an architect. They didn't have that course at the university that I attended, so I said, "What am I going to major in?" I looked at my cousin, who was a psychologist, who was ten years older, and thought about what a good life he had and how he helped people. I liked this idea of helping people, and I liked this idea of interacting with people. I thought maybe I would be a psychologist, but then, when I actually served a year as a volunteer in a children's psychiatric ward, in an indigent hospital in Tampa, I decided this is not really for me. I didn't see that people got better. They stayed the same, and I thought what could I do?

About that time, I took a history class as an elective. But I ended up with B.A.s in zoology and psychology, but I loved the history. I said, "I need to do what I love," and so I started taking courses for graduate school, got admitted to the M.A. program at the University of South Florida, and then went on to do a Ph.D. at Emory University in Atlanta, and that is how I came here.

In the 1970s, there weren't many college positions, so I abandoned the idea of being a college professor and went onto working in the business world, but I missed interacting with people, and I missed history. I said, "Why don't I try this high school idea? I came here and I liked the first year, I liked the second year okay, but it was in the third year that I committed. This is what I am going to do. At that point, I had no idea that I would permanently be here.

When I came here, it had many pluses that it still has as an institution, so I think that I saw those positive aspects of it and related to what we are talking about, here. When I came here, I wasn't out, but everybody knew I was gay and had a partner.

Andrew. Some of the kids have said to me, "Oh, I don't know how much Spanish I remember, but the life lessons, the things we talked about, stuck." As teachers, we have to remember that it could be an offhanded comment, but that is what they are going to remember, in 40 years. I don't want that. I want them to think about the good things, so I try—but I am human. We are all human. Sometimes we have said things we regret, but I am getting better, 20 years on, at not doing that. Certainly, I want them to be who they are, because I am who I am.

We talked about once we revealed our marriage plans to the community, it was not to make a statement other than I love Edward, and he loves me, and that was it. It kind of became a little bigger than that, but if I can be who I am, in my classroom, I want the students to be comfortable, being who they are, too, even if their opinion is different than mine.

Edward. When I first came here, it bothered me a lot that I couldn't actually be completely open, then. I wasn't bothered that people knew that I was gay, and there were quite a few gay faculty members, and I am sure that the president understood that. He was a bright man. He was a very progressive and forward-thinking man. It was never an issue, but it was all quiet, and it's nice to see the way it is now because I think it's so healthy for someone to be a whole person and not to have one's life segmented. It's healthy not to have the business life and the school life, in which you are partly in the closet, and then you have your other life with your gay friends and family. That is not good, psychologically. It's very liberating, and it's very positive to have all of this as one life. The people here all know that we are married and that we enjoy each other's company, and it's not a mystery. This is really good.

As far as in the classroom, I think Andrew is the best at giving kids what they need to grow up. He communicates so well with them. I try. I would love to say I am successful. I like my students. Sometimes I criticize other things about teaching, but the kids are wonderful, and I think that serving their needs and getting them ready for college is important—I don't worry so much about how much history they remember. I want them to be ready to perform well when they go to whatever college they attend. They all go to college, and they understand that that's what I have in mind. I do not ever want them to feel overwhelmed in here. I want them to enjoy it. I want them to leave here liking history but a little bit stronger in reading and writing skills than they were when they came in the door.

How much history they remember is not as important. In terms of the interaction with the students, I enjoy them, and I try to get them to be involved in discussion, and I love discussion. I love to talk with them, but when we finally get to the point where we do some group work, then we will move these desks around. I like to be among them, rather than to be standing up, overlooking the room. I like to sit there with them, rather than reading notes or holding forth in a traditional way. I like to have a discussion going, so you sometimes have to have a point of discussion, which the kids relate to. Sometimes they are sneaking a look at their iPhone or their iPad, but that's okay. That's human. I don't think that's a problem.

The kids embraced the fact that we're gay and the fact that we got married so positively. We had three classes that threw parties for us. The faculty threw a party for us. The vice president, principal, the assistant principal, all came to the party. We got a "congratulations" from the president of the school. So many parents have sent us their well wishes, and they have even given us nice gifts, and it has been so good. I am very much devoted to the community and the kids, especially. It's all about the kids.

Andrew. I don't really think now there is much distinction between my persona here, in the school, and out. Like Edward mentioned, we don't have that constant thing that many LGBT people do of stepping into and out of the closet all day long, not just weekly but every day. The faculty always knew that I was gay. The kids questioned. You always keep them guessing, to make it fun, but outside of school, being gay is part of who I am, not all of who I am.

Unfortunately, when I first came out in my early 20s, it was all of who I am. I was trying to be super gay and change the world, but I think I am the same person, really, outside of school that I am, and it has really come through this process of coming out, come hell or high water. Being married has really lifted a lot of that pressure, in every aspect of my life.

Edward. I agree with everything that Andrew said. When we are outside of school, it is fun to tell people you encounter, be it the waiter in a restaurant or the person behind the counter at the pharmacy, or whoever. It is good to tell people about how wonderful it is here at this school. We were so happy about getting married that there wasn't a person that we encountered that we didn't tell. It was not the original intent.

I proposed to Andrew on the beach in Florida, Cocoa Beach, near where he grew up in Merritt Island, and I decided it was the right place to do it. I had no idea what I would do if he said no. I didn't even think about that, but it was a very private thing. It was just the two of us, but then as it unfolded, it was exhilarating.

Yes, my life has been pulled together here in such a good way so that what I am outside of school and in school can be the same thing. That is a happy thing. We sent the announcement of the wedding to some of his fundamentalist relatives, and to our tattoo artist and our doctor, it was the same, "Hey, I am getting married" as it would be to tell the kids here. It was nice. It was just the way it ought to be.

Andrew. I don't want to use the word activist by any means, but there are things that are important to me, as it would be to any teacher, be it human rights or vegetarianism or the fight against GMOs or whatever. Those things I talk about outside of school with whomever we like to have the conversation, and then those subjects present themselves in context, in my Spanish class, often.

Like now, in my third-year class, the first chapter we are doing is all about personal relationships, and they are using vocabulary words like proposing matrimony, divorce, personality types. I don't think twice about including LGBT couples in that conversation. I think that was one of the activities in the book, and it was just following that sociology norm, the traditional way, and it put it in a male/female context. It did kind of make me pause for a second. So, as I am talking about the activity and explaining it, I added a little injection of inclusivity to the book; not in a militant way, but to let them know that the editor put it together this way, not to exclude anyone. They had to choose what to put in print, and that is what they chose, and I don't get into that explanation with them, but I inject that little bit of inclusivity, and the kids are—they are already there. They are the MTV culture. They take it, and they run with it.

One of my new students this year had a question, and in answering it, I said, "Have you met Dr. Edward?" He hadn't, and I said, "Dr. Edward is my husband." He paused for a second and said, "You're kidding." I said, "No," and then I thought I put him on the spot. I hadn't met this boy before, but that wasn't, of course, the intent, but I spoke to him the next day in private. I said, "I didn't want to make you feel uncomfortable. Not everyone is aware," and he said, "Oh, don't worry, my aunts and my cousin goes here, and it is not a big deal." It wasn't a big deal at all.

I think that part of my identity, regarding those things that I care about, I have complete freedom to share with the students now, and it is very empowering, and it is empowering them to be able to share what's important to them. They have a forum to do that in my room, be it in Spanish or English.

Edward. I am very fortunate in that I teach history, and historians have been pushing the envelope here for years to try to include all people and to try to look into all aspects of history. That is where it's at, and social history is such a strong part of history. It is my background in education, in history, and my preference, so it goes together really well.

When we look at history, we look at the great diversity of people who are in this country, and we do it from the get-go and try not to leave people out and try not to be unrealistic. We try to be realistic. It allows you to continue interjecting a little bit of what you feel to be true, but most of the students at this school accept this idea of tolerance and respect of others.

Compared to maybe some of the other independent schools in the Metro area, we are in a unique situation in terms of our history, our geographic location, the values of the people who work here, the leaders, the governing board. The inclusivity here is special, so it was my good fortune that I came here, as opposed to maybe one of the other schools, though Atlanta is a good place on this. Atlanta is a progressive, modern city, and it is possible to be who you are and what you are in the city, I think. As you move farther out, that wouldn't be true.

In 2014, things are changing. We chose to get married in Vermont because it has the history of being tolerant and open-minded, and that appealed to us, so we picked that place, and some of the kids or parents or others that we encounter ask, "Why did you go there?" It is a beautiful place, and if you go there, you are going to a place where there is true acceptance of everyone, where people are educated, open-minded people. The freedom you feel there, to me as a gay man, is really palpable. You can just feel it in the air. It is almost like, "So you are married? So am I." It is so normal. You are just average. I hate that word, normal, but it is average. It is status quo, there.

Edward. Yeah. New York City is down the road, and Boston is over there, and Montreal is up there. It is a really great feeling to be there, but you get that here in the heart of Metro Atlanta, too. There is that attitude, but it goes away, once you go farther out. This is a great place. We are sort of an island within the island of tolerance and progressivism.

Andrew. Coming out for me was rough. I grew up in Florida, but still from a very Southern kind of family, so there was always that fear of what's going to happen, and you test the waters, of course, before you finally decide to tell who you tell. Mom made comments like, "Oh, I was watching MTV the other day with your dad, and asked, 'What would you do if Andrew were gay?' and he said, 'It would be the only thing to kill me.'" What are you going to do with that statement? You don't want to kill your father by revealing this, but luckily, it did not. My fears were not true in any sense.

My friends, of course, say—and this may be a cliché—but they said it was about time: "If you knew all this time, since junior high school, you could have said something and made my life a lot easier." But I had great friends that didn't want to push it, and it turned out well. I struggled. About the same time I came out, I converted to Roman Catholicism as well, so that was a strange dichotomy there, but I have since given that up for Lent, years ago. I am actually the atheist in charge of the Jewish students club nowadays.

Edward. When I finally acted upon it (being gay), I was about halfway through college, and it was by accident. I knew what I wanted, but I wouldn't do anything about it because I had this idea. I think a lot of gay people have it: "I don't have to live that life. I will just be straight because it is probably easier, so I will just be straight." But then I had a roommate who I then had a relationship with, and he couldn't cope with that and ran off and got married after a couple of years. But I decided, then, that ain't going to work for me, that I can't lead that straight life.

I am so glad that I didn't fall into what so many people in my generation did. They got married because they thought they were supposed to and have kids, and then that didn't work, and then that was a mess, so I never was married to a woman, and I decided that when I graduated school here in Atlanta, that Atlanta would be the place for me because it already was known for having a gay community. This is in 1973.

When I came here in 1973, it just seemed so exciting, and I had a friend who had gone to the University of South Florida, who I then moved in with, him and his roommate, who was also from Florida. The three of us lived in the middle of Atlanta, and we had a good time. I was in graduate school, but every weekend I would go out to the clubs and dance. Soon enough, I met a fellow in graduate school with me, at Emory, who then later became my partner, and he came to work here, and that is how I found out about this place. But I was leading that two-life kind of thing, and I had gay friends, and there were instances where others knew. I decided it would be nice to have a gay physician, for example, which I did. From the late '70s to the present, I have had gay physicians. At this point, I am on the fourth one, and he is really wonderful. I realized that my little brother was gay, and we then have that that we share. But it was two lives going on, side by side, this closeted life that, I didn't like. I never did like it, so it has been very liberating to abandon that approach to living, which really didn't happen completely until we got married.

Andrew. I dated a guy back in Florida, when I was teaching, and he was a first-year teacher at the time and had a picture of a female friend on his desk and actually wore a wedding band. He created this whole scenario about himself, and then the first summer that he worked there, he got a divorce and came back as a divorced teacher, a divorced straight man, the whole while that we were dating.

Of course, I was still more in the closet then than I was out, professionally or even privately, but the kids see pictures of their teachers' families on the desk or around the room. You can see them here that Edward has, and in my room, and it is amazing to be able to. Not that we talk about the photographs, but just the kids be able to see that, and it reinforces it.

We had conversations about whether we should send wedding announcements or do we not, because we were going to have a very small ceremony. Our family wasn't able to come and travel with us to Vermont. My cousin, who is younger and like a little brother to me, actually traveled with us, and we had him certified by the state to perform our marriage and solemnize it, so it was just the three of us and this co-ed who happened to be sitting in the old library while we were there. I said, "We need to send these wedding announcements because it legitimizes what we're doing." Not that I need anyone to agree with the fact, but it just further legitimizes and normalizes what we have, with what's already established. When they walk into their straight math teacher's room, and they see her family or his family in the photos, they now see the same thing in my room. It is great to not lead that double-standard, that double life, anymore.

Last year I tutored both of this lady's sons, and I was actually in her home tutoring, and we were waiting for the young man to come back from a Boy Scout outing. It was around the time when the Boy Scouts had started the conversation with letting gay students in, and gay Scout leaders, and I asked her what she thought of it. I hadn't outed myself to her at this point and really didn't before she received the wedding invitation, but I think she had concluded it, and she said to me, "I really wouldn't want a gay Scout leader in the tent with my son." Had I not been sitting at her dining room, I may have had some stern words for her, to maybe kind of help her redirect her paradigm.

But now I think being fully outed, open, and her having know what she knows and what she knew of me, is helping to shift some of that paradigm. She made a $100 donation to HRC on our behalf. We are established in our lives, so we really didn't need a wedding gift registry, so we said, "Let's talk about HRC, Southern Poverty Law Center and Atlanta Legal. If you so choose, and as you are able, make a donation, either in our names or without," to kind of help give other people the opportunity that we have or that we have taken.

A good many of our colleagues took that opportunity and did it, so I think being able to be out is super important because I can inadvertently help some individuals maybe change the way they think. One of the kids last year, in one of the classes, gave us a party, said, "You know, Señor, you are the talk of the town." I said, "I hope it's good talk," and she goes, "Oh, yeah, everyone is so excited. We love it." I told her, I said, "Just understand that not everyone, even in our community here is going to be perhaps as happy about it as you and I are, but don't let that become your issue." I said, "You have to let them find peace with their soul, and someday, hopefully, they will. They will come around, so don't let this positive thing that you are helping celebrate be a point of negativity for you." They understand that. It's been great.

Richard

One thing I still feel a lot of anger about is that there were no openly gay people in my life. I didn't know gay people could be smart or respectable or contribute to the community in exciting ways or have happy lives or be loved. I just didn't see that. I had no model of what an adult gay life would look like.

Teaching really was an accident for me. I went to grad school to do an MFA in creative writing and we had to teach as part of the assistantship I got. I thought I would hate teaching, and I really loved it. I was like, "Wait—my day job is I get to talk to people about Faulkner, or Flannery O'Connor or Toni Morrison? Like you fucking pay me to do that? That sounds ridiculous!" I just really, really liked it.

At the time, I was like, "Well, I definitely don't want to teach high school, so I better go and do a Ph.D. so I can teach at the college level. So, I went to university and did the Ph.D. and went on the job market. I'm sure you know the academic job market is just a nightmare. The director of graduate studies at the time, her husband is an English teacher, and he shot this thing to the job seekers about this job here. I was like I need a job. You know? I was like where is the money going to come from?

I kind of lucked into this job. I applied for it, and I thought there is no way this fancy elite private school is going to hire this openly gay guy who wrote a dissertation on sissies and whatever. So I was like, "I'll just be out on my application materials, and then they won't hire me." But I was hired, and the whole thing went from there. And it's been a really tremendously happy accident. It's been a really great experience. I'm really, really happy to be where I am. I feel rescued from that kind of like I don't want—to move to Nebraska and teach with no health care kind of thing. I felt like that was kind of the thing that was next, and this job kind of rescued me. It's been lovely.

I was right up front in the application letter about my fields of study. My dissertation is called "Sissies!" I can't remember if I was any more out than that. I may have said something in my teaching philosophy about as a gay man, blah, blah, blah. I guess my thinking about that was like, "I'm not interested in being in the closet." If they didn't want an out teacher, I just wanted them to know upfront, and they could not call me back for an interview. That'll be fine. If that's the reason they don't call me back then I don't want to work there anyway.

I read this book a number of years ago called *Teaching Literature* by Elaine Showalter, who's at Princeton or Yale, one of the Ivies. She has a chapter in that book about teaching as a performance and that really helped. That really changed the way I thought about teaching. Her point is it's not a performance like wearing a fake mustache and a wig and have a fake French accent, but it is a performance in the sense of Dr. Richard is a character that I play in the classroom. He's me.

He's very much like me, but he's an exaggerated performative version of me. The truth of me is that I'm a huge introvert—being around people and being social. One thing I learned about high school teaching is it's 24/7. I went from being a graduate student where I had a tiny little closet office in some big building on campus that no one ever came to—where I could have had a heart attack and died and it would have been three months before anybody came to look for me. High school teaching is like you're never alone. People are in your room 24/7: students asking questions, colleagues stopping by, meetings all the time. That's been a huge thing to adjust to. Oh my god, the meetings we have. Meetings to talk about having meetings to talk about planning meetings. That's an aspect of the job that wears me out.

When I say Dr. Richard is a performance, it's like Dr. Richard is outgoing and friendly. When my kids come by, I try not to be like, "I'm really tired, people! Go away!" I try to be on and welcoming. I guess I try to blend. I have a little speech I say to students at the start of the semester. I tell them, "I want this room to be really comfortable, and I want this class to be fun. I want us to have a good time here, but I have really high standards and expect a lot out of you. There is a lot of stuff I have zero tolerance for, like lateness and disorganization. You've got to do the work. That's the price of admission to be in here, and I'll do my best to make it a fun, exciting place, and I'll try to connect to stuff to your lives. You're 15 and don't understand what romantic poetry has to do with your life."

I grew up in North Florida in the '90s in a really conservative family. I felt very alone. High school was super miserable. I couldn't wait to get out and be done. I didn't know at the time if I was going to have a relationship with my family...if they were going to disown me. Things worked out super positive. Things are good now.

High school was really rough for me. One thing I still feel a lot of anger about is that there were no openly gay people in my life. I didn't know gay people could be smart or respectable or contribute to the community in exciting ways or have happy lives or be loved. I just didn't see that. I had no model of what an adult gay life would look like. So on the one hand, because of that, I feel this really powerful responsibility to be out. Enjoy this class if you think I'm a good teacher, if you think I'm smart.

I want kids to know I'm also gay. That's a part of this total package. On the other hand, I feel pretty strongly. I had a really bad experience TA'ing for a professor in a film study class. He was very invested in being the "cool" teacher. The class is a joke. It was really horrible. His desire to be cool, please them, and be friends with them meant they learned nothing. We had no standards. The whole thing was a joke, and the students knew that it was a joke. I believe pretty strongly that I want to be friendly, warm, and welcoming to my students, but they're not my friends and we're not peers. I do want to maintain that distance, and I think that's really healthy to maintain. At the end of the day, I'm going to give them a grade. You know sometimes they don't like the grade you give them, and you have to have a broad conversation about that. It's nice to have that sense and separation.

One thing that's always been on my mind, and I guess I have different answers to it at different times in places of teaching, is how out should I be? On the one hand I want to be out. I want them to know that I'm gay. On the other hand, they don't need to know a great deal about my personal life. Trying to strike that balance is an ongoing struggle for me in ways that I'm sure straight teachers don't ever think about.

In those few minutes before class, they'll come in and make small talk with you. And they'll be like, "What'd you do this weekend?" If my partner and I went to a movie, am I going to say? If I was married to a woman, I would never have to think anything about it. I would just say, "Oh my wife and I went to see the *X-Men* movie." On the other hand, I'm a pretty private person, and I do want there to be some kind of distance.

I started coming out to my friends at 17 or 18. I would say I was 16 or 17 before I could come out to myself. I came out to my mom at 18 or 19 and my dad at 20 or 21. And I was pretty much totally out then. I was really scared to come out to my dad. I was like, "Well, I don't give a fuck who knows!" I came out to my dad so I could care less what everybody else thinks about it.

It was rough. My parents are very conservative. They're both from a little small town in Tennessee. Very conservative. Did not have openly gay friends. The guy who cut my mom's hair was gay. I remember when I was ten or eleven my dad taking me aside and was like. "Ben's a nice guy, but that's no way to live your life just remember that."

It was rough for a long time. I came out to my mom, and for a couple of years the only way we'd talk about it was that she'd send me articles that ran in the Tallahassee newspaper about HIV and AIDS. She would cut them out and send them to me. If they had any demographic information about gay men like infection rates about gay men or whatever that would just be highlighted. They would be sent to me. Just the article folded up in an envelope. No commentary. No nothing.

Fast forward everything is fantastic. They've really grown a lot in the intervening years. They really love me, they really love my partner, and they made it abundantly clear they see us as married, that he is a part of the family. We're actually going on family vacation this summer. God help our souls. We're going to New York City. We're super flattered that they want to take us and spend money on us, but it's also like, "What are we going to do with my parents for five days in the city?" So, things are great now, but it took a long time. It was a long process.

I told them separately. I was sort of cowardly about it in retrospect. I told my mom because I didn't think my mom was going to disown me. I knew she'd be upset, but I didn't think she was going to disown me. And I told her hoping she was going to run and tell my dad so I didn't have to, but she didn't. For about two years, she knew and my dad didn't, and they're still married and live together. So, that was a really weird fraud for a couple of years. I came out to her, and she said, "Well, I snuck in your bedroom in high school and read your journal." I was like, "Oh, thanks mom." I was enormously hurt by it at the time, and now that I'm older, and especially now that I'm at teacher, it's like, "I was depressed as shit my senior year; she had to know something was going on." I can't blame her for being concerned. There was a lot of weeping and tears.

I have a cousin that's much older than me who died of AIDS in '84 or '85, which was right at the beginning when it was a total death sentence. I think that's what they knew, and I think for a long time for them it was like, "You're going to get HIV and AIDS and you're going to die. Your life's going to be short, sad, and miserable." I think it just took them time to see I was still me; I was still they're kid in a lot of ways and that their values are still my values and that I didn't have a unicorn horn or a tail.

I think back to early gay and lesbian rights movements and the emphasis they put on visibility in the hope that if people knew us in the full complexity of our lives, knew us as sons, brothers, uncles, cousins, fathers, they wouldn't be so horrible to us. If you put a face on gay people, then it's a lot harder to discriminate against them. It's a lot harder to go to the ballot box and take away their rights if you know them as your coworkers, your friends, your family members, that kind of thing. I think about how alone and how invisible it is for a kid, and I do feel some small obligation to be out in my life for that reason.

The very first interview I had before I even got hired, I talked very openly about my dissertation, and at the end of the interview, when he asked, "Do you have any questions for us?" I said, "I'm openly gay, and I'm not interested in being in the closet. I hope that's not a problem for you all." We had a nice conversation about it. There had been a guy who worked in the college admissions office who had been openly guy and the kids really liked him, and he had a good relationship with them. But there is about a quarter of the school that is very religious, very Southern, very White, evangelical, conservative that probably is less thrilled about me being at the school.

I've been very surprised at how little grief or hardship there's been about it. Some of that is probably self-selecting. I'm sure there's homophobia here. The kids come and tell me about it. Because I'm openly gay, I don't hear a lot about it; people aren't going to say that shit to my face. I'm sure there must be a few parents that are freaked out and don't want their kids to take my classes. I'm sure they just go to the registrar and get their kids moved out of my class and that doesn't come to me directly.

The school has a gay, straight alliance (GSA). It had one before I got there, but there wasn't an institutional history of them having a GSA putting on an annual assembly. One thing that we did this year that went over really well that I've seen a lot of this done at college. At university, I had that safe zone training thing, and I used to volunteer and do that. There was a segment of the safe zone training where they'd get openly gay, lesbian, bisexual, trans people to come in talk about their lives. People in training could ask them questions. So, we basically did that for assembly this year. We got a panel of LGBTQ people and one ally—a senior who's straight but has been raised by two moms. She talked about her experience being the kid of two moms.

I said, "This event isn't about me, but if you want me to talk about my experiences in coming out, I will." The GSA was like, "You have to speak." So, I spoke. I was one of the panelists. I talked about my coming out experience and the long slow growth of my parents. Were there kids that were grossed and freaked out? Probably, but I didn't hear about it. We got a lot of really positive feedback, and there were a lot of kids that sent me emails saying thank you for sharing that. I won this magnificent faculty award this year, which students nominate faculty for. When they gave me that award they were like, "We really appreciate your attempts to remind us it's okay to be different in a place that's often really homogenous. The language of that award they gave me reflected that the assembly had been powerful.

I'm coming from a background of seven or eight years in queer studies and feminist studies and gender studies. So, I have to going in be like, "I'm gay, and what that means is I am romantically and sexually attracted to people of my own gender. People who are attracted to both genders are called bisexual." To have to do that kind of work has been eye-opening to me. That work feels really basic to me. That work needs to be done, even here, which is by and large pretty progressive.

I think our school is in the process of changing. I think historically it has been the "country club high school." And I think there's about half of the student body and parent body that would be perfectly content to let it remain that. I think the other half is the half that I like better. That half I would call the new global elite: they're really high-powered, they've traveled the world, their kids maybe speak a language other than English at home, they're from multiracial families, they're interested in being a more inclusive place. They're more inclusive in terms of class, they're interested in better relationships between the school and community, better connectedness between city and school.

I read queer studies that talk about this. In some ways, maybe I'm part of the problem because they get to hire me, and they get to hire another white dude, and they also get diversity. So, last year, my first year I got hired, one of the classes they asked me to take over was AP Gothic literature. I have a huge amount of leeway in terms of how I design my courses and how I teach, and so when I was talking to the English department chair, I was like, "I kind of want to take the Gothic course and tweak it and make it a Southern Gothic Literature class. I know the book I want to end the year with is Randall Kenan's *Visitation of Spirits*." It's a very Gothic piece. It expands the territory of the Gothic into sexuality and the ways we are haunted by sexuality. It's a ghost story. It was perfect. I thought that would be a great contemporary example. It is in this state. It's set in this city. There's a reference to local towns. And neither my chair or the head of the upper school had read that before. They were like, "What its content like?" I was like, "Well, it does have an openly gay protagonist." And they were like, "We trust you to make this call, even though we haven't read the book. But we'd like you to put a disclaimer in their syllabus about teaching this book."

So, I had to put this disclaimer in. It was, "The last book we're reading this year is *The Visitation of Spirits*. It has an openly gay protagonist and has a few brief but not especially graphic depictions of gay sex. If you are uncomfortable reading this, come talk to me at the start of the semester, and we'll work out an alternative assignment." I really hated doing that. It really made me mad, but I just was like, "I'm the new guy—what am I going to do? Bottom line, they're going to let me teach the book. So, the second year, I went and had a conversation with them. I didn't ask. I just told them: "I'm not putting this disclaimer on my syllabus when I teach this class the second year. One of the books 11th graders read is Toni Morrison's *The Bluest Eye*, which has graphic descriptions of father-daughter rape. We don't have a disclaimer for that. There's no opting out of that. So, what we are saying is that being openly gay is worse or more controversial or more upsetting than graphic rape." And they were like, "Yeah, don't put the disclaimer on there."

As far as I know, I never heard about any complaints about it, and I've taught it two years now. The students complained about the book. They were like, "It's hard." We read *Beloved* this semester. *Beloved* is hard. This is not that hard.

And I remember that first year, I thought about having that disclaimer on my syllabus because I went to the school musical, which was *Oklahoma!* In those conversations about the book, my chair was like, "Well, this is high school. We have to be very careful about how we talk. We kind talk about sexuality period. It is not gay sexuality. Sexuality in general is a controversial thing to talk about." I saw the school musical, and one song is, "I'm just a girl that can't say no." Here's a high school junior or senior girl up on stage singing a song about being a slut with all these thinly-veiled double entendres about sex. Everybody's like, "Aw, it's so great! We love the school musical." That was one of those moments where I was like this is straight privilege because it absolutely is. Nobody thinks that play was really talking about sexuality, but of course the whole thing's about sexuality.

There's homophobia at school. Kids come and talk to me about it. I had two really smart guys who were lacrosse players come and talk to me about homophobia on the lacrosse team. And "fag" this and "we're going to beat these queers." Gay as an adjective to mean bad. I told them, "The fact you guys are willing to have this conversation with me is hope for the future. Y'all are seniors. You are going to have to take the hit. It's not comfortable to stand up for social justice, but nothing's going to change until you're like, 'Hey, stop saying that!' The fact that you care about this at all kind of boggles my mind. I can't imagine senior jocks from my high school being concerned about that kind of stuff."

And that is what I like—when all the bullshit drops and all the meetings and planning drop away, and you're in the room with really, really smart kids and you get to put good art in front of them and watch them wrestle with it. I was really super spoiled this year. I had a fantastic honors American Lit class. I'm doomed next year. It will never be as good. I like to go in every day and watch these super smart kids dive into Fredrick Douglass or dive into Toni Morrison, dive into Tennessee Williams or dive into poetry. That's my favorite thing. To get to be in the room and facilitate that when it happens.

Kevin

I would go to bookstores and to libraries and try and find information on homosexuality, and there were some of these 1950s textbooks talking about it being a mental illness and a disorder.

As a child I would use my Fisher-Price toys. I was acting with them, and I was also using them as...I don't know...let's say they were teaching each other things. My mother noticed it. My elementary teachers on the report card said I'd be a great teacher one day.

In college, whenever I was going to review for a test, I would find an empty classroom, and I would reteach the material to an empty room to review. It was my way of going over all the material. It was just an instinctual thing. I didn't do it on purpose; I didn't plan for it. It was just what I needed to do to get it into my brain to review all the material. Eventually, the pieces came together.

Once I graduated from ACT, American Conservatory Theater, I got a master's degree in theater and I wanted to start acting a lot. For some reason I just started teaching on the side to make money, and then it just steamrolled into being an education director of theater companies, and then finally this job became available, so I just threw my hat into the ring. Fifteen years later I'm still doing it. So it's kind of like what it was supposed to be.

I'm an advocate for the arts and for students. This is a really intensive math and science school. It's really hard. It's $40,000-plus a year tuition. The kids, of they're in regular, want honors; if they're in honors, they want AP. They want five AP classes. Their parents are pushing them; they're pushing themselves. It's really intense. But there are no desks anywhere in my room. I have twinkly lights on the ceiling. I have candles. I just want it to be an environment that the students feel safe and no pressure—it's creative and right-brain.

I feel I am allowed to be exactly who I am in the classroom. In high school, I took a psychology class, and I wrote, "I think I might be gay." Then I tore that piece of paper out and ripped it up in small pieces and threw it away. It took me about three more years to allow myself to accept it.

After 20, there was no turning back, but then a guy told me he loved me, and I ran away to Guam for six months to work in a hotel. Back in the '80s it was scarier. I would go to bookstores and to libraries and try and find information on homosexuality, and there were some of these 1950s textbooks talking about it being a mental illness and a disorder. So, it took me a while. If the internet were invented then, I would have come out in an afternoon. It would have been a very, very different world. I was working in a retail store, and that guy gave me his number. I went on one date with him. It was *Karate Kid 2*, I think. In the first case, I was shaking so much. The second I felt him kiss me, just this little scrub of his facial hair, and all that, was the moment it happened; everything clicked in; it all aligned. I knew exactly who and where I was. I went to Guam to process it. I came back, and then I just came out of the closet.

I was overwhelmed with work and a lot of stuff. I was tired. So, it was one of the reasons why I left. I really just wanted to go to an island and just work in a hotel on the beach and lead Japanese tourists on snorkeling tours. And there were gay guys there. I began to make out and test the waters and see what it was to be with a man. It was perfect.

I feel lucky to have been raised in the time I was—when I was able to hear about AIDS and not to take risks. I feel I'm alive today because I was born two or three years later than other people. So that saved me; I was able to be safe and not contract AIDS, first of all.

I'm married in California. I was able to be out and happy. I've been with my partner now, for 17 and a half years. I feel I've been allowed to be exactly who I am the entire way. It's not that easy for people in the Midwest and in other cities, or even my neighborhood, and I live at the corner of "Gay and Gay." Yeah. So, I feel really lucky.

I'm out to everyone, and their reaction is mostly a yawn. I'm a dean of students for a class. Right now it's the sophomores. I got married seven years ago. I had gotten married multiple times but they were annulled. I got married again to my husband in 2008. When I got married then, the students, my entire class, got me a wedding cake and threw a celebration. I got a gift from the entire faculty. It almost is a non-issue, other than being cool. But some people don't have it that way. I get to ignore it. I take it for granted, in a good way, because it doesn't seem to be a huge deal. No one seems to care.

There are another eight or ten other out gay teachers. One of them runs the GSA. When I got here I got involved in the GSA, and then I realized that I didn't have time for it. I didn't need to have time for it, because it's almost a non-issue. The GSA is a little bit boring.

Even the phrase "That's so gay" is not an issue any more. There's no anti-gay talk. Some of the students have a hard time coming out when they're here. There is some stress at home, because we have a very racially diverse, culturally diverse student body, and their Asian and East Indian parents can be very conservative. So there's some stress at home for those kids.

I think in some ways, I get to be a role model and say, "It's okay to be out. Once you graduate, once you leave home, you can be exactly who you are and be happy." We don't talk about it as openly; we don't push it, but being who I am and being happily open I think is a bit of a role model for some kids.

We do bring in guest speakers, such as Kevin Jackson and Kate Kendall from the National Center for Lesbian Rights. Other speakers come here every other year and address the kids with gay issues. Again, no one seems to really worry about it. It's great.

Speaking forced me to learn about myself, and I think that made me a better actor, first of all. When I talk about integrity, I'm empowering the students to be fully themselves, to express themselves, to be honest, to be truthful in their work as a performer. I think that comes from my need to be honest with who I was with myself, with being gay. I think that being gay myself has made me a better theater teacher.

We had a transgender teacher here. She didn't reveal it. I think people had suspicions, but she was such a powerful math teacher. Her emails kicked ass. She was so good. She would be in a faculty meeting and say the exact right thing. She was a power teacher, and she was trans. Just before she left, she became public about it and had a meeting with about two of the students about being trans and GSA. This is a school where everyone yawned again. No one seems to care.

I came out early on, 14 years ago, in a class. Something came up about how all the theater artists, so many of them seem to be gay. I just mentioned I was a gay man myself. And then a conservative Christian girl called and told her parents. The parents called the office, and then they called me in and said, "Why did you come out of the closet?" I said, "It was part of the academic discussion." They said, "Okay. Cool. Thanks," and that was it. It never came up again.

My goal this year is to empower students, even if they're not an actor. I have so many non-actors this year. I empower them be free to be who they are, whether in a character or not, and presenting in front of people, to speak openly and truthfully, to speak what they need to say, to not feel the need to edit who they are. That's my theme for the year, and I'm realizing now that my being gay is infusing that in a really great way.

Olivia

I felt like I wasn't butch enough, I wasn't sarcastic enough, I wasn't funny enough. It was not an easy process as I'm sure it's not for most people. In some ways, I think it was harder. My straight friends were a lot more accepting than I found the gay community, initially.

When I tell stories about myself as a teacher, I call myself Ms. Olivia. I definitely have a persona at school, whereas if I'm telling another story about myself, I will say Olivia. I think the kids find me approachable, but not their best friend.

I think I'm a better high school teacher. I covered a middle school class earlier this year when somebody was sick, and the kids were doing batteries and stuff. I'm like, "Don't put the battery on your tongue." I shouldn't even have given them that idea to do that. I think I'm definitely much better with the older students.

Clearly, the physics that I'm teaching is not high-level physics. I don't think I've yet turned into one of those people that's like, "Come on! Don't you get this?" I forget that I've explained it 50 times or 150 times, but they've only heard it once. What keeps me going is I like the kids as people. That's why I like teaching high school, not college

I also like to think about how they learn. I love reading books about cognitive psychology and how that connects to having kids retain material. I think perhaps my biggest fault might be that I absorb their energy. If they're too stressed, I might slow down my class a bit. I'm not somebody who's always, "Let's move forward." I don't like to ask people to do things that they don't want to do. Sometimes I don't think I push my kids as hard as they could be pushed.

The thing that's the biggest part of my identity is being from the Midwest. I don't think it's being gay. I didn't come out until I was in my late 20s. But in my formative years, looking back, I can understand how being gay was part of all that stuff going on. What's important to me in terms of standing up is my own identity is being from a culture where, heaven forbid you'd have somebody clean your house.

Growing up, we didn't go out to eat. Part of that was financial. You did for yourself. Now, I have a garden. I hem my own pants. Friends from high school have jobs in a factory and work in a supermarket, and they know everybody in town and everybody's job was important. That is the biggest part of my personality. My identity is that identifier.

It was definitely an asset in that I coach an engineering team at my school. That is how stereotypically some of the farm boys, most of the boys, would move off of the farm. They say, "I'm comfortable fixing a tractor. I'm going to go to Purdue and study engineering." In that sense, it's an asset that I maintain lab equipment.

If you asked kids what's important to Ms. Olivia, I don't know if they would know. They can say that so-and-so's a Boston Red Sox fan or so-and-so likes to ride horses, but I bet they don't know about me, other than that I coach the engineering team. Every once in a while, I might say I'm from the Midwest, but I don't think they get it as much. They are no easy things for them to appreciate about me.

Growing up, I was in this small town and Catholic with the fear of sex and being pregnant. People in my high school got pregnant and it was easy for me to be like, why is it so hard? I went to college. Where I went to school, it was very sorority and fraternity oriented. Being gay was not even an option. I bought into the whole math/science geek identity. I didn't have the same socio-economic class as a bunch of people at my school.

I thought I was socially awkward. I was in grad school with mostly men in physics. It wasn't until I moved here and had some gay friends and then realized, this might be something that maybe I am. It wasn't like I dated a lot, but it was very hard for me to meet other women. Even when I thought I probably was, it wasn't like when people say, "I went to this gay bar and these are my people."

I felt like I wasn't butch enough, I wasn't sarcastic enough, I wasn't funny enough. It was not an easy process as I'm sure it's not for most people. In some ways, I think it was harder. My straight friends were a lot more accepting than I found the gay community, initially.

We had a head of school at the time, and he was rather homophobic. The culture was not to talk about it. I was so relieved that this was going to make me feel more comfortable with myself that I told some of the people I worked closely with who were straight. My sister lives in town. She was very accepting. In a way, it was a huge relief. I was like, "This explains a lot."

I was living with my best friend from high school who is supportive, but not very emotional. I moved into a lesbian group house and bought a car. It was helpful. I thought, "This will help me feel more comfortable with who I am and living here." For the most part, it was a mix of feeling relieved that I'm not a social nerd—I'm just gay. Yet, trying to figure out how to navigate was hard. I got how to be straight: you go with your girlfriends and you talk about guys. Everybody together looking for the same thing. I thought, how does that translate? With everybody dating each other, how does that work? People would say, "You should join a softball league." I'm like, "I don't like softball. I like theater." It was exhilarating and confusing, I guess.

The lesbian group house was good for me to claim my identity, but I didn't end up being best friends with anybody in that group. Because I was so frustrated by how to meet people, I did join a coming out group. That was super helpful. In the coming out group, there were one or two facilitators and maybe ten people. We would go around the group every week and talk about what was going on. Some people were not out to their families. Some people had been in long term relationships for a long time and still not out to their families and trying to deal with that. The facilitators would give us readings about homophobia, racism, and coming out. Afterward, we would often go out for dinner or something. Occasionally, people would say, "I'm going hiking this weekend. Would you like to do that?" That was nice to have other people, like a freshmen orientation, where we're all clueless and we're going to give each other permission to be clueless together. There's no such thing as a stupid question.

Now, the biggest thing being openly gay means to me is when people say, "We don't have any out kids." I'm not very political, but I say, "Every year I know of kids who have told their college counselor, have told their good friends that they are gay." You don't have to wave the rainbow flag as a student every day to be out. That's asking a lot of a 16-year-old. For myself, it means talking about my partner to people that I know. To me it means not hiding it from my doctor, not hiding it from my friends. All of my family knows.

We had a commitment ceremony. We're not legally married, because we live in the South. I was asked to be on the diversity task force and help with the gay/straight alliance, and it has meant claiming a culture. Being out is telling the world publicly and owning who you are, but a deeper level of out is feeling that that is part of you culturally. Learning about the history and learning about what it's like now. I've been asked to do more to help plan coming-out days at school, and the more I do, I've really felt this is also part of who I am culturally.

I first came out to my department chair. I think she knew. I think she was probably the first person I told. The head of school now knows. But I don't think I told the old head of school because of the feeling that I had gotten from them. When she became the new head of school and we had introductory meetings, I wanted to tell her; it was important to me to explain it to her, but I can't remember why I didn't.

When we were thinking about our honeymoon, we were planning a trip to Hawaii and one of the kids said they were going. I said I'm going next summer. The kid said, "You're really planning ahead, aren't you?" I said, "No, I'm getting married. We're going there for our honeymoon." This kid said, "I didn't even realize you had a boyfriend, Ms.

Olivia." I said, "I don't have a boyfriend. I have a partner." The kids all felt, in a good way, respectful. The rumor that got spread is they were like, "We're special. That may not be something she wants to tell other people. She told us this. We want to honor that."

As time went on, the woman who teaches civil liberties said, "Would you give a presentation about the Stonewall riots to my class?" That became, "Will you do a presentation for the whole school?" The students all know. But I don't know how much the parents know. It's not something that I try to throw out there, but I don't know how many of the parents know. I think all of the students are very aware.

At first, what I was afraid of was the kids saying that she favors the girls more than the boys. I was afraid of that. I was not afraid of them saying that's gross. We did have a student who was from Jordan, and it was against his religion. He was pretty open about that. There've been some kids who've been in various discussions because of the gay/ straight alliance who have say, "It's against my religion, but I'm open minded." Occasionally you will hear about a straight person favoring, not necessarily inappropriately, but still having a preference for either people of their own gender or people of the other gender because of how they connect. That made me anxious.

To be honest, when the girls wear those low tops, and I'm trying to go around the room and help them with their problems. I'm like, "I'm going to kneel down on the floor next to you." I'm not going to lean over. That makes me uncomfortable.

I am sensitive to the students who might be struggling with their real identity. I can think of one boy in particular who was incredibly anxious and very annoying in terms of wanting to memorize the formulas and very needy coming in for help. I'm sitting there thinking I know where this kid's struggle is coming from. This fear of being wrong is connected to this other fear in his life of having the wrong sexual orientation, and I was a lot more patient with him. I'm a patient person anyway, but there was definitely another layer of understanding of that.

I think, even if I was straight, I might be a feminist, too. I'm definitely always thinking about girls can do math, girls can do physics, girls can be on the engineering team. That's probably more connected to my own personal experience in the science field and not necessarily being gay.

Being a lesbian definitely affects my identity as a science teacher and being a role model for girls. We don't have a lot of girls on the engineering team. I'm wondering what are we not doing for them? How is it that I say this is important to me and yet we haven't taken the steps? Next year, we're trying to do more low stress activities where we invite the freshmen to come so they don't show up and feel like everybody already knows how to use all these tools.

I grew up in a gender-stereotypical town. I went to high school in the '80s. My sister, who likes to dance, joined the school dance squad or whatever. They did the rifles and the flag corp during the football game. They were given football players and basketball players and they were supposed to decorate their lockers. I tell this story at my school now, and we don't even have cheerleaders. If we told the girls, "You have to decorate the male athletes' lockers and bake them cookies," there would be an outrage. This was not the '50s; this was the '80s!

There are occasions when I am angry because I did not want to be a teacher. I wanted to do databases and computer science. My school hadn't figured out how to be liberal arts and do computer science. There are days when I'm pissed off. I'm like, "Damn it, I didn't want to be a teacher." Girls are told, "You can be a teacher, a nurse, and you can be a mom." I'm not a mom I'm not a nurse. There are days when I feel like I wanted to fight this. I didn't want to end up in a traditional female role. What I try to do is try to be as professional as I can be. That's how I fight that feeling.

This past year, another gay teacher and I started an affinity group for kids that meet at lunch. The kids who came the first week have continued to come. We have a gay/straight alliance, but that was always well-meaning straight people trying to talk. I'm sure it's how I sounded when I was trying to be on the side of the people of color at our school. Meanwhile, you have no idea what you're talking about, or you're trying to step into our shoes and that's not the same thing.

We do have a gay/straight alliance, but the leadership on that has been uneven. There have been years where they have hardly had meetings. One year, when it turned into watching *Glee*, and the other teacher and I were like, "Okay. This is really not what we think this used to be."

Now that we have the affinity group, we know who they are. Next year's leaders are going to be two gay kids, who aren't vocally out, but by stepping out next year, they are in a way being more out. The third leader, she's an adopted kid from two moms. We definitely have same-sex families here, and most of the students know. They own that as part of their identity, as a child of same-sex parents.

More recently, we had a girl who was pretty out, and a little bit different on top of that. She was into the fur community, where they dress up like animals. She liked costumes, and she was an artist. I don't think she was into the sexual side, although she may have been, I don't know. She was always marching to her own drum. There was an incident where somebody posted a very hateful comment on her Tumblr, saying, "If you take a girl to prom, I will kill you." It was anonymous, and the school tried to trace the IP address, but could not get that. That was three years ago. We had a town meeting about that. A straight kid came to me and said, "Why isn't the school doing anything about this incident?" Then I went to the administration, and they were doing something about it but doing it behind the scenes. The student didn't know that was happening. Then we did eventually have a town meeting, with the victim's permission.

Like I said, it was popular to say, "Oh, I like your sweater, homo" a couple years ago, but I have not heard that as much lately. At one of the gay/straight alliance meetings, some of the girls said that the boys in the senior lounge were saying, "Would you rather have this horrible thing happen to you, or this gay sex act, or be gay?" I know it happens, because the kids will occasionally tell me. If they're telling me, then I know that they're only going to tell you a fraction of what there is. I know there are also kids who are standing up when they hear that, and saying, "That's not okay."

I am someone who gets very frustrated when I am going into a situation, and I don't know what's going to happen. I hate it when, like my college counseling job, you're going to be in charge but not necessarily given you the tools you need. Not because they're trying to make you sink or swim, but because they don't have it. I hate that feeling. I had an older sister who got A pluses in school, and I hated feeling inferior to her. I have a very high sensitivity to helping kids feel confident. I did enough activities, labs, exercises, and worksheets to know what I'm doing. It helps me feel I know what that's like to be in a situation. I'm a good explainer, so that they get that.

I love having students come back as alums and finding out who they are as adults. I find it funny when they make up nicknames for each other that are appropriate. I find it cute. I love the high school age, where they're really saying, "I'm trying on some hats and gaining some confidence and learning that I'm a self-sufficient young man or woman."

Brian

One of the things that's really difficult about this school is that we have not had a lot of kids who are openly gay here. We have kids who are gay who will tell a select few people that they're gay, but not a lot of kids who are out and proud as it were.

I was offered a number of different jobs when I was looking for work, and this was the only school that had a statement that included nondiscrimination based on sexual orientation. That was a big part of my taking the job here. Other places said, "We don't discriminate, sex, whatever, race, creed," but this school actually had a sexual orientation statement, which made me think it's probably an okay place to work.

I came out in the heat of the AIDS crisis in the early '80s, so I'm more of a kind who doesn't make a lot of noise. I'm not like screaming about my sexual identity a lot with the students and families. It's work, you know? To me, it's more like this is my job. I don't avoid questions about my personal life, but I also don't say, "Hey, let me talk about my personal life with kids." I truly think this is a generational thing in some ways. I grew up in Texas, too, so I grew up in a pretty conservative part of the world at a pretty conservative time.

When I first came to this school, my partner had been an administrator at a university in Michigan. He's older than I am and had made conscious work choices. He was never going to deny the fact that he was gay at work. When I moved here, I said, "You know what? I'm not going to do that either. I'm going to be honest with people." The very first day of work, we had this stand up, sit down activity. Stand up if you're this or that. One of the questions was stand up if you're gay. I stood up, and that was a really big moment for me. From the beginning, I was out to the faculty. That night there was a party at the head's house for the new teachers, and I brought my partner and introduced him to my boss and then to both my department chair and my boss. With the faculty, I've been out from the very beginning.

Subsequently kids have been over to my house and have met my partner, and I introduce my partner to them when I run into them in the street, but I don't spend a lot of time talking about political issues in class. I try to be pretty neutral about most of this. I just don't talk about it a lot.

I teach a human development class, and we talked about sexual orientation in that class, but I don't really say, "This is how I feel. This is how I knew I was gay. This is when I knew I was gay." I never talk about that stuff. I truly think some of it is because of my age and my background. Some of it is also because of my philosophy of teaching is that you don't say, "Hey, this is how you should think."

Coming out was pretty rough. Again, I came from a family, a loving family, but very conservative, Southern Baptist, the whole drill. Lots of tears. Lots of emotions. Lots of disapproving from my father. But, it's great. It's funny. We weathered that storm. We never had, "I am never going to speak to you again." There was never that kind of thing, but that was a rough patch.

For me, being gay is kind of a passive thing in that when I have to go to dinners with our board of trustees, I will bring my spouse and introduce him as my spouse, as opposed to walking around the hallways saying, "Hi, I'm gay." I would never introduce myself, and say, "Oh, I'm gay."

I was at this event last night that was for our new teachers. It was the same thing I went to 15 years before. It was interesting. I was telling a story to the new music teacher, and I was saying how I play the piano, and my spouse plays the stringed instrument, and I found myself hesitating to reveal the sex of my spouse. Even after 15 years! And also, what I think is really interesting, is that I am in a little bit of a position of power as this person, even though, compared to her, I have a lot more power and access in the institution, I still found myself hesitant to tell her, "Oh, it's a he that I live with. I'm talking about him." It's kind of sad, but it's still true.

This is a pretty sophisticated school and school culture. I have a friend who is a physics teacher here who's gay, and she talks about her partner all the time and shows pictures from their honeymoon and all that kind of stuff. I don't do any of that with my students. Some of it is personality of not wanting to share a lot of personal information with people. Some of it really is disproportional. I just don't think anybody cares about my life.

There is sort of a group of gay teachers at the school, but it's a very diverse group of people. There's the physics teacher. There's me. There's a person who is an athletic director and who was very closeted when I got here. I have said it took her a long time to say that she's a lesbian. She's like ten years older than I am, and so there's another generational thing. Donald is ten years younger than I am. It's interesting that there's this diversity of ages because I think most of us kind of play to the stereotypes of those ages.

I had a colleague once who mimicked the way I walk. Like seventh-grade bullying kind of stuff. Just once, I said, "No, that's wrong. That's terrible," whatever. Once I was in a meeting with a lower school teacher, and this was a long time ago, and the lower school teacher said, "That's so gay," in response to something that she thought was stupid. When I confronted her, she burst into tears, and I'm suddenly the bad guy.

We have a blood drive that comes every year and, for many years, there was no acknowledgment that gay men were basically banned from giving blood. That has been interesting, how those conversations go somewhere or they don't go somewhere or they create real disagreement within the gay community here at the school.

One of the things that's really difficult about this school too is that we have not had a lot of kids who are openly gay here. We have kids who are gay who will tell a select few people that they're gay, but not a lot of kids who are out and proud, as it were. There's been a lot of special pleading for that: "Oh, we're so small," or whatever. That conversation has evolved over the years. I think because people have pushed harder, but that's a way that I think that I have made a difference here.

What's hard about it is you kind of have to balance your own feeling of paranoia and whatever. It's hard to know how much of it is my own paranoia and how much of it is real. I think that's been challenging. There have been specific people who have done things that I have found problematic or offensive, but some of it is—this is not the right word—a hunch. It's just like a hunch. It's hard for me to put my finger on some of it. I think some people trivialize the relationship that I have with my partner because there's not a child involved. I work with teachers who say things like, "Well, you don't understand. You don't have children." Okay. That to me feels homophobic.

I think that's also one of the dangers of being a teacher is that I still remember things that my teachers said in second grade, and I understand that some things that I say thoughtlessly are remembered by my students.

I grew up poor and gay and those things make me feel alienated from the school culture at large, which is affluent and straight. For a lot of years, I thought, "That really gives me an insight that is a really important one," and I hadn't really thought (although I was interested in equity and racial justice and all those kinds of thing), about how in interacting with Black families or Latino families or whatever, they don't know that I grew up poor, and their first thought isn't about the fact that I am gay; instead, it's probably that I'm White. So that has been a real revelation to me in the last five years and thinking about sort of claiming my Whiteness when I'm talking in some situations.

Our culture is White, affluent, and straight. Although I think this is a school that likes to reflect, I think to be honest, it's a pretty self-congratulatory place. It is a very nice culture. There's lots of celebration. I think that that's all good and everything, but what happens is I think it creates complacency: "Let's talk about how sensitive we are and how wonderful we are and let's talk about this one kid who had a great experience, but let's not talk about the kids who maybe didn't get acknowledged at all."

Here's an example. The footballer, Michael Sam. Everyone was like, "Oh, it's great. It's great." But then he gets drafted, and he kisses his boyfriend, and all of a sudden everyone is like, "Oh my god, what the hell is happening?" I thought that was really interesting. Theoretically, that was fine that he was gay, but then when they actually saw him kissing someone, it was knock-your-socks-off crazy.

I haven't been in many other school contexts. When I worked in Texas, certainly no kid said that he was gay. And when I worked in the university, they weren't really talking about that kind of stuff at that level.

I notice a lot of kids will come out as bisexual, and then may bring a person of the same sex to the prom or something like that, but that is very disturbing to the community. I think that some kids react strongly. The faculty is actually fine. I truly believe that the faculty is good. The thing that I think is really true, though, goes back to my question of niceness. Nobody wants to be a jerk. Educators really do want to do the right thing and be good people. What I think, is hard is when I have confronted people with things that I really think are wrong or are homophobic or heterosexist even, and the defensiveness is just incredible. I think it's hard to own mistakes. For example, nobody wants to be like, "You know, what I said was homophobic. I must be homophobic in some way." Nobody wants to think that. So, what ends up happening is that there's this huge defensiveness that occurs that then puts the burden of the problem back on me, as it were, and I feel like I'm apologizing for upsetting someone for pointing out what an asshole they were, which is not great.

Lisa

*We don't have any "out" students at school,
which is really fascinating when paired with how many "out"
faculty members there are.*

I had a really great experience in a private school. I went to boarding school when I was junior, and in the faculty there, there were a few specific adults that really just supported me and changed my life. I got there wanting to be a writer and left after two years knowing that I wanted to be part of a school community, and I wanted to have that same impact that these people had on me.

I think being a teacher is a big part of who I am. I think having the summers off and having that time to explore and go after my interests has really played into who I am. I like being outdoors. I love playing basketball. I think that's one of the things I found the most success at in my life. Family's really important to me, so I'm a daughter, and I have a sister. I'm a wife now; I got married a little over a year ago.

Most of the time, I'd say an awful a lot has changed. I think the responsibility that comes with being out, I have felt that a little bit more. I am very aware of my gender and of my sexual orientation. I think that's something I want to make sure people know, and I sur-round myself with people who support me. I feel really fortunate to have a lot of support in my life.

I think the person I am at school very much resembles who I am as a person. I definitely am a big kind of self-discloser, and the kids know a lot about my life, and I think that's important to build those relationships. It's funny because my wife used to work at the same school as well, and she was definitely much more private, so that was an interesting balance to find for a while. Like I said, I am a big family person who has a really tight-knit group of friends, and I think that focus and importance on relationships carries into my role as a teacher.

I was dreading going back to school more than I actually ever have for some reason, but when I saw the kids, I just...I don't know...it was great. I really thrive on those relationships, and I think that's true outside of school and in my life as a teacher.

I started dating when I played basketball in college. I started dating one of my teammates for quite a while. It was one of those things where I'd thought about it for a year, and kind of kept it at bay. I had a boyfriend at the time and kept saying, "No. This isn't true. This isn't true..." and then the second it happened, I knew that this is who I am.

All my friends were very supportive. That really important person in my life from high school was super supportive. She was my biggest fan. Had a pretty horrific reaction from my mom at first, who has since come around completely, but the rest of my family, extended family and everything, were all very supportive. Like I said, the second it happened, it clicked, and it didn't take me long to start talking about it. I told a lot of my closest friends. I called some of my friends from high school, things like that, so it became a pretty big part of my life pretty quickly.

Mom came up at the end of the year to help me move some stuff out, so I ended up telling her on Mother's Day, which wasn't necessarily fair, looking back. I actually thought that she would be fine, and that my dad was the one that I was worried about. Her youngest brother is gay, and she's been super supportive, and the whole family has been really supportive, and she's seen how much happier he has been since he came out. For some reason, it was just a lot of, "I don't support you. I'll never support you. I don't agree with this." Just to make sure I understood that, she sent follow up emails just being like, "I want to make sure you didn't take anything wrong away from our conversation. I want you to know that I don't support this relationship," blah, blah, blah.

It went on like that for probably for a year. We didn't really talk about it, but we didn't get along anyway before all this, so we just didn't talk about it for a while. When she met my now wife for the first time, probably three years later, it kind of all clicked the second she met her. The second she met, she said that she knew and it made sense to her and that she can't imagine a better person for me. Since then, she's like my biggest fan, but there's a part of her that is embarrassed; she thought maybe it was a reflection on her, or some reason.

I'm out to everybody. My wife worked at the school first, so I already knew quite a few people just from coming to social events and things like that. I think in one of my first new faculty meetings, I told the story, "Oh yeah, I was traveling in Europe this summer with my girl-friend," and kind of just let it be known that way. A lot of the kids have kind of figured it out just how they are. They notice everything.

I think we finally started talking about it specifically with the kids once we got engaged, but I have pictures from our wedding and things like that. It's definitely not something that I necessarily talk about a ton with the kids, but I definitely put it out there.

There are a lot of out faculty members here which is neat, specif-ically a lot of gay women, so I think I wasn't the first. One of my col-leagues who just left this year, she'd been there for 20 years, sounded like she was kind of the first. It sounds like, 20 years ago, the school was entirely different, and the school kind of asked her to get up there and talk about it and things like that, I guess it's not as big of a deal now. It's not something that you feel like you need to handle delicately, which I really appreciate.

We don't have any "out" students at school, which is really fasci-nating when paired with how many 'out' faculty members there are. I try to talk about it, or try to just kind of share this part of my life, to make that space a little bit more comfortable and to model for kids what it can look like, and that it is an okay space. I think it says a lot about the school that there aren't out students.

I feel very supported. People go out of their way to, maybe when they're around me, but even when they're talking with other people, go out of their way to say "girlfriend or boyfriend" or things like that. I think we're evolving to include more LGBT-friendly language and assumptions and things like that, at least within the faculty. I don't think that's true within the student body yet.

I think I carry myself in a certain way, but I'm not sure if that is because of my gender expression or my sexual orientation. I'm an athlete, and I think I've always had this certain confidence, and I dress in a certain way. What I put out there maybe comes across as a little bit more confident than some of my other female colleagues. I don't know if I necessarily am confident. I don't think that's the case, but I think the way I carry myself is different. Again, I don't know if that's because of my orientation or how I see myself as female, as a woman.

I've experienced a lot of homophobic language. Usually, just like, "That's so gay" or hearing people call each other "faggots" or things like that. I was in a classroom once, and a kid said like, "That's so gay" to someone and then he saw me, and he left. He came back, I think like an hour later, and he looked mortified. He was like, "I know you heard what I said," and I appreciated that. It was really hard for him to do that, and he recognized what he had done. I don't take that to mean that he'll never do it again. He's a kid who just knows how to play the game.

We had an interesting email last year after our Day of Silence speaker who was Tim McCarthy from Harvard who runs the Carr Center. He talked a lot about race. He talked a lot about sexual orientation. He was a big athlete in college and has since come out, and he was just kind of talking about a little bit of the history of the LGBT movement and focused a bit on bullying and the ways that he didn't stand up for people growing up and ways that he wasn't stood up for either.

We got a parent email saying, "Why this bullying fad? What's so different about LGBT bullying?" Things like that. I think the parent meant well, and the head of school forwarded it to me and said that he asked the parent if we could share it with the GSA, which we did, which was nice, and the head of school came. We just discussed the email, which I thought was really neat, and it kind of gave the kids a way to talk about it, in a real-life context.

Parents push back for certain things. We also have something called Day of Consideration, which is a day we take off school and usually have a bunch of workshops. We did it for the second time last year. It's a day to look inward at your identity and to look out. It's different every year. We usually have a keynote speaker and a performance. And last year I think we had, for a school with 400, we had 100 kids called in sick that day, which made me want to quit my job. I went home at the end of the day and almost in tears.

Then we found out or saw that a lot of kids were tweeting things about it that were really racist and really homophobic, and that was really disappointing. I think it kind of told us where we were, where we are. I think the school, the community, the administration, the faculty, supports a lot of the work, but it's not necessarily well received by all the families. There were a ton of kids that were there, but a quarter of the school not being there sends a pretty clear message. I don't blame the kids. I blame the parents. I think that's part of it too: it is the parent population that we're working with.

James

By virtue of walking this journey, I would say that I am more sensitive to students who feel they are at the margins in any number of ways; sexual orientation, for sure, but also students who are from historically underserved populations or students who are of different language origins or religious background.

I've always known teaching was going to be something I'd end up doing. I fought it for a while. At the end of the day, for me, I realized how important teachers were in my life. That's really where I felt most at home, was in the classroom. I'm a nerd, and I own that fully. For me to give students a chance to explore ideas and to see and play with novel concepts or talking about authors and their own world views is really powerful. That was one of the reasons I think I got into teaching.

The other reason, I think, is to be a mentor to people, to help people on whatever journey it is, walk through that journey with them and be supportive. I help them with their growth and learning, about self and personhood and what it means to be a citizen in society.

A lot of my students would say I'm kind of their friend before teacher, which is interesting and somewhat of a blurred line to walk. We are all about boundaries in teaching, but at the same time if I can't be authentic with students and can't be transparent, I feel like nothing will really happen in the classroom the way that it should.

I am not a content expert. I don't value content in the way that other people do. It has its place, but I care much more that students can do and perform and have confidence in things and also have IQ that is strong and developed. I want students who can write and become authors of their own thoughts and ideas about the world. For us to really be in that heart and mind space, I think I have to be more authentic, transparent, more of a friend, as opposed to someone who is teaching. That sort of distance between myself and my students is much less than some of my peers.

I am someone who believes that classroom is community and needs to be built. It has to be intentionally done. It can't be, "Here is your roster, go to it." It is how can we create something in this classroom that feels a certain way. Not everyone believes that is important, but that is pretty fundamental to my belief about education.

That classroom space is one of the most important things and it has to be thoughtfully done. There are times when students or myself make mistakes with that and we have to repair those things, and that is time away from content, but it is really important time to spend.

My junior course, I teach about all kinds of issues with identity, and students are just learning for the first time things about, let's say, white privilege. They may say things that sounds messy or sloppy or irresponsible, and it is not from a place of being malicious but a place of just not knowing. They are trying to fumble through ideas, which is good and encouraged, and we have a safe space that they can do that in, but there are times people are offended. Just from not knowing, they have said something that unintentionally has some bias or maybe a rude statement. Or I may say something inadvertently.

I think here in this place, being religious, I oftentimes made light of religion. I also forget that, for a lot of students, this is really important to them and their family—faith is exceptionally important. I would definitely put my foot in my mouth a few times about religious things, so I have to tend to that as well.

My students here and outside know my struggles with being multiracial. They know about my struggles being openly gay in this community. There are times I struggle in this city, being openly gay and being multiracial, and I get frustrated with the community a lot. My students, kind of by virtue of what I talk about in class, know some of the struggles. So it is nice of them to see it and understand from a first-person narrative that this is what it is like for me. I can share some things with my students as I walk through my daily life. I offer a kind of commentary on issues of race, issues of sexuality. I can talk openly with my students about that. When I first arrived here seven years ago: no way, no how. Couldn't share those things.

I think part of my growth and my identity can be more okay living in my skin being multi-racial, being gay. Being somebody who kind of considers themselves an intellect. I am at ease with those things now, and seven years ago, I wasn't. I think this place has change me. I have read the cultural landscape here, and I think families are a bit more accepting.

The role I can play in students' lives by being openly gay in a classroom or in school is, for me, a modeling thing. I can be support. If you are questioning, if you are not sure, if you are sure whatever it is, you know there is someone who has walked a walk similar to yours. Not exact similar, but it is, "Oh yeah, Mr. James, he is gay, so he must know." Or if you just need to talk about it. It is nice for them, I think, to know there is someone out there, so in a way, it is my way of serving the community.

I always was gay but didn't have the word for it when I was five. I knew the word and put it all together when I was 12. I was reading a book, and it was called *A Boy's Own Story*, and it was a very vivid coming-of-age story for this young gay boy. I am like, "Oh, my god this is it. That is it! Got it." I remember I was in a car coming back from Memphis with my family after shopping. That is when I knew and had the word language to put with it. That was 12, then the next six or seven years, I struggled with it. I had a girlfriend in high school but was still acting on kind of the homosexual stuff on the side.

I made out with guys. It wasn't really experimentation for me. I was like, "Yeah, this is what I want." Then I came out when I was 19 to a friend in college. Then family when I was 21. I don't know if it is hard for me to tell where I fall in the spectrum of early or late in life. I think fairly late, from what I hear now from students anyway and what I read in the literature and popular culture.

Friends were great. I think it wasn't a bad for me with my friends because people already assumed I was. So, it was really more of a validation of what I think the world thought. Which was interesting, and it took some of the pressure off. I had this grand vision of what it would be like to come out, and I expected this very glamorous kind of debutante moment, and it was not that. I thought, "Okay, whatever. That sucked." But it was fine. I was supported for sure.

For my family it was a little bit harder. I am from in a little town in Missouri. I told my brothers first, and they again had a very similar response to friends. It was more of a confirmation, "Yeah, we know. It is okay. Everything is good." I told my parents shortly after, and my parents were accepting. My mom cried, I remember, but I think moms typically do, and I remember her comment to me was, "I am not crying because of you. I am crying because of how I know the world will view you and treat you and it is harder." She said, "I am frustrated for you because I know what it will mean."

My dad didn't say a lot. My dad is very religious. Fortunately, his sister had come out a couple years prior, so that kind of paved the way a little bit. My mom told me that she talked to my father soon after, and she said, "You know you have two choices here. You can either love him for who he is or you lose him entirely. You take your pick. I am not telling you what your answer should be." But really at that point, he was good.

I know people have had struggles with coming out to family and what that can mean for people, so I am very fortunate to have none of those traumatic moments where I am disowned or kicked out. I have been thankful for those things.

I think depending on the context and how we define it, I think coming out to students it is just sharing who I am. I make a declaration on day one: "Just so you know, you may have heard I am gay." Even my sophomore, I tell them, "You may have heard and you may not have, but I just want to share this part of me with you. If you have any questions about it or comments or concerns, please talk to me about those." That, again, was not the case seven years ago.

I remember it was a strange thing. I asked permission to come out. I asked my head of school at the time, and I look, "I want to live in this school and this community, if you think this place would be okay with it." He said, "I am okay with it, so it is fine." So that was two years into my career here, and since then, I have been open.

There were a couple of people, I think, who weren't thrilled with it or okay with it, given some of their religious background and beliefs. I have had a colleague of mine say that an anecdote she heard from a family was they were worried at first when they hired me but were really glad I was there and a part of their daughter's life. She has never really been around an openly gay person who had everything together, which was interesting.

This place is a series of contradictions, given is Episcopal nature. The Episcopal church is inclusive, and homosexuality has been something that has been a topic of conversation in front of the church for a long time. It has come down on the side as being inclusive and accepted. When I first arrived here, I didn't necessarily feel that right away. I feel that the needle is pointing more and more towards that now, which is good.

Being openly gay in this particular place doesn't feel marginalized necessarily. It doesn't feel stigmatized. I am able to move throughout my day as a professional at ease. I don't have to worry about it. I always worry about parents who have a bit of curiosity or maybe a bit of dislike or disdain for it. That may be a small worry I have.

I think the other piece, as I am walking around my day here, is students who are careless with language. I hear it from other people as well. It is a symptom of something deeper I think. My students and I have these conversations in class about have we moved to a place where words like "gay" and "fag" are commonplace, and they don't really have the loaded meaning that we associate with them. We have never settled the debate. Gay for them maybe be a perfectly innocuous word; for me, I still hear it and I feel something.

Most of the time, I confront it for sure. I will speak up and say something. Not in a reprimanding way. I don't think students respond when you are reprimanding. It is more of coaching, coaching through language and thinking about what could you say, or how might this sound? Or what was your intent in your choice of words? As opposed to, "Don't do that." It is really kind of training to, pardon the phrase, make it a "teachable moment," where students think, "Oh, okay, just think of how it actually may sound to the external world based on who is in your presence." Those moments happen a fair amount.

By virtue of walking this journey, I would say that I am more sensitive to students who feel they are at the margins in any number of ways. Sexual orientation for sure, but also students who are from historically underserved populations or students who are of different language origins or religious background. I think I am acutely aware of where they are in the community, how they find place, and how they find somewhere or something to connect to in this space. That is what school should be for everybody. It should be a place where you can connect and feel a sense of home. I really worry about those students because I know I have walked that walk myself throughout school.

I think it affects me in that way. I approach a lot of teaching from more of a coaching standpoint. It is not about scolding, telling what not to do. It is about encouraging and your reflection of the moment. I want them to be more equipped and better able to handle the situation. I want them to be more inclusive people in this world, and I can get there by coaching and facilitating and encouraging and reflection.

Generally, there are probably two things I would say about how my sexual orientation has really impacted or influenced my identity as a teacher. The way I see it manifest itself most obviously is that the students who approach me are the ones I feel most comfortable with.

I think at any point in time, if you walked by my office, you would see it more than likely filled with far more girls than boys. I think young women have gravitated toward me.

I think I have been given a pass by being gay. "Well, he's gay, so nothing to worry about." I coach a girl's sport. I think that, over time, I have been able to build relationships with guys here. I would say it is harder to build them with guys. I think it has probably made it a bit harder by being openly gay with some of our guys in this community, particularly those who haven't been exposed to it and don't know; they may have some stress and anxiety about it or be just somewhat prejudicial in their actions or beliefs about it.

Nothing has been directly aimed at me. There have been only anecdotal things passed to me. I had one young man—and here is where I mean intersections get crazy—an African American male, who was high achieving but had been underserved by all accounts asked a peer, "Does Mr. Walker act faggy during class?" I think those kind of interactions may get hatched on me. I think they do have motivation. But it has been nothing confrontational per se with a student directly.

I think, if anything, it has enabled me to work through the nuances, and I think about them a lot as I'm just living this somewhat straddled life and identity. I think when I work in small group or larger setting facilitating conversation around sexuality with minority students, it is very different given what our African American population in this school by and large thinks about sexual orientation. It is an inconsistency they get to grapple with.

I agree with this idea of racial equality for all. That is what they talk about and they think about. It is a topic of mine, so I understand. But at the same time, we don't have the same kind of equality for those who are in the sexual minority. They have a hard time grasping what that really means, and they don't necessarily attach meaning to it the same way. They are not as quick to say, "Yeah, sure, equal rights for all." It comes out more as, at least in this community, "My religious teaching tells me this is right and this is wrong. That can't possibly be right." They have to really grapple with that kind of dual piece of equality at odds in their adolescent minds; whereas I have been able to view those things and be at peace with both of them, being multi-racial myself.

I don't know what students would label me as. I think most students here would label me as Black, and that is it, which is even a switch from when I first got here. The Black students wouldn't necessarily talk to me or approach me for support. I wasn't black enough to offer support. I think the more I have been here, the more they start to see and realize that we can talk.

I think, if anything, coming from the Episcopal tradition that we are a part of, we do a good job of teaching all inclusively. That is something that I think students can get. We have very few students that would say anything negative about homosexuality. I also think they haven't had a chance to put anything into practice yet by knowing people. If you walk around, you will see on different doors there are safe spaces here. That was invented by a couple of us five years ago; we made a pretty big push on campus. We expected a little bit of flack, and we really didn't receive any, which was good.

What we have not been able to successfully do is create any kind of gay-straight alliance here, and that has been a fight for five or six years. Different people feel differently about, if it is going to start, how it should start and when it needs to start and how to populate it. Given that my read of this landscape is that it is still largely heterosexual and pretty skittish around issues of sexual orientation, I come at it from a place where, as an adult, I need to provide a safe space. I think other people here think it needs to be treated as another student club where students come forward to create something. I have been at odds with some other colleagues with that for years. I am always on the losing end of that, but it seems to always been student led, student driven, and I know my question always is, "If there is not a student who feels safe enough doing that, then we will continue to have nothing for these students."

Daniel

I also grew up in a very homophobic family and a very homophobic culture, and always had school, sports, school ... a lot of aggressive homophobia, a lot of aggressive, "The gays are going to give you AIDS and rape your children" talk. It had a big impact on me, so I was very much afraid of being gay.

I'm definitely a different person when I'm not at school. At school, it's essential that you're professional. My circle of friends outside of school and my professional circle are not the same. There's maybe a few overlaps.

I live in Los Angeles, West Hollywood, California. There are tons of different circles that we run with socially, and some of them are not ones I would necessarily invite into professional settings, for sure. There's leather crowds, there's sports crowds, there's bar crowds, there's my nerdy crowds that we go to concerts and stuff with. If I go to West Hollywood, and I walk through, I'll see about five people that I know, and so I totally feel integrated into a lot of different groups of people in Los Angeles in terms of gayness, but most of my circle of friends are gay. Me and my partner meet with a lot of couples, especially. And now that we just got a place in Palm Springs, we're starting to meet a lot of other people.

Certainly, there are some gay colleagues that I talk with, but I would say I definitely don't feel like I'm seeking out a cohort of gay colleagues professionally. There are a few that I really like, and a number of whom I don't professionally align myself with. In terms of a professional stance, there's a number of gay colleagues. We're certainly cordial and collegial and professional with each other, but they're not like my buddies that I hang with. I'd say the gay/straight balance is pretty proportional.

I definitely censor myself professionally the older I get. There's less of this going on, and this is probably true of everyone. You have a personal life that you share selectively and appropriately. You're working professional colleagues, and you're working with adolescent kids, so obviously you need to be appropriate and selective about what you share.

That's, I think, true for everybody. I'm probably much more hyper-sensitive about that than the typical teacher, because there are kids that are fascinated by what you do, and who you are, and what your life is outside of it. I don't talk a lot about it, like, "Oh, we went to this party, and let me tell you what happened." That doesn't happen. It doesn't happen often with many teachers there. I probably am much more inquisitive about their lives than I let them be about my life.

When I finally kind of got over myself and really had to own it, it wasn't probably until my first year of teaching. That was like 22, 23. I was sharply in denial through college, through graduate school, growing up. Certainly, looking back, what I was turned on by was men. But, I also grew up in a very homophobic family and a very homophobic culture, and always had school, sports, school...a lot of aggressive homophobia, a lot of aggressive "the gays are going to give you AIDS and rape your children" talk. It had a big impact on me, so I was very much afraid of being gay, and turning out gay, growing up. My house was not a place where I felt happy.

You know they say people had a heart attack when they find out? My mother had a heart attack. Literally was in the hospital with a heart attack. Didn't tell me that she knew. Didn't find out she knew about it until probably a year later. She said, "Daniel, I think there's something very important we need to talk about." "Oh, the fact that I'm gay? Yeah, as long as you're ready to hear it, yeah." But then, I didn't find out that she had known about it until even after that conversation; I found out from my sister. To be honest with you, with my family, there's so much lack of transparency, lack of openness about so many things. I tried to make a joke at the time, I was like, "I'll continue to not tell you much about my life after this" because it was just the kind of family dynamic, when I look back at it now.

Our family just had a very closed way of relating with other, and my coming out as gay was just one part of that. My father had alcoholism. There was a huge related issue in our family. There was a lack of love between my mom and father, so there are all sorts of things. My coming out as gay seems like, "Whatever!" But I was so out of there at that point that I didn't think much about their feelings. Even now, I don't sweat it too much. For me, I was very much about forging my own path.

My being gay is such a known fact at my school, because I'm always talking about things—the things you like and the things you talk about, and the television shows, "Oh my God, I saw that too!"—it generally becomes pretty clear. I think there are a lot of different ways that people know that I'm gay, such as alumni connections. Kids that had been there four years ago that have family members at the school now. Kids are totally Facebook connected with people three and four years their junior or senior, so it's a pretty continuous thing. Now maybe ten years ago, we had this kind of phenomenon of coming out every year. I don't sense that anymore.

I think there's a little bit of a freedom because I don't really sweat it too much, I guess. I don't know why. I think there's something related to the fact that when you first come out as gay, especially my family finding out, you're at the point where you're like, "You know what? Take it or leave it." I think that part influences my identity as a teacher. I don't suffer the trappings of playing the game that sometimes the moneyed, the powerful, and the privileged play to keep the people they want in the system, or put into the system. I don't. I just don't support it.

I remember seeing a lot of this in Connecticut. There's a lot of talk about open-mindedness, there's a lot of talk about inclusivity, and then there was a lot of actual behaviors that I would notice, that I would bring to particular people. People would pull me aside and say, "Maybe tone this down a bit, maybe do this?"

This year, I really felt proud; I'm really happy with what was achieved this year. I generally feel that. It's a nice feeling. We're always excited to start the year brand-new. We get treated well. As much as we criticize some of the commodity-driven attitudes, it's a pretty nice culture. I like it. I feel totally supported in terms of all the LGBT things; it's a great place to be. They're incredibly supportive, and there are a hundred different ways to be gay at our school, and I really dig that. When you have gay and lesbian and transgender students and teachers at the school, and bisexual teachers, there's everything you need. We have the whole alphabet soup within our student community and within our faculty. I feel very much at home in terms of that.

Mary

> *I make it a point to identify myself as gay at the outset for students in the room who have people who are gay in their lives; maybe it's themselves, who knows.*

I think from the time I was very little I always loved language and words and loved being read to, loved reading, loved writing. Somewhere, maybe in high school, but certainly an undergrad, I realized that the way for me to truly engage with language in a way I wanted to would be with kids in high school. I wasn't as interested in the politics around Ph.D. programs; I was in one, but I was more interested in sharing and finding a common ground around the work I love, but not because it had to be certain literature. It just was a place to be human.

Literature was like this humane platform to find a connection, and I came alive when I did my student teaching. In my first years of teaching, it was amazing. It didn't matter what I was teaching literature-wise, as long as it spoke to the kids in some way. That's where my identity work and diversity has been so rewarding: the more it really mirrored the children, the more it opened up new ways for them to think about themselves and others. It's this perfect marriage of getting to be with the language I really care about and getting to be with kids. I teach kids now from upper elementary school on up in creative writing, but the place where I'm really comfortable is with kids between about 15 and 18.

I came out 11 or 12 years ago, but I knew that I was at least bisexual, and I've been able to identify it certainly from the time I was a teenager. In the classroom, I always do believe you teach as who you are, so I think I've identified definitely as a woman. I have never taught at a single-gender school. I identify as a woman, definitely as a white woman, now very much so as a lesbian woman. At the beginning of my teaching career here, the very beginning, I was at the end of a marriage to a man, so that's also been a part of that identity. It's hard to keep that out of the classroom, especially when I'm teaching stories of people and interacting with the stories of children—it's hard not to bring that in. I think now, when I am in my classroom, I'm very much in my classroom as a mother, as a woman, as a white person, as a gay woman, as a colleague. There are so many aspects of who I am that I do bring to the room; how much I bring that out overtly sometimes depends on the day.

Two of my children are on this hallway as tenth graders this same building. I teach a lot of their friends, and I work with a lot of their friends. I do the LGBTQ affinity group (it's not a GSA, it's an affinity group), so several of their friends are in there. My identity is pretty tied up into the school for better or for worse.

I'm a mother, I'm a spouse, I'm a woman, I'm definitely a white person, that's unavoidable, and I suppose I'm Southern. I'm a writer, and that's something that's hard to integrate into all of my life, but I think it is very important in my classroom and outside that students see me writing with them, and that they understand that I understand some of what that exposure can mean when I share what I do with my peers. I'm not sure if my identity is much different outside the classroom, to be honest with you.

My identity makes me highly conscious of who is in the room, and, on one hand, I operate on making sure my classroom reflects who's in my room. I have a quote on the board that says, "everybody needs with windows and mirrors in their lives." The classroom is mirrored and windowed for them as much as I can make it. Granted, I'm a white woman sitting at the front of the room, which is what they've seen for the most part going through. I make it a point to identify myself as gay at the outset for students in the room who have people who are gay in their lives; maybe it's themselves, who knows.

We don't "out" people ourselves unless that's what people want to do. I don't think I'm always a great role model, but I want to be a model of someone who's going to be brave to show the children that there is someone here for them. On the other hand, I'm conscious more and more of how much I do give because there are people in the room who are in different places in their own families, in their own identity development. It's not about becoming a test case for them, and I don't need for children to see me feeling victimized, that's never a goal.

I think it's also good to celebrate difference, just like, "I am the way I am, and I love the way I am, I love my family," but it's not the centerpiece of the conversation—that's established at the outset. I choose my curriculum very carefully around who is in my classroom. I've been at the forefront of making sure that I have a really diverse reading list, and I've pushed for that more than anyone in my department personally because of the diversity kind of work that I do. I'm constantly pushing them on the curriculum here; it doesn't stop, and I think that's good.

I need to be that resistor, in terms of identity but also in terms of engaging with literature, giving the kids the skills. Creating diversity of space for them is important. No one is ever required to read their own writing aloud. I hope it's safe for them. I also teach things I love that speak to the issue of identity, and I teach a lot of the poetics of rap and hip-hop and spoken word. Not because I have a few guys of color in the room—who knows maybe they hate rap and love Mozart—but I like it because it spoke to me as someone who was different and wanting a voice. I do a lot with spoken word here.

The magazine I founded about seven years ago here is called *Evolution*, and it's a no cut magazine. Any idea can be submitted as long as you're willing to workshop it. It's a really diverse collection of voices, and my head writers are always several kids of color. There are a lot of kids who are publishing in there who are saying things in their pieces that, if you read really closely, I would probably get shown the door.

They're speaking out about things like President Obama's first election, talking about what it was like to be here through that—kids of color, kids who are biracial. I'm really interested in voice, kids feeling like they can have a voice whoever they are.

The school is really connected to my coming out. I don't know how to describe it, but when I got divorced, it was very generous to me monetarily with fellowships. Not that I didn't earn them, but I could tell they were paying attention. I was able to really educate myself as a poet; I was able to kind of nurture parts of my identity that I really cared about while simultaneously being aware of the school's own struggle with embracing sexuality spectrums and any issue of diversity.

I think there are stages of identity development for being a lesbian, as much as being white or a person of color. For me it was Karen because she came out when she was 18, and she's 50 now. We met 33 or so. I'm 44 now, and it wasn't that I needed to be in bars. It wasn't that I needed any of that because I had a child. I'm out, and I was definite: "This is my girlfriend. This is my spouse. This is my wife." We got married in 2007.

I am out to everybody. I say, "Yeah, I am Mrs. Mary. Let me tell you a little bit about myself." I do it knowing what it's like to come through here and watch kids, and I do this also with the parents. I will be honest with you: that's actually the point. I did tell the kids, "I'm married to Jackson and Katie's mother, and that's why I have this last name: we're hyphenated because I want to represent my son and my older two children." Again, another conscious kind of sign of us being together.

I think sometimes it can be lonely, there are a few of us at the school, but I think for a long time there really weren't. It was just me and one other woman down in middle school, and she wasn't out to her students particularly. She was when she felt like she needed to make sure her partner had credit. This is a very southern place, and I don't know if it's a different place, but I would think in some ways it is. No one is going to really show it if they're uncomfortable with me, but it's just that I have so many identities in this place, as a parent and as a teacher.

My worst experiences have occurred as a parent in the lower school. The teachers there and my child's third-grade experience here was horrible. He was in a class of two pretty evangelical teachers, and I felt all right there; he's had religious teachers before, and he really connected with them, so who am I to gauge? They're not specifically bringing that into the classroom, and I'm coming from a certain perspective, too, so I hope people won't take people out of my class. I let it happen and hated myself for it for a long time: these were people who I found out later had been really cruel to the kids of gay friends of mine. They were about as uninvolved as they could be when it came to interacting with my kid, and the irony was that I was teaching one of those woman's children at the same time and being very kind and thoughtful. She was going through a divorce at the time and never told me. She let me feel like my child was so horrible, while I was trying to care for hers. It's hard to put your finger on it, but there were things that definitely happened. But I don't interact with those parents, and I don't go to their socials because they're all in this neighborhood.

I've had them change the language on the admissions materials here. I've done a lot of systemic things to help, but as a parent, I've felt very lonely here. There's one other gay family here, but they're not out and do not disclose why they're divorced. It's extremely hard to be a gay parent here. On the other hand, as a teacher, I haven't had any issues until this year. I have a lot of seniority. I'm respected as a faculty here, so I feel confident. If you can make it through the first four, five years here, which were nasty, you're okay.

Two things happened. One is the book I was teaching with two colleagues in the senior year, a couple of liars broke it up, and they banned it when I was midway through it. There were two pretty abrupt references to a young girl being raped by a man (explicit descriptions just of his penis, not of even the rape itself). That kind of took me aback a little bit—the way we're still so afraid to touch on rape, and it's tied into race because we still teach *Beloved*. Black kids have to experience it, but the white kids? Heaven forbid! One of my black students was like, "We have to read *Heart of Darkness* and we can't read that?" I thought, "Yeah, you noticed it too." That made me reconsider: should I be so open? I talked to the head, and I was like, "Are these people still out there?" referring to the people who came out of the woodwork to get rid of the book. They were parents, and those parents are pretty rabidly anti-gay. However it's confusing because some of their children are pretty close to my children.

The other issue is when I had a student when I was teaching the book *Passing*, who is a cheerleader. I called her out for lying to me about something. She was mad I wouldn't lie for her for missing practice. She went down to my colleague, who is a woman of color, who is teaching my daughter, to say, "I feel like when I'm in that classroom, I can't talk about my opinions about sexuality, and I can't voice my opposition."

When people brought up sexuality around *Passing*, I said let's look at the text, and I said could that be homo erotic or could it even be homosexual? Then the kids said, "Well what are your experiences?" I mentioned a few things. I said, "That is not a signal to you that any other voice doesn't matter in this room, I welcome your voice." I said, "Some of my closer friends on this campus are Evangelical Christians who battle with these issues." That cheerleader is also one of the mean girls in class, she's very cruel to people, and I'd be the first to call her on it. I lowered the participation grade because she's mean to the kids around her; she rolls her eyes when they talk. I am like yeah...you are getting docked for that. You are mean. That was a first time anyone has taken it somewhere.

I also do this LGBTQ affinity group, and one of the freshmen in it has just come alive. She showed up right out of the blue all by herself—brave kid. She's awesome. Like her face is like brighter, hair is back off her face. The mother is like, "Do you think this group is making her do this?" I'm like, "Oh boy, here we go. Like kind of convert her?" I've taught long enough to know, and I've been a mom long enough to know, that fear is what that mom is feeling. I didn't feel personally attacked at all. I was like, "Frankly, I would have been going anywhere I could just to grapple with it."

The young lady who came at me has had hell on earth in her own family and is looking desperately for someone to love her. When someone challenges her in the classroom, which I do, she was going to come up to me. Some of the kids, when they come out, because they're in such horrible situations at home about coming out, have lashed back at me. Like at one point, when we were starting the GSA, which is now separate from the LGBTQ group, my boss said you can't use the word "gay." I was like, "Are you kidding me?"

I am one of the last standing people, and I would say the main reason is for my children, and that's sort of selfish, but if I'm here I'm going to make sure that this culture feels okay to them and any other child who is here. What I really love is that there are kids in there, Hispanic kids, Latino kids, several kids of color, all these kids, who are at different intersections with their identity who feel safe to come in and have the conversation.

I love my life. I love being gay. I think being joyous about that and not falsely is really important in the classroom, but it doesn't necessarily have to do with me being joyous because I'm gay. I just published a poem about my daughter, which is about how much strength she gives me, and she showed everybody. That infects, in a good way, my demeanor in here. It is what I bring to the classroom; it just makes me so much more human.

6

ADMINISTRATION

Elizabeth

When I talk to prospective families, I say that it's mostly like coming to work in a giant living room every day. I think the thing we do well is culture because we take the time to develop it.

I went to a large public school. Coming out was not an easy process. Actually, I was dating my first girlfriend, and we were in the process of breaking up, but we were arguing about how we weren't "breaking up" because we hadn't been dating because we weren't gay, but a breakup was really what it was. Once I got through that first experience, I realized this is who I am and started to come out. I came out actually to my high school English teacher, who was kind of the first adult that I told.

I came out to my friends, and then it wasn't until college that I actually officially came out to my parents. My parents are Catholic, and I was raised in a fairly conservative household. I met my partner in college, and we were getting ready to move to New Hampshire so that I could go to graduate school, and it was like, "She is going to move with me to New Hampshire, and we need to talk about this as a family." I came out, and then my parents said, "Well, we knew. We just didn't know how to talk about it." They've been supportive, and not to say it's been easy, but they've been supportive of us.

Students will ask me now about coming out, and sometimes I don't profess to have any of the answers, but I say that sometimes just working through it together without talking about it can work. That's an odd thing to say, but that's kind of where we were. We were in a nebulous "don't ask, don't tell," but that worked for us; whereas, I think if I had tried to articulate it when I was younger, I don't know how it would have gone over.

I came out to my parents once I felt established. That was part of my fear. I didn't come out almost until I graduated college, so I was established on my own, as my own person, and I wasn't as dependent on them in part because I feared what would happen. I wanted to make sure that I could take care of myself if things went south.

I wrote them a letter because I couldn't figure out how to articulate it at first out loud. I wrote them a letter, and then they responded with an email. The written correspondence allowed enough distance between us but also enough connectivity that we were able to kind of work things out in a better way. I think that is my parents' style. As the relationship progressed, my partner and I moved across the country together, we moved back together, we're going to have this child together. We started to talk about it more, and I think it has all worked out fine. We have more of a dialogue now about just being a family, and not who's gay and who's straight.

When I started to work here, a northern suburb in probably the most conservative part of the metropolitan area, I was new to independent schools. I didn't know the culture and the climate, so I didn't come out right away because I was afraid and didn't want to be open. My partner was working in a rural school district, and it wasn't that I thought I would lose my job here, but it was a very real concern that she could lose her job. I did a lot of deflecting, maybe not denying but deflecting questions. I didn't talk about who I was with, I didn't talk about our family life and then, when I came out, I was much more open. I brought Portia to things, and we became known as a couple, and there was much less hiding.

Right now, I am fairly out to everyone. I first came out to the head of school, and I was working closely with him in this secretarial role, his assistant basically. Then I came out to some other teachers that I was close to and some students that had asked that were also questioning themselves and I wanted to be supportive to them.

What really kind of pushed everything to the forefront is when we decided to have a child. We had an anonymous sperm donor. I mean it was going to be very clear that we were in this relationship together now. I actually talked about it at a faculty meeting with everyone. I said, "I know most of you know this, but if you did not, here's where I am and I appreciate the school's support." And everyone did, for the most part, support me. The school actually threw us a baby shower that I think rivaled most wedding receptions.

It doesn't mean that every family has been okay with it, but I did get a lot of anecdotal evidence. Teachers came to me and said this parent talked to me and said, "We're giving Elizabeth and Portia a gift, and we're coming to the shower. We don't know how we feel about gay marriage, but I know that Elizabeth takes care of my kids, and I want to help her take care of hers." It was nice to see outward support, and then hear those secondhand stories as well.

For the most part, the kids are supportive, the parents are supportive, and my co-workers are supportive. We are not a progressive school, but we are probably the most progressive independent school here, for high schools at least, but we will get criticized for being a liberal school, and sometimes I think that comes from the perception that I'm here and I'm out, and therefore the school condones all things liberal and leftist.

My personal experience being a lesbian feeds everything that I do. The process of struggling to come to terms with who I am myself, struggling to tell my family, my friends, and people I care about. I bring that to everything I do. Discrimination I faced at various times in my life, I think that all feeds my understanding, particularly because I teach humanities, and I teach how to tell one's own story, and how to develop a written sense of who you are. That becomes part of my teaching. I feel as though I am very sensitive to that struggle for identity, that struggle to be heard as a minority group. I think it shows up in the classroom.

I think that the message is you can be gay here, you can be out here and be accepted, certainly by the adults and mostly by the students. We still have trouble around language, such as "that's so gay" and people saying the word, "fag." We have to transition every year to reorient people to not using that language in shared space.

I think for the most part, our students feel comfortable being openly gay, and they receive the message that that's okay. It is interesting—I've noticed over time that we have far more open lesbian students or girls who have said they're bisexual than gay or bisexual male students. Partly I know that because I will have students that come out to me on an individual level but who don't come out to the school and oftentimes that's our boys. I don't know exactly what's contributing to that, but my sense I've gotten from a few of these individuals is that it's a peer-to-peer thing that they don't necessarily feel as accepted by other male students at the school to come out fully the way that some of our girls have.

Initially, we had some students who asked if we can have a GSA, and the faculty talked about it. The school was still very young, I think we were in our fifth or sixth year. The faculty and the administration were nervous, "What is it going to mean to have a GSA and to say that we accept this here?" We were still living with a fluctuating enrollment, and we were in portable classrooms. Is this going to taint the school?

Sometimes I go to GSA, which I sponsor, and another straight male faculty member also sponsors. I go to the meetings, and the kids plan the meetings, and they plan the topics. Sometimes they will turn to me like I have some expertise or wisdom, and I often say, "Here's what I feel, but I don't think this is the only way we can feel about this topic," and they value that. Sometimes they'll say, "All we want to hear is your story of your life, and how that played out for you." They want to see kind of that it's okay. Our state has had many debates about gay marriage, and we don't have a constitutional amendment prohibiting it, but it's not legal, so we're in this middle ground. I've talked a lot about my relationship with Portia. I was able to adopt our child, so we both have custody of her. At the end of one day, I said, "I feel like all I'm doing is telling stories about myself," and the kids said, "That's what's important. We want to hear that."

When I was at school, there was a lot of awkwardness and I guess, shame—a need to hide myself, the gay part of my identity, which was a less than worthy part of my identity. That doesn't exist here for a number of our students, and our school makes it less able to exist.

I have this memory, and I tell this story to kids in GSA. I was dating a girl my senior year in high school and we broke up, and I vividly remember it because I was an English department aide, and I was in the room where we kept all the books. She and I were in there, and we were talking about this, and she said, "We have to break up because I just want to date someone whose hand I can hold in the hallway." I was heartbroken and crushed. I felt like, "Here I am: this failure as a girlfriend because I can't hold your hand in the hallway." She wanted to go date a boy that she could take to prom and be prom king and queen with in this very kind of public way. I felt really bad about that. It was like one of these crushing heartbreaks of my life in the way that when you're a teenager you have these great emotional experiences. It's not that we don't have messy breakups between straight and gay couples here, but we don't have that kind of devastation. I felt bad that I was gay at that point in my life, and I don't feel like our students have that experience here.

Getting to see how kids expand their experience of the world is great. Our mission is to expand the hearts and minds of our students, and it really is an expansion for them to consider a point they've never considered before or see how someone else's experience is similar to theirs but different. To see them start to grow as individuals, that's what I like about high school. They do come in as kids and they're adults when they graduate. They're not fully perfect adults, but they're grown. Them starting to establish themselves as people separate from their friends, separate from their parents and separate family—not to say those influences aren't important, but seeing their individual role beyond a collective role is great.

Charles

It's certainly assumed that everybody's heterosexual and that everybody wants to get a date for the prom and those relationships.

I think I went through high school basically doing the asexual thing. I went to an all-boys high school, so there wasn't a lot of pressure on dating and romance. That wasn't a big deal for most of my friends. It was a big deal; they wanted it but it was not available.

Toward the end of high school, I just realized that the way that I had always felt about other boys was really completely analogous to the way that my best and closest friends talked about feeling about girls. I felt like they had to get girlfriends, and I had to experience what that was, hearing from them, before I realized, "Oh, that's what those feelings are."

The coming-out process really started with a conversation with my best friend at the time. Still my best friend. Kind of quickly, we shared that news with our friends. It was convenient timing, I think, going off to college. It was a nice time to open up, be someone different. But I was able also to share that news with my folks before I left for college and have that out of the way. College, and I would say through graduate school, was just a process to figure out, "All right, what does this mean? Where does this put me?"

My best friend is straight. It was kind of a funny conversation. We were hanging out after dance, waiting for an express bus back to the Bronx. I was staying at his house. We were talking about our prom dates, and I had gotten this girl to go with me. It was a total pity date. She was a girl that I had loved from afar. She happened to be the sister of this boy that I just was obsessed with. So, we were talking about our prom dates and how excited we were, and I think I just offhandedly mentioned something about how I'd be a lot more excited if I could take her brother instead of her. We both kind of laughed at that. It was just a light comment, but as we were laughing we were looking each other in the eyes and realizing, "Oh, wait a minute. This is a serious thing." I don't think until that moment, I had ever thought in my own head, "I'm gay. These feelings mean that I'm gay."

I feel lucky in that way. I discovered it right at the same instant that my best friend did. We spent this whole two-hour bus ride to the Bronx, and I remember very explicitly there was an older church lady sitting across from us. We just had this whole conversation about my sexuality, and she was looking at us like, "Why are you telling us?" I felt like she was like praying for us the whole time.

It was shocking, I think, to my parents. I think there were some tears. I felt like my mom cried. In those days, that's just what parents would believe, I think, that there's no way to be happy. That's just such a set thing. You're not going to have any kind of life. So, there was that. My dad asked some good questions, though. They were kind of silly questions at the time. It was like, "Are you going to be wearing dresses?" And that kind of stuff. He had a very vague sense of what that identity might be. Once I clarified the dresses thing, he was totally fine with it after that.

What does being openly gay mean to me? That has changed over time. I think in college it was important to me that everybody that I might possibly encounter would know that I was gay from a hundred feet away. I guess more and more over time, it's more about who I am in the world. Am I hiding something or not? Being out is like not hiding something.

When I was looking for this job, I was sure to include on my résumé a couple of volunteer things that I was doing or had done with gay and lesbian youth groups because I thought, "People don't have to call me for an interview if they're freaked out by that." No direct conversation about it, of course. I feel like the leadership, the people who hired me and stuff just kind of knew that and assumed it.

The first few months I was at school, the drama guy, who I got to be good friends with, wanted to put on Laramie Project, which was a big deal for the school. I really helped with that and we put together a panel, we brought in a bunch of speakers, we brought in some folks from GLSEN and from GLAAD. For me, it was great being part of a new community and wondering, "How am I going to negotiate here?" It was this totally positive, just wide open accepting atmosphere, which was great. It gave me a chance to be out without having to make some kind of awkward announcement.

From that, we started a GSA. So that was Gay-Straight Alliance. I was leading that, and that has continued. And we started doing the Day of Silence my second year at the school. The Day of Silence, that was the day for me when I explicitly said in public, with a bunch of other teachers and students, that I'm a gay man. To use that sentence, which I hadn't used before—I don't think it surprised anyone in the room, but I don't think I had said it before.

It was an assembly at the end of the Day of Silence. One of the teachers was talking about how she feels like, as a straight woman, it's really important for her to be here for everyone in this community, students and teachers, regardless of their sexual orientation. I felt like that was a really nice opening for me to say, and I happened to be standing next to her, to say, "And as a gay man, I feel exactly the same, Mary. I feel like that's my role here as well." It felt kind of organic. I'm a little bit hesitant, especially working in a school. There's always that sense of am I doing this for the benefit of the community and the students? Or am I doing this because of some personal, internal need that I have? I think that maybe gay teachers think about this more than straight teachers do.

That wasn't the easiest moment for me to come out and say it at that time, but it did feel right. It got a positive response from the campers, and any sense that I was less than or to be joked about just vanished. If you're not keeping a secret, I don't think people gossip in that way.

I feel like being gay helps me not take for granted or not assume that I understand the ways that people connect and the ways that people's feelings connect with each other. I feel like that's a big part of the work that I do as a counselor. I also feel that working in an educational setting, as opposed to a mental health setting, with kids who are just discovering who they are in the world, whether that's gay or straight or anything, means I'm still very connected to that struggle. Although it was a very long time ago for me, I feel like it stands out in my mind because it was a pretty major struggle for me to figure out.

I feel like part of being a nerdy white guy is that it works anywhere, right? You can go anywhere with that presentation. In a way, that kind of makes things easy. I think it also makes it's more challenging, though. In all the conversations that we have in our school about diversity, I feel like that's something that I care a great deal about. Personally, I think sometimes my motives there or just my understanding is a bit suspect because what's a nerdy White guy know about real diversity? I certainly coast on being a nerdy white guy. If I put on a blazer, I look like I can go anywhere and have that air of authority. I've been told since I'm a kid like, "Oh, you're really smart," so I coast on that.

I feel like I can hold my own if things do get, at times, a little complicated or challenging or difficult with students or with parents or with teachers. I feel like I have certain things in my back pocket that I can just coast on, and I would say being a smart, nerdy, white guy, and having a Ph.D., those are things that make it easier. I feel like I coast on those things, and that is partly why I think I have the comfort level that I do with being openly gay. I feel like there's a balance there, in a way. I don't like it, and I don't like saying this either, but in a way, the credentials that I have are formidable enough that I feel like somebody would have to think twice about taking me on in that way.

Dorothy

My freshman year, I really came out to myself because I was in a space where I could. It was okay. It wasn't like this big thing.

I actually don't teach any grade. I started out teaching kindergarten, but I've switched into administration, so I actually created a position of Director of Diversity and Community Life. This is still not a full-time position because it's new. It's half of my time. Next year, I'll be doing that half of my time and the other half will be middle school dean of programs.

I run the middle school diversity club, and I lead a upper school diversity club. That's the only way I directly, right now, teach. I'd like to actually teach a class. I just don't know which one yet. I do miss teaching. For eight years, I used to teach third grade. I do miss being directly in the classroom, but I still interact with students, do clubs, do conferences, and there are other ways that I interact with students.

I'm a pretty open person. I think I'm often like a mediator for many different people. I am into creating space and safety and community for truly everyone. I'm a listening ear. I'm an activist, a change agent. When I think about my role in my own family and my own community, and what I care about—that's who I am. I mean, I'm also obviously a person of color. That's also part of my identity. I am out at school as I am with my family and my community. It's really all the same. I don't find myself having to switch or be a different person at school than I am at home or with my family, which is quite amazing.

Things can get emotional with the diversity work and change work, You can get offended or things can hurt in a different way when you put yourself out there. At the same time, it creates space for greater change to happen and for real understanding when you put yourself out there. People see that. People notice that and appreciate it. I think it encourages them to be their whole selves. I think it's a benefit just as much as it can be a little bit of a struggle or a challenge at times.

I just feel pretty lucky to be able to do all of that. It strengthens my work. I guess I'm a person of high integrity in that way. If I'm going to be an activist and push for change in the school and push for safe communities, I need to be doing that too. I need to be that example. Otherwise, I feel a little bit hypocritical. I need to continue to challenge myself and be all of myself as an example for the students and for the faculty and staff, and for parents, and for everyone in the community. I have to push myself if I'm going to expect them to push themselves as well. I feel like for me, that's important.

I think being out and open does make a difference. I've noticed it in the workshops I've done with adults and students. They see that I bring my whole self. I've heard that in their feedback: "We see that you bring this, so we feel comfortable and challenge ourselves to do the same. If you're doing it, okay then maybe I can try this too. Even though it's a little hard or it's a little different or this is new. I've been doing this for 30 years like this as an educator, but I'm going to try because you're leading an example." And, in a way, that's inviting. It's not like beating them over ahead with it. I am just truly bringing myself. They see that it's genuine.

I'm the oldest of three. I always have taken care of my younger brothers. I've always loved taking care of people. That's how I was raised. I was babysitting at a young age for my own family and then others. I used to work in a lot of camps and other programs as I got older. Working with kids and being an educator was always something I did on the side. I never thought of it as a profession, but it was always something I enjoyed. Then I was always an activist. I spent half my life growing up in Philadelphia and the other half in Vermont.

When we moved to Vermont, it was a very different social, racial, emotional, everything dynamic. It was hard, and it was challenging, but I came from the very activist-type family. In my family, it was, "Okay, it's difficult, but then what are you going to do about it? How are you going to change this? How are you going to make it better?" Even in high school, I was an activist to change things, to have confrontations that were hard to push people. That was my way of surviving. That was my way of dealing with things. I did the same thing when I was an undergrad. I always continued that trajectory. Both of those things intermeshed. Literally, it was happenstance. I was, "I'm interested in working with kids," so I applied for this fellowship with the Stepping Stones college program because I wasn't sure I wanted to teach.

I grew up in a time when the AIDS crisis was still happening, so there was a lot of talk about that like health stuff. I remember my health teacher in seventh grade or something throwing a scenario at us like, "Oh, we're going to have a kid come to our school and he's got HIV." It was a mock thing, but they were trying to educate us. I remember language being around that and gay people and men, but I never heard the same for women.

There was always something different, like, "I'm not really into these guys." I didn't know if it was because all the guys in my school were White. I was the only brown face. I was like, "Maybe there's just nobody interesting here to me." I was never like crazy like my girlfriends were in middle school about dances and all that other stuff that was going on. I was never really into guys. It wasn't until public high school that there were some girls who were out. I was part of many different groups. I was with artists. I liked theater and I played the violin. I used to sing, but I was also a really big athlete. I had friends across the board. I got to watch different social groups.

I remember watching that one social group or being close to those girls. I mean like, "Oh, girls can like girls." That's something that dawned at me. Then it terrified me. They were outcasts, but no one made fun of them, but they were on their periphery. You're at high school, you don't want to be on the periphery. It was already hard enough. I was already the only one of two Black people in a class of 450. I don't need something else. At the same time, it still was there. I was still attracted to some of my friends, and I couldn't name it.

It was scary. There was no language for it. Then I think it was my junior year in high school, and my dad was working at an organization. Two of his coworkers were getting married, two women. We went to their commitment ceremony in Vermont. It changed my whole perspective. Then I saw it was being validated. This was like a community event. These were my dad's coworkers. I knew these women, Alyssa and Kim. I was just like, "Whoa." I was starting to swallow it: "I think this is what I am. I'm still too scared to talk about it." Then I also learned in that experience, my mom grew up in a more religious family than I was raised. She did not believe in gay people. She's like, "That's just the lifestyle choice." She didn't believe it was a real thing. That was also hard because I was very close to my parents.

I started to slightly come out to myself, but I don't think I really came out to myself until I was in college. I was away from home. Then I went to Swarthmore College, a very liberal space, very open and accepting space. My freshman year, I really came out to myself because I was in a space where I could. It was okay. It wasn't like this big thing. Then I came out to my parents at the end of my freshman year. That was hard for my mom. I knew it would be, but it was harder than I thought it would be.

I wrote a poem to come out to my parents, and I published it in literary magazine. It had been published. It was spring of the end of the year. I sent it to her. It was a coming-out poem, all dramatic. Then I confirmed it when they came to pick me up at the end of the year. She was just, "It's my fault that you're gay. We lived in Vermont too long. There weren't any older Black men." She really took it there. "This is just lifestyle choices. You're just discovering yourself in college." My dad was different. My dad said, "I love you, and you can love whoever you want. I'm going to love you anyway. You're always going to be my daughter." He was just like, "I love you. It's cool."

That hurt me when my mother was just like, "No. That's not what it is." I told her, "I felt like this when I was in middle school. You just didn't know it. I didn't have the language to talk about it. Now, I do." Then, over time, she became accepting to it. She never pushed me away and was like, "You're not my daughter." She just didn't believe me. She was just like, "This is a phase," and trying to blame herself, which made us a little distant. Some of that just happened. It was hard. We never really had a hard time when I was in high school. We always got along.

That was the first time I didn't get along with my mom or my parent. I was a pretty decent kid. That was a hard thing. At the same time I was like, "This is who I am. I couldn't deny it." I actually tried dating a guy the beginning of my freshman year. I was just, "Ah, no. This is not it." Then I had different girlfriends.

It just took time coming out. Just like it took time for me to come out to myself. It took Mom time to recognize that that's who I was. She actually works in a university now. She does diversity work as well. She didn't at the time, but probably end of my college time, that was about on the time she started working in the university. She started getting surrounded by different community and people. I think it's true that through relationships, people can learn to understand and see something different.

When she started working at the university, she started to have to work with the women's center and do other things, and work with different people, and LGBT, the Q Centers or whatever. It changed things for her. She was doing diversity work, so she had to be an advocate for all that. Through those experiences and her relationship with me, she's now a cool advocate, like total ally. No problems whatsoever. People grow.

Being openly gay means that you're not denying who you are. When you're in public space, the public spaces that are safe. You will share that part about yourself. You won't edit. I'll say "my wife"; I won't say "my friend" or deny she's my partner or deny she's my wife. When it comes up, as it naturally would in a conversation or in a space, you don't edit that out. You just are who you are. I say it in a safe space because if I don't feel I'm safe, I won't do that. I actually worked abroad in Sudan for two years. There were certain places where that was not safe for me to do that. I just omitted it. In any safe space, you are who you are. You don't deny that to yourself or to the people around you.

I think I'm out to everybody. The reaction is pretty benign. It's a pretty normal thing in our school. There are a lot of out faculty and some administration as well. I feel like it's almost a non-issue. It's almost like, "Oh, cool. When did you get married?" It's not like, "Do you have a family? Do you have kids?' It's not something I honestly think about. Even with students, I'm out with students, and they're also pretty cool with it because it's normalized at our school. I'm not the first openly out person that they met whether they know parents, friends, of their parents or their own parents or other teachers. It's not a new thing.

I don't think about it honestly. In another way, like I said, I can be my whole self. I really can. When I first got there, I was surprised by that because I had just come from Sudan. When I first came there, and I knew that about the place, I was a little hesitant at first, but then when I noticed other people doing that and it being a non-issue, I was like, "Oh, I can actually do this with everybody and anyone. It's not an issue." It's not like I talk about all the time. When it's relevant, I'll say something. I won't edit myself when it's relevant. I feel like it's just like being an educator on any other campus. I can easily share my personal life when it's relevant or not. I won't get a reaction from students. I won't get questions. I won't get weird looks. It's just roll on to the next thing.

When I taught kindergarten, there are some kids who have not been exposed or don't understand different families other than their own, which is totally normal for a five-year-old. When I would teach with my co-teacher in kindergarten and we mentioned something came up about two moms or two dads, one little kid said, "You can't have two dads," or something. We were like, "No, actually you can." He just didn't get it. He didn't know. We took the opportunity to talk to him about different kinds of families. We read some books about it. Then he was like, "Oh, okay. You can." To me, that's okay. You're five. You're still learning that. Then later on, when they're 12 and in middle school, it's really a non-issue.

I mentioned times with my wife or just different pieces that would out me. The kids don't even blink. It's just like, "Yeah, right. My dad did this. My aunt did this." Occasionally, a kid my find affinity and will say, "Oh, yeah. I have two aunts," or something. It's exciting to them because there's an affinity. Then in the high school kids, they really couldn't care less. It's just very normal.

I visit different groups like affinity groups that we have from time to time. The kids know who's out. It's normal. It's a normal thing in their world now, especially in our school, our community. Really, it's like being in any other teaching space. There's no backlash.

I think, because of my own identity as a lesbian, I'm aware of a lot of things, like kids being safe and feeling comfortable. Just in the way the language that I might use. I'm not going to say, "Take this home to your mom and dad." You know what I mean. I'm going to be more inclusive, "Take this home to your parents." That could be anybody or parent or take it home to your family.

I have gender things, too, not just sexual orientation. We are a friend's school and we're co-ed, but we always address everybody as friends. We don't say girls and boys or boys and girls. We say, "Friends, line up. Friends come to the circle," or whatever. It's neutralized. It's to include everybody. Yeah, I am more aware of that. I always have been just because of my own identity. That's going to travel forth in the language that we use in the classroom and make sure that everybody's being included and that there are space for kids and their own identities. Yet, kids express their gender identities in different ways.

We do have kids in our school who are gender nonconforming and identify differently as not boy or girl, or the gender they were assigned at birth. We as a school have to be more aware of that. I am aware. I was already aware, but that's just because of my identity in the world that I'm in and my peer groups outside of school. I'm thinking about that. I'm thinking about making sure it's really inclusive. Then at the same time, when I hadn't been inclusive, someone called me on it. I'm very open to that and saying, "Oh, yeah. I'm sorry I didn't see that. Sorry I may have offended. I'm going to think about that in the future." I was raised in a heterosexualized world, so I still do some of the things such as not including everybody and being heteronormative.

I think I'm also open to growing and being aware that I can make mistakes too even if I'm a lesbian woman. That doesn't exempt me as a multiracial, as a Black woman. We all have bias. It's impossible not to. I'm also open to constructive criticism, so that I can grow as well. Yeah, I am aware of those kids and those families. I'm sure more hyper-aware to make sure they feel included and not otherwise or not included.

I have to create spaces for myself to vent and outside my school. I have affinity group space with other university directors and other people. I can really let go, so I can go back to work the next day. That doesn't happen so much around being lesbian at all at least in my community.

I probably think about being Black first because being a lesbian is really a non-issue. I think about being a person of color. There are times in my day, when sometimes I'm not representing myself as a person of color because it's not safe. I don't want to lose my job. I'm never having to do that being a lesbian. I'm pretty out. It's really accepted. I can be as out as I want to be. I'm not even super flamboyant in any way, but I never think about that. I do think about myself being a person of color. That's the thing I'll edit out or have to put on the back corners, so I don't freak out and get fired.

Karen

> *I made a decision then, in college, that being out was a political decision that I had to make in order to demystify this notion that "I don't know gay people." Like yeah, your teacher's gay, your neighbor's gay, your friend is gay. I'm gay. I'm the person that you know in this intimate way.*

I think the first thing that comes to mind is I'm an anti-bias educator, and that was also stemmed from an experience I had in my first independent school, which was as an assistant teacher almost 25 years ago. I was young, teacher of color in a predominantly White school with many White students...three-year-olds, mind you...and a few kids of color. One little girl, a little African American girl, decided that she wanted yellow hair and white skin and blue eyes, and so when her parents and I convened about the experience she was having and what she was talking about, I realized that I didn't know anything about how to raise, how to teach really young children around identity issues and around these systems of oppression that were huge concepts for young kids.

I just started getting my feet into the work and really became an anti-bias educator, and that led me to become the diversity director about eight years ago. In all the schools that I've worked in, it's been my mission to really teach from that social justice perspective.

When I describe myself, I'm a Latina, a lesbian, mother of two, single mom of two, although currently in a relationship, which is nice, and those are the primary identifiers, and also call myself a New York Rican.

My educational identity now is different than it was 25 years ago when I was first starting. I didn't think I could be the Latina lesbian. I thought I had to blend in, you know, because my first experiences were really in independent schools, and then it didn't take long for me to realize that there were lots of interesting people with interesting identities and interesting personalities and ways of being, and I just thought, "Let's make some room for this Latina lesbian then."

I was really well received in the first school and the second school and now where I am, so I don't find as many conflicts around that. I feel very well embraced. During National Coming Out Day during my first time at the school, I wrote a letter to the whole community saying thank you for being a warm community for me to feel that I can be safe in coming out. For about seven years, I wrote a National Coming Out Day letter every year, and was, again, well received around that.

I talk openly, not only when I was the classroom teacher at the school. I taught third grade there before I became the director of diversity. I also talked openly around issues of discrimination and issues of race and ethnicity, identity, and that sort of webbed into the work that I do now with the students around identity development. I'm as out as out can be in my school community. Everybody knows I'm a lesbian, and when they don't, they find out pretty soon.

The founder of our school, who passed away in the 1940s, was a lesbian. The school, about 35 years ago, outed her because back in the 1920s, she was a closet lesbian. Everybody in the school community knew, but nobody in the neighborhood knew. She was a political figure, and she worked with John Dewey and worked with other political figures to try and reform schools. Being out wasn't an option in the public sphere, but in her private life, she was. I came into the school after they had already outed her in the larger community, both in and out of the school, so that's how it felt like a natural space for me to work in and a natural place for me to be who I wanted to be, or who I am, rather.

I started to have some thoughts around fourth to sixth grade. I sometimes say fourth, but really, the language and the idea of what that meant, probably emerged in elementary school. By seventh grade, a neighbor moved in across the hall from me who identified as bisexual, and at first, I thought that was what I was. Then by eighth grade, certainly before I entered high school, before ninth grade, I knew I was a lesbian, and then had my first kiss in ninth grade with a girl and thought, "Yep, this is it." This was it.

I dated two boys, though I wouldn't call it dating but maybe they would. And I think I kissed three in my whole time, and I just didn't like it. This was like, "What is… this is it? Oh, man, I'm so not enjoying this." So yeah, after that first kiss in high school, it was like, "Ah, this makes more sense."

It was challenging growing up in a Latina Catholic household, but also very interesting. My mom is Puerto Rican, and she came to this country when she was 19. Her family situation was her mom and her twin sister died at birth, so she was raised by lots of different people, and so the notion of rejecting anybody in your family didn't make sense to her. You just embraced everybody because everybody embraced her. While she had a hard time, when I came out to her, it only took her about three months before she realized, "Well, this is my damn daughter. What am I supposed to do?"

She gave me a hard time. I was living back at home when I came out to her. I came out when I was about 19, and I had moved from a college dorm back home to save some money because I was in graduate school, my first year of graduate school. And so I came out to her, and she was shocked; she cried. We had to call my sister who was in nursing school to calm her down, and it was like, "I raised you the same way I raised your sisters." I'm like, "Yeah you did, exactly the same. This is just more information."

She didn't talk to me for three months, and that was really hard, but prior to that, I had come out to my brother and he was fine about it. I came out to my sister in a funky way, and she was upset about how I came out, but she was fine about it in the end. I was in my sophomore year of college, and I pretended that I was doing a study, a paper on people's reactions to finding out that their sibling is a lesbian or gay or whatever, so I said, "I am working on this, so if I told you this, what would you say? What's your reaction?" She wrote down her thoughts. I said, "All right, thanks, I'm going to go ask my other sister. I'm going to go ask Janet," and she looked at me funny, and I just ignored it and wrote notes like I was writing this factual paper. She had, at that point, moved on to Columbia University for nursing school, but she was still connected to some of her friends at the college that I was going to, because I went to the same college. One of her friends said, "Hey, did you know your sister's a lesbian? She's dating this girl in college." I'm like, "Oh, man, busted." So she came to me afterwards, and she's like, "I'm really upset that you didn't tell me, that this is how I had to find out. Why'd you have to go around in this circle and stuff?"

Then my other sister, who at the time we didn't know, but she has been diagnosed as having bipolar disorder, so we had a very odd relationship growing up. Like I said, nobody knew this about her until much later, and so I came out to her. She was not talking to me, and we did the silent treatment all the time, so we would have these moments of not talking to each other, and then when we would break the silence with each other. One of us would write a note about something we needed or wanted, which was funny, nothing rude, and then throw it to the other person. I don't know if I threw the first note or if she did, but I remember that's how I came out to her. I wrote it in a note, "I'm a lesbian," and I threw it at her.

I used to tell my fifth-grade students that being out is a political decision that I've made in order for me to have a personal life that I prefer, because my sexual orientation is personal. Nobody has to know anything about it. I don't need to know anybody else's sexual orientation. It's not relevant to how I interact with people, particularly at my job. It's not relevant to how I interact with my friends. Their sexual orientation doesn't affect me in that way and mine shouldn't affect them.

However, in college in particular, when I was coming out and feeling more confident about who I was, I began to read books, just getting to know what does this mean? I realized that the more people are closeted, the harder it is for people to realize that they know gay people, and so I made a decision then, in college, that being out was a political decision that I had to make in order to demystify this notion that "I don't know gay people." Like, "Yeah, your teacher's gay, your neighbor's gay, your friend is gay. I'm gay. I'm the person that you know in this intimate way."

I'm gay. I'm a lesbian, and that's something that you don't need to know about me in order to figure out how to function. And I think the other piece of it, and this is something I learned after coming out to my mom and her huge disappointment in those three months of hell, she felt that I was different. What she ended up saying eventually to my sister, and my sister told me years later, is she realized that I was still in college, I was applying to graduate school, and I was wanting to be a teacher: I was a good person. She realized her image of me didn't really change. She just had this layer that she now knew about me, and that's the thing that I really took out of that journey with my mom, which is, I want people to see my multi-layers. Lesbian is just one of them. I'm also a social justice activist. I'm also a really good teacher. I'm also a very good friend. I'm an amazing parent. Like there's just some great things about me. This is just one of them.

I'm out to everybody. I mean, everybody. It's a school of 650 students and all their family members. We have a number—not a whole lot—but we have a number of gay/lesbian families in the school. I just had this conversation recently with the head of the school. While I gear towards more feminine clothing, I don't ascribe to a gender identity in terms of gender expression, and so every once in a while, I'll get my groove on and I'll need to wear my shirt and tie and flats and all of that. There was this one day I wore a shirt I had gotten on sale in the men's department of Urban Outfitters, and I wanted to sport my shirt in the spring, but I got to work and found out that there was an evening event that I had forgotten to put on my calendar. I went to the head of the school, and I said, "Look, I'm going to have to leave work early because I have to go home and change for this event tonight." It was the new parent gathering, and he's like, "Why?" and I said, "I can't show up in my 'lesbianhood' for the new families just yet." He looked at me, because he and I have great relationship, and goes, "They need to know you first." I said, "Yes, particularly for the families of color and for the Latino families, but also my daughter's entering into high school, and I don't want her first reaction to be 'you can't be friends with that kid.'" For families who don't know who I am, I can't afford to lose the respect—I don't know if it's respect, but maybe that's the word that's coming to me—of families of color who have never met a lesbian of color or not in the workplace and not out, who is going to be their go-to person if something happens in a racial way with their child or they need support around race issues and that kind of thing.

I need them to know that I'm going to be there for them without the roadblock of them saying, "Well, she's a dyke," or "She's a lesbian." That's a split second. That's a one-time closeting moment that I will give myself for the benefit of what happens afterwards, and then after that—once they've signed, they're in school and school's starting in a few weeks—that's it. That's all they get. They get that one time of me wearing something that's traditionally girl clothing, to just be accepting of me, and then after that, it's just whatever. They get me.

It's a hard one to describe what it is like being an "out" lesbian because I don't know anything else. It's like saying, describe what it's like to be a woman. Describe what it's like to have your two legs. Like, it just is. There isn't any other way of being. I think I'm grateful for the fact that the school did some work around LGBT issues before I got here 12 years ago, and I was doing workshops on LGBT inclusion with young children for about ten years before I started working at the school, so they knew me. The principal who hired me, she and I would show up at the same conferences and attend the same workshops around these issues because she was also doing the same work.

From the perspective of a principal, that was really powerful for me, so she and I knew each other through this work around LGBT inclusion with young children, and so she hired me knowing that I'm a lesbian. That just made that process even that much easier.

If I were male, I might have a different story, especially if I was male of color, gay and teaching three-year-olds, which is what I was first teaching. I think perhaps I'd have more stories around the challenges. But as a young Latina who was a caretaker in many ways, teaching three-year-olds and four-year-olds, there was nothing that was challenging, nothing around the career choice I made with my family that was challenging.

When I told my mom in elementary school that I wanted to join the junior corps and wear uniforms, she was like, "Hell, no," in her Spanish way, and when I told my sister in high school that I wanted to join ROTC, she said, "No, you're not." So, those were not career choices that I could choose. The military was something that was calling my name, but it's like, "Nope, you're not doing that." Being a teacher and being a female go hand in hand.

I'm just aware of being female, and then I just have to un-psych myself out of feeling intimidated by it, but that's probably where I feel my gender the most, in those spaces. Then there are times when it's hard to separate, again, because of intersectionality; it's hard to separate my female, my gender from my ethnicity in particular, and there are times in my leadership meetings or the senior administrative meetings where I am very much feeling something, as a woman, as a woman of color, as a Latina, but everybody else at the table's up here, in their heads. I'm feeling it raw in my heart, and that's really challenging for me. I don't want to not do that. I don't want to stop being that way, but it's hard because I have to find a safe way of sharing who I am in those spaces without feeling like I'm going to be seen as inappropriate.

You know what it reminds me of? It reminds me of the chatter that Hillary Clinton had to deal with because she cried or didn't cry, that she was too tough or not tough enough, and it was like, yeah, I feel that.

I'm the only Latina administrator, but not the only administrator of color. There were more, but they just left the school for other great reasons, so it's now going to be myself and one other woman, an Indian woman. But one of the things that I've been grateful for is the work that I have been doing with this team, this administrative team, and so I feel like they're aware of their whiteness. They're aware of privilege, male privilege as well as White privilege. They're aware of who I am and who they are themselves, and its less of an issue than it was eight years ago, but that's at work.

The challenge then became when I was an administrator because once I became an administrator, particularly in the independent school sphere, there are many more White male administrators than there are White female, and certainly females of color, very, very few. That's where I felt my gender in lots of ways, particularly doing workshops.

There are two conferences that I present regularly. One is an annual conference for the National Association of Independent Schools, and that's geared towards administrators, and the other one is the People of Color Conference, which is geared towards educators, particularly educators of color. So there, I'm just me, and there's not an issue. But at the annual conference, I feel my femaleness. I feel my lesbian-ness… I pick my clothing. I feel my race as well. I feel the fact that I talk with my hands, like all of me is heightened, and I'm very, very aware. It's like what Claude Steele says in terms of stereotype threat. It's like it's right here, all my identities are like inscribed on my forehead as I walk the halls.

DISCUSSION AND IMPLICATIONS

The purpose of this qualitative study was to examine the ways in which sexual orientation influences the identities of LGBTQ teachers in independent schools. The study consisted of forty self-identified, LGBTQ teachers. This chapter will discuss the interpretation of the findings and link them to literary works that address sexual orientation, identity development, teacher identity, LGBTQ teacher identity, and the intersectionality of race, gender, and sexual orientation.

This study examined the discourses and norms related to sexual orientation that LGBTQ teachers experience in independent school settings. The key findings were developed from a thorough review of the data, and they represent themes that emerged during data analysis. Each finding addresses the primary research question and provides additional insight into how LGBTQ teachers in independent schools perceive the relationship between their sexual orientation and their identity as teacher. This chapter discusses and draws conclusions related to the data presented and is structured into three sections: (1) discussion of key findings in relation to research questions and relevant literature; (2) implications for future research and practice; and (3) summary and concluding statements.

Discussion of Key Findings

Data analysis revealed six findings resulting from the primary research questions that guided this study: "Do LGBTQ teachers in independent schools view their sexual orientation as informing their teacher identities? If so, in what ways?" Secondarily, the research focused on the following question: "How do LGBTQ teachers in independent schools perceive the relationship between their sexual orientation and their identity as teachers?"

Sexual orientation development was a critical component of the conceptual framework for this study. The shared experiences of the participants in this study echoed a key concept: the process of coming out is critical for creating an authentic life for LGBTQ teachers. The results of this study support the continual nature of coming out and identity development. This process occurs in different stages of life for each person, and regression between stages can occur based on life experiences and environments.

Revisiting Trodien and Jackson's Sexual Orientation Identity Models

Trodien's 1989 sexual identity development model and Jackson's 2007 gay teacher identity theory provides a backdrop for understanding how internal and external factors impinge upon homosexual and teacher identities and influence the professional practice of gay teachers in independent schools. The teachers identified a wide range of factors, including school culture, bias, perceived homophobia, heteronormativity, and messages of acceptance and tolerance that influenced their identities as teachers. Birden (2005) and Evans (2002) discussed the implications of negotiating sexual orientation in educational settings. Notably, both Birden and Evans argue that gay teachers navigate their sexual orientation within the heteronormative confines of education. Participants in this study felt that being out and open would help to create a safe and collaborative classroom environment, as well as provide support for students who were questioning their own sexual orientation.

Similarly, the results in this study also found some validity in Jackson's 2007 theory of the duality of gay teacher identity. Jackson's study found that "the more gay teachers integrated their full selves into their teaching, the more student-centered their teaching became" (p. 173). The participants in this study shared various perceptions of their identities as teachers. When asked how they describe their identities as teachers, they gave a range of responses that were categorized as "out," "role models," "student-centered," "authentic," and "having high expectation for their students." However, being student-centered was critical to the way many of the participants identified as teachers. Kevin and Olivia both gave examples of paying close attention to the way the students show up to learn and adjusting their classroom practices to meet the needs of their students. The participants' instinct to create a student-centered approach to learning fits Jackson's conclusion that gay and lesbian teachers who manage to incorporate their sexual orientation into their teacher identity become more student-centered.

Due to the small number of participants (nine), Jackson's 2007 results cannot be generalized to the greater LGBTQ community. In addition, Jackson's study is limited by the fact that all of the participants in the study were White. As a result, the author does not address the influence of the intersection of race and sexual orientation in the identity development of gay teachers. The LGBTQ community has been critiqued for the omission of non-White perspectives.[73] The lack of racial and ethnic diversity presented in Jackson's model perpetuates the social and cultural normative of White images of homosexuality that fail to acknowledge the experiences of people of color.

---

73   Balsam et al., 2011; Han, 2007; Harper, Jernewall, & Zea, 2004; Kudler, 2007

Sexual Orientation Development of LGBTQ Teachers

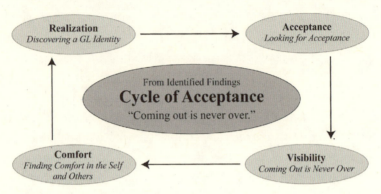

Figure 3. LGBTQ Teachers: Cycle of Acceptance

Sexual orientation identity development is in constant evolution. LGBTQ participants were purposely chosen for this study in order to explore the reflective logic of the coming out process. Figure 3 presents a revised conceptual framework for exploring homosexual identity development that emerged from this study. The model incorporates the models of Troiden (1989) and Jackson (2007) for stages of development that are presented on a more linear continuum. Jackson and Troiden equate coming out to distinct stages of development. In an attempt to address the fixed nature of the stages model, Troiden acknowledges that homosexual identity development is "emergent and never fully determined" (p. 112). Therefore, coming out cannot be consistently aligned with developmental stages; rather it is a continuous circular process of acceptance. Figure 3 represents an attempt to allow for those who identify as LGBTQ to revisit moments along their development as they pertain to their current context and the complexities of coming out.

Discovering a Gay Identity

Troiden (1989) indicated that the first stage of realization typically occurs during the sensitization stage. Sixteen of the 40 participants fell in line with Troiden's model of becoming aware of their sexual orientation before puberty. For some participants this stage of realization was not so clear. As such, the remaining participants reached this stage at various ages from ten and up. Discrepancies existed throughout the stages with no clear indications that gays and lesbians had to pass through each sequence of the model to complete the process of homosexual identity formation and adopt homosexuality as a way of life.

Looking for Acceptance

The participants in this study described unique challenges on their quest for self-acceptance and validation from others. The complexities of sexual orientation are heightened as the participants described the complex messages they had to navigate during the early stages of development. Matthew shared a story about the role that religion and his family played in his quest for self-acceptance. He shared, "That process was difficult because I was raised in a very conservative Christian home with those 'traditions.' For lack of better terminology, I tried to fix myself."

The participants confirmed the complexity associated with developing a gay identity. As a result, there were varied accounts that highlighted the barriers associated with stages of development, such as Daniel's:

"I also grew up in a very homophobic family and a very homophobic culture and always had school, sports, school...a lot of aggressive homophobia, a lot of aggressive 'the gays are going to give you AIDS and rape your children' talk. It had a big impact on me, so I was very much afraid of being gay, and turning up gay, growing up."

There is no clear path to complete acceptance. Development can often have periods of regression when individuals go back and forth through various cycles. It was noted that participants viewed being out and open as a form of self-acceptance. For example, Keith shared about the need to deny his sexual orientation:

"I temper myself wherever I'm at. I live in the city. We have a lot of gay people. I'm completely comfortable here. But then, if I'm home or with my partner in his home state, I gauge who I am and how I need to be."

Many pointed to times in their adult lives where they still did not feel sure about who they were or felt sure about who they were but did not feel that they would be accepted because of their sexual orientation.

Finding Comfort

The stories presented details regarding the level of comfort participants acknowledged when identifying as LGBTQ. Comfort was often found through self-exploration and experimentation with gay-identified social groups. Participants corroborated this stage with stories of actively seeking out gay support groups as well as building up levels of defiance in claiming their sexual orientation identity. Olivia's story speaks to this point:

"I was living with my best friend from high school, who is supportive but not very emotional. I moved into a lesbian group house and bought a car. It was helpful. This helped me feel more comfortable with who I am and living here. For the most part, it was a mix of feeling relieved that I'm not a social nerd. I'm just gay, yet trying to figure out how to navigate."

Finding a place to confront the challenges of sexual orientation comfortably is crucial in the process of sexual identity development.

Visibility

The visibility associated with coming out of the closet is crucial for creating an environment in which everyone can be their most authentic selves. The concept of coming out is used to describe the acceptance of identity development for many marginalized groups within the LGBTQ community. However, for the purpose of this study, it applies specifically to the experience of LGBTQ individuals. Participants' sense of self was connected to their coming out experience. Indeed, 38 of the 40 participants shared their coming out experience and expressed the importance of the coming out process to their sexual orientation identity development. As a result, the participants worked hard to be in a constant state of awareness, to be sensitive to issues of inclusion, to use their outness as a way of connecting with others, and to feel empowered through their sexual orientation.

The results of this study support the continual nature of coming out and identity development. This process occurs in different stages of life for each person, and regression between stages can occur based on life experiences and environments. Barbara shared, "It is a constant process being out and living out and practicing 'outness,' and it looks different at different times." Through analysis of the stories participants shared regarding their coming out processes and their sexual orientation identity development, the results of this study confirm that developing a gay identity is a process of realization, self-acceptance, social acceptance, and social visibility.

Empathy, Awareness, and Sensitivity: Integral Components of an Authentic Gay Teacher Identity

LGBTQ teachers believe that their sexual orientation informs their teacher identities. Thirty-five of the participants declared that their sexual orientation absolutely influenced who they were in their independent school settings. The participants cited empathy, awareness, and sensitivity as important qualities that allow them to relate to the needs of their students. Furthermore, they referenced the qualities of authenticity and visibility as being key components related to their sexual orientation that influence their teacher identities. Their stories related experiences of acceptance, struggle, affirmation, and authenticity. These findings are consistent with the literature associated with identifying the challenges of gay people working in education.[74]

The influence of sexual orientation on LGBTQ teachers in independent schools is tied to their ability to empathize. When they are empathetic, they are able to understand the internal and external conflicts of their students better. This ability is connected to the process of gay teachers coming out and coming to terms with their sexual orientation. Additionally, a heightened level of awareness and sensitivity are integral components of their authentic identity. Being authentic then becomes about having a sense of the ways in which their sexual orientation identity development can be used to create and expand learning opportunities for their students and their extended learning environment.

LGBTQ teachers have had to defeat heterosexist values impressed upon them from an early age. Being LGBTQ requires individuals to successfully integrate homosexuality into their identity. That necessitates the ability to think outside of the heteronormative mainstream of expectations associated with sexuality. When LGBTQ teachers authentically enter a classroom in an independent school, they have struggled with, rejected and pushed beyond heterosexual imposed truths and cultural values to arrive at a thoughtful integration of self, sexuality, and teacher identity. The ability to think and engage critically with their otherness creates an intellectual and emotional challenge that is at the core of their identity as teachers. That awareness and sensitivity gives them the ability to empathize with their students' struggles

---

74. Birden, 2005; Epstein, 1994; Irwin, 2002

and impacts their capacity to make what they teach relevant to their students and not the heteronormative cultural expectations that are reinforced in independent schools.

The most effective teachers are those who are able to connect learning when students struggle with new concepts. Those moments call for teachers to integrate the students' edge of understanding and to try to expand the students' knowledge and belief in what they are capable of discovering. LGBTQ teachers in independent schools are most effective when they are able to use the complexities of their identity to challenge the resistance of sexual orientation identity development and negotiate relationships with their students for them to become empowered learners.

Intersectionality of Race and Sexual Orientation Identity

Race was embedded in the findings as a vital component of how the participants perceived their teacher identity. The intersection of sexual orientation and race highlights that almost all of the White participants (26/29) indicated that race had an impact on their identity as LGBTQ teachers. The candid and forthright reflections offered by the White participants were different than hypothesized when conceptualizing the study. It is not often that Whites have the opportunity to experience otherness. Traditionally, Whites have benefited from the privileged status of their race in independent schools. The comparison between the intersection of race and sexual orientation concludes that White teachers in independent schools, who are LGBTQ, benefit from an elevated status of otherness.

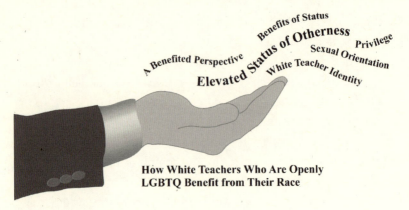

Benefits of Status
Benefited Perspective
Elevated Status of Otherness
A Benefited Perspective
Privilege
Sexual Orientation
White Teacher Identity

**How White Teachers Who Are Openly
LGBTQ Benefit from Their Race**

Figure 4. Elevated Status of Otherness

Privileged Status: White Participants, Race, and Sexual Orientation

The White acknowledgment of privilege represents a benefited perspective of otherness. In the most typical ways, White teachers who identify as gay benefit from the cultural ideals and expectations of their racial identity as White people. For example, White teachers who also are gay have the benefit of knowing that they represent the cultural ideals of America. Those ideals have been established from cultural norms associated with being White and a historical narrative of hegemony and oppression of other cultures that lead to the evolution of racism and the construction of otherness based on race, gender, class, sexuality, and difference.

The expectations associated with a White racial identity are limitless. The marginalization of groups has been so successfully normalized in our mainstream culture that Whites will never experience the devaluation and limits imposed on others by the dominance of their race. Whites have not been systemically subjected to the low expectations associated with failing educational systems, discriminative hiring practices, or the threat of police violence. They will never operate within the sphere of the injustice of Jim Crow laws or experience the inhumanness of slavery. Policies and practices have been disproportionately set up in various sectors of our society to reinforce White superiority and the inferiority of otherness.

The same culture of privileging sameness has relevance in independent school settings. Independent schools have a longstanding history of privileging sameness, with many independent schools mirroring the hegemonic construct of a White and affluent society. As a result, it is easier for White, LGBTQ teachers in independent schools to embrace and anchor themselves in their racial identity as recipients of the inheritance of the imposing power of the dominate group without having to suffer the repercussions associated with their deviant sexual orientation identity.

White, LGBTQ teachers in independent schools who are fully aware and explore their privilege have the perspective of an elevated status of power. Their sexual orientation combined with their privileged racial identity place them in a unique position to use their otherness to connect and advocate for students and other marginalized groups. The critique of White privilege is that White people are not aware that they have a privileged existence. Furthermore, many do not understand the benefit of not having to think about the societal inequities associated with their racial identity. Their perspective of their otherness creates opportunities for them to align their status with the atonement for people of color who identify as gay and lesbian in independent schools and have not been able to move beyond the confines of the intersection of race and sexual orientation. Having the dual status of White and gay allowed those teachers to use race to cover their otherness and move between the two identities into spheres of influence to seek out ways to connect and advocate for other oppressed groups. The intersection of race and sexual orientation in the context of White teachers actively exploring their privilege lead to teachers using their influence to challenge various forms of oppression and to speak out against systems of inequity in independent schools without fear of retribution. This advocacy is influenced by the shared experience associated with sexual orientation identity development.

White teachers who identify as LGBTQ in independent schools are unable to fully assimilate into a marginalized identity—the implication being that they still benefit from their otherness at the expense of others. Although, they can never feel the full impact of the systemic nature of oppression, White teachers who fully integrate their racial and sexual orientations benefit from their perspective of otherness. The inherent benefit of this otherness is that White teachers who are LGBTQ have a sense of how other stories are told and lives are lived. They have the vantage point of privilege to work through the paradox of their otherness and to leverage their influence on policies that govern independent schools and impact the collective identities of LGBTQ teachers.

Limitations of the Study

Inevitably, the study design had limitations. The generalizability of the results is limited by the independent school requirement of the study participants, self-reporting of data, and the absence of teachers who are not open about their sexuality. The study did not include teachers from public schools or transgender teachers. The goal of this study was to explore LGBTQ teachers' perspectives on sexual orientation and on their identity in an independent school setting. Moving forward, it is important to expand the research to include conversations that represent the vastness and complexities of the LGBTQ community. The experiences of LGBTQ teachers in general and of LGBTQ teachers in public schools are in equal need of careful and detailed examination.

Many areas touched upon in this study warrant further research, including the relationships of LGBTQ teachers to students, LGBTQ teachers as role models for other LGBTQ students, and the intersectionality of race and sexual orientation as it pertains to White LGBTQ educators and their ability to identify with groups of people with marginalized identities. Opportunities to examine the cultural relationships between the missions and philosophies of independent schools in order to better understand the influences they have on LGBTQ teachers, administrators, and families—and more importantly students—and their various identity constructions would help further the advancement of LGBTQ issues.

Implications for Research

Many studies have examined the experience of gay and lesbian teachers and how polices in education affect LGBTQ teachers and students, but few have explored the sexual orientation and identity construction of LGBTQ teachers in independent schools. Independent school culture plays an integral part in understanding the influence of sexual orientation on the identity of LGBTQ teachers. Independent schools have traditionally been implicit in their reinforcement of heterosexual ideals and traditions that often exclude the possibility of anything other than heterosexuality. The assumption is that heterosexuality is privileged over homosexuality.

This study was designed to elicit participants' reflections on every stage of their development that led them to a place of openness and "outness" within the context of an independent school setting, with the understanding that an "out" LGBTQ identity is an ongoing process of advocacy and safety. Independent schools have spent time thinking about the issues of diversity and inclusion. School leaders are being charged with creating learning environments that are more inclusive as diversity and inclusion continue to challenge independent schools.[75]

---

75   Hall & Stevenson, 2007

In reflecting on their independent school cultures, the participants recognized that personal responsibility requires exposure to and respect for diversity, different people, and various points of view.

The participants addressed the assumed expectations of being heterosexual in an independent school setting. Participants spoke to both positive and negative cultural messages about homosexuality. Many stated that their schools had adopted policies and established support to address the shifting landscape around sexual orientation by way of creating Gay-Straight Alliances and other advocacy groups. Some noted that their schools' mission statements were filled with patterned language of shared meaning, emphasizing the value of difference, the whole person, and creating global citizens, with limited support to implement the stated goals particularly as they relate to sexual orientation.

The participants gave examples of making progress in recruitment efforts targeting students from more diverse social, racial, cultural, and socioeconomic backgrounds. This supports Patterson's 2001 research that chronicled and described in detail the injustices surrounding access to education in which he notes the interplay of race and economics. Participants in this study shared concerns that though the efforts were commendable, the institutions were far from where they needed to be in order to mirror the diversity of larger society. The participants gave the impression that publicly, independent schools appeared to be creating more inclusive learning environments, but some shared that, privately, the history of privileging heterosexuality, racism, segregation, male hegemony, and elitism was ongoing.

Analysis of the data collected during this study pointed to areas for future research. A comparison of LGBTQ people in independent schools with LGBTQ people in other fields would be useful in determining if there are shared experiences associated with sexual orientation identity and to gauge the levels of awareness in similar communities. It would also be beneficial to investigate the attitudes of heads of schools, board members, and other administrators in independent schools toward gays and lesbians and the broader LGBTQ community. Future studies would contribute to the literature on gay perspectives in education and encourage other voices to be heard.

Further Research: LGBTQ Teachers as Role Models

A majority of the LGBTQ teachers identified key role models regarding their decision to become a teacher. The participants in the study describe the importance of being authentic and student-centered, and the significance of establishing themselves as role models in their schools. Almost all of the respondents reported that being gay informed their identities as teachers and noted that it was important for their students to see them in the fullness of their lives.

In addition, further research is needed to determine how students perceive their relationships with their openly LGBTQ teachers and the implications these relationships have on student identity development, both inside and outside of the classroom. It would be helpful to know how students who identify as LGBTQ are informed by the presence of openly LGBTQ teachers and administrators. Do they view those teachers as role models? What are the comparisons to teachers who are heterosexual? Do they feel safe, or at least safer, in the classrooms of LGBTQ teachers?

Further Research: Finding Security In and Out of the Closet

This study provided detailed accounts of LGBTQ teachers and their processes of coming to terms with their sexual orientation. Participants in the study communicate the benefits of being out and open and the positive effects this had on their students. The perception of a welcoming school environment may reflect the fact that respondents were openly LGBTQ, and it would be valuable to assess the perceptions of closeted teachers and students to gain a better understanding of the perceptions of those who do not feel safe or welcomed as compared to those who do. A study that addresses views from the closet and of other marginalized groups could yield valuable information for future interventions and research.

Participants also note the difficulty of being completely out and open all the time, citing safety, job security, and stigma as reasons to return to the closet to conceal their sexual orientation. A study examining the relationship between finding safety in the closet and LGBTQ educators would constitute an important step toward understanding the dynamics of being out in an educational setting. Additional research would yield a deeper understanding of how teachers who identify as out and openly LGBTQ find themselves back in the closet. Additional questions to consider include:

- What if teachers do not want to or do not feel the need to be out?
- How do LGBTQ teachers come out? To students? To peers?
- How do teachers navigate the association of out and open LGBTQ educators as threats to student safety or the stereotype of gay men as pedophiles?

All 40 of the participants identified as being "out" LGBTQ teachers. It is unclear if these sentiments shared in the study were associated with being out (versus being closeted) or with being gay (versus being straight). Additional research using mixed methods to compare openly LGBTQ teachers to closeted teachers in independent schools and LGBTQ teachers to heterosexual teachers could help clarify those questions presented earlier.

Implications for Practice

This study confirms that teachers who are LGBTQ have to find ways to incorporate their sexual orientation into their teacher identities.[76] Moving forward, how can information in this study help struggling and closeted gay teachers and educators in the broader LGBTQ community develop a stronger teacher identity that is informed by their sexual orientation? In particular, how can these educators use their experiences coming to terms with their sexual orientation to become aware of all students generally and support the marginalized students specifically? How can teachers' status as LGBTQ individuals make them more effective as educators?

Policies that Support and Protect LGBTQ Teachers and Students

The role of independent schools in establishing procedures and policies to support and sustain welcoming environments for gay people and other marginalized groups is evident in this study. Respondents frequently mention that they feel their school environments are open and accepting, but more than half recognize the prevalence of negative cultural messages at their schools. The research suggests that existing educational policies to support gay educators need to be stated and explicated. A clear policy regarding the acceptance and treatment of gays and lesbians in independent schools has the potential to enhance and create support networks for educators who feel alone or silenced. Such an initiative would substantiate mission statements of inclusivity. In addition, with such a vocal presence, this would then allow for a curriculum and other initiatives based on gay issues selected to expand the community knowledgebase regarding human rights.

---

76   Kissen, 1993

Knowing that the NAIS encourages in-depth approaches to promoting inclusiveness and stamping out bullying and discrimination, LGBTQ teachers could reach out to NAIS to create a series of professional development trainings focused on building learning communities that are free from discrimination. This should include schools, students, and parent leaders, as well as board members. There should be extensive discussion about homophobia and other forms of oppression, particularly as they relate to educational practices and policies. The overall message that intolerance is not acceptable in an educational institution that strives for excellence in academics and service should be voiced by school leaders and echoed by every member of the learning community.

Many respondents note diversity as a point of concern for their independent school settings. This highlights the ongoing challenge of creating learning environments in independent schools that are true representations of real-life diversity. As issues of diversity become increasingly relevant to education, the need for initiatives that help independent schools successfully manage diversity also increases. Given this increasing need, independent schools should create initiatives and programs to educate their communities, develop policies that are specific to sexual orientation, and support and protect LGBTQ teachers, staff, and students. Several institutions have established policies to address diversity and inclusion, but independent schools could benefit from LGBTQ-specific policies and curricula that are in compliance with the United States' progress and support concerning issues of sexual orientation and identity.

Conclusion

LGBTQ teachers face many challenges when it comes to disclosing their sexual orientation in school settings. This study highlights the lives of 40 teachers who identified as LGBTQ in an independent school setting. This study was designed as a quest for authenticity in education. The goal of this study is to create a dialogue around the experiences of LGBTQ teachers in independent schools. The stories offered vast, complex, important, and significant information regarding gay identity development and regarding advocacy for LGBTQ teachers, administrators, and students.

LGBTQ teachers have had to endure school-based homophobia as a part of their fight for integrity and respect. This study chronicles teachers who were open about their sexual orientation and identity. By being out and open about their sexual orientation, the teachers challenged existing prejudice and homophobia and helped to establish schools as safer environments, not only for themselves, but also for their students. From a systems perspective, teachers being open about their sexual orientation and identity forces educational institutions to address homophobia and the institutionalized mistreatment of marginalized people.[77]

My research with LGBTQ teachers in independent schools has helped me to understand that it is critical for those teachers to create conditions where they can be open about their sexual orientation. As LGBTQ teachers, we must hold ourselves accountable to the students that we serve and create spaces of learning in which they have the opportunity to see themselves reflected in the lives of their teachers. Sumara (2008) described being out as a creation of more expansive places of learning and teaching against the limits of heteronormativity. As teachers, we have the opportunity to have a positive impact on the lives of our students. We are shaping their views of themselves and the world simply by how we walk into a classroom and the identities we bring with us.

---

77 Ferfolja & Hopkins, 2013; Gregory, 2004; Jackson, 2007; Kissen, 1996; Takatori & Ofuji, 2007

APPENDIX

Participants and Interview Dates

Name	Interview	Name	Interview
Kenneth	August 18, 2014	Steven	August 20, 2014
Elizabeth	June 19, 2014	Joseph	June 22, 2014
Mark	July 5, 2014	Kevin	August 27, 2014
George	August 20, 2014	Mary	June 25, 2014
Brian	August 21, 2014	Olivia	July 6, 2014
Christopher	June 24, 2014	Andrew	August 25, 2014
Thomas	June 23, 2014	Jennifer	June 17, 2014
William	June 20, 2014	Lisa	September 3, 2014
Joshua	August 22, 2014	Anthony	July 9, 2014
Nancy	August 25, 2014	Linda	June 14, 2014
Jessica	July 7, 2014	Dorothy	July 11, 2014
Robert	June 24, 2014	Donald	July 7, 2014
David	June 20, 2014	James	June 10, 2014
Sarah	August, 20 2014	Betty	August 26, 2014
Edward	August 25, 2014	Michael	June 11, 2014
Barbara	June 26, 2014	Karen	August 22, 2014
Matthew	June 26, 2014	Margaret	July 6, 2014
Charles	June 23, 2014	Patricia	June 14, 2014
Richard	June 22, 2014	John	June 10, 2014
Paul	July 5, 2014	Daniel	June 25, 2014

BIBLIOGRAPHY

Akkerman, S. F., & Meijer, P. C. (2011). "A Dialogical Approach to Conceptualizing Teacher Identity." *Teaching and Teacher Education, 27*(2), 308–319.

Andersen, M. L., & Collins, P. H. *Race, Class and Gender: An Anthology* (5th ed.). (Belmont, CA: Wadsworth, 2004.)

Anderson, J. D. *The Education of Blacks in the South, 1860–1935*. (Chapel Hill, NC: University of North Carolina, 1988.)

Balsam, K. F., Molina, Y., Beadnell, B., Simoni, J., & Walters, K. (2011). "Measuring Multiple Minority Stress: The LGBT People of Color Microaggressions Scale." *Cultural Diversity and Ethnic Minority Psychology, 17*(2), 163.

Bernstein, M. (1997). "Celebration and Suppression: The Strategic Uses of Identity by the Lesbian and Gay Movement." *American Journal of Sociology, 103*(3), 531–565.

Birden, S. *Rethinking Sexual Identity in Education*. (New York: Rowman & Littlefield, 2005.)

Blount, J. M. (2000). "Spinsters, Bachelors, and Other Gender Transgressors in School Employment, 1850–1990." *Review of Educational Research, 70*(1), 83–101.

Blount, J. M. *Fit to Teach: Same-Sex Desire, Gender, and School Work in the Twentieth Century*. (Albany, NY: State University of New York, 2006.)

Boswell, J. *Christianity, Social Tolerance, and Homosexuality: Gay People in Western Europe From the Beginning of the Christian Era*. Chicago: (University of Chicago, 1980.)

Brosnan, M. *The Inclusive School: A Selection of Writing on Diversity Issues in Independent Schools*. (Washington, DC: National Association of Independent Schools, 2012.)

Brunner, C. C., & deLeon, M. (2013). "Cycles of Fear: A Model of Lesbian and Gay Educational Leaders' Lived Experiences." *Educational Administration Quarterly, 49*(1), 161–203.

Cain, P. A. (1993). "Litigating for Lesbian and Gay Rights: A Legal History." *Virginia Law Review*, 1551–1641.

Cass, V. (1979). "Homosexuality Identity Formation: A Theoretical Model." *Journal of Homosexuality, 4*, 219–235.

Chambers, S. A. (2007). "'An Incalculable Effect': Subversions of Heteronormativity." *Political Studies, 55*(3), 656–679.

Collins, P. H. (1998). "It's All in the Family: Intersections of Gender, Race, and Nation." *Hypatia, 13*(3), 62–82.

Collins, P. H. *Black Feminist Thought: Knowledge, Consciousness, and the Politics of Empowerment*. (New York: Routledge, 2002.)

Crenshaw, K. W. (1995). "Mapping the Margins: Intersectionality, Identity Politics, and Violence Against Women of Color." In K. W. Crenshaw, N. Gotanda, G. Peller, & K.

Croteau, J. M., Talbot, D. M., Lance, T. S., & Evans, N. J. (2002). "A Qualitative Study of the Interplay Between Privilege and Oppression." *Journal of Multicultural Counseling and Development, 30*(4), 239–258.

Thomas (Eds.), *Critical Race Theory: The Key Writings that Formed the Movement* (pp. 357–383). (New York: The New Press, 1995.)

Datnow, A., & Cooper, R. (2000). "Creating a Climate for Diversity? The Institutional Response of Predominantly White Independent Schools to African-American Students." In M. G. Sanders (Ed.), *Schooling students placed at risk: Research policy and practice in the education of poor and minority adolescents* (pp. 207–228). Mahwah, NJ: Erlbaum.

DeCuir, J. T., & Dixson, A. D. (2004). "'So When It Comes Out, They Aren't That Surprised That It Is There': Using Critical Race Theory as a Tool of Analysis of Race and Racism in Education." *Educational Researcher*, 26–31.

DeJean, W. (2008). "Out Gay and Lesbian K–12 Educators: A Study in Radical Honesty." *Journal of Gay & Lesbian Issues in Education, 4*(4), 59–72.

DePalma, R., & Jennett, M. (2010). "Homophobia, Transphobia and Culture: Deconstructing Heteronormativity in English Primary Schools." *Intercultural Education, 21*(1), 15–26.

Doan, P., & Higgins, H. (2011). "The Demise of Queer Space?" *Journal of Planning Education and Research, 31*, 6–25.

Donahue, D. M. (2008). "Rethinking Silence as Support: Normalizing Lesbian and Gay Teacher Identities Through Models and Conversations in Student Teaching." *Journal of Gay & Lesbian Issues in Education, 4*(4), 73–95.

Donelson, R., & Rogers, T. (2004). "Negotiating a Research Protocol for Studying School-Based Gay and Lesbian Issues." *Theory into Practice, 43*(2), 128–135.

Duberman, M. B. *About Time: Exploring the Gay Past*. (New York: Gay Presses of New York, 1991.)

Duyvendak, J. W., & Krouwel, A. *The Global Emergence of Gay and Lesbian Politics: National Imprints of a Worldwide Movement*. (Philadelphia: Temple University Press, 2009.)

Eisen, V., & Hall, I. (1996). "Introduction." *Harvard Educational Review*, *66* (Summer), v–ix.

Epstein, D. *Challenging Lesbian and Gay Inequalities in Education (Gender and Education Series)*. (Buckingham, UK: Open University Press, 1994.)

Evans, K. *Negotiating the Self: Identity, Sexuality, and Emotion in Learning to Teach*. (London: Routledge Falmer, 2002.)

Ferfolja, T., & Hopkins, L. (2013). "The Complexities of Workplace Experience for Lesbian and Gay Teachers." *Critical Studies in Education*, *54*(3), 311–324.

Fischer, E., Imi, T., Färberböck, M., & Munro, R. *Aimee & Jaguar*. (Cologne: Kiepenheuer & Witsch, 1994.)

Fleischmann, A. & Hardman, J. (2004). "Hitting Below the Bible Belt: The Development of the Gay Rights Movement in Atlanta." *Journal of Urban Affairs*, *26*(4), 407–426.

Foster, M. *Black Teachers on Teaching*. (New York: The New Press, 1997.)

Gee, J. (2001). "Identity as an Analytic Lens for Research in Education." *Review of Research in Education*, *25*, 99–125.

Giddings, P. *When and Where I Enter: The Impact of Black Women on Race and Sex in America*. (New York: Bantam Books, 1984.)

Graves, K. *And They Were Wonderful Teachers: Florida's Purge of Gay and Lesbian Teachers*. (Champaign, IL: University of Illinois, 2009.)

Gregory, M. R. (2004). "Being Out, Speaking Out: Vulnerability and Classroom Inquiry." *Journal of Gay & Lesbian Issues in Education*, *2*(2), 53–64.

Griffin, P., & Ouellett, M. (2003). "From Silence to Safety and Beyond: Historical Trends in Addressing Lesbian, Gay, Bisexual, Transgender Issues in K–12 Schools." *Equity & Excellence in Education*, *36*(2), 106–114.

Hall, D., & Stevenson, H. (2007). "Double Jeopardy: Being African-American 'Doing Diversity' in Independent Schools." *The Teachers College Record*, *109*(1), 1–23.

Han, C. S. (2007). "They Don't Want to Cruise your Type: Gay Men of Color and the

Racial Politics of Exclusion." *Social Identities*, *13*(1), 51–67.

Harper, G. W., Jernewall, N., & Zea, M. C. (2004). "Giving Voice to Emerging Science and Theory for Lesbian, Gay, and Bisexual People of Color." *Cultural Diversity and Ethnic Minority Psychology*, *10*(3), 187.

Harbeck, Karen M. *Coming Out of the Classroom Closet: Gay and Lesbian Students, Teachers, and Curricula*. (New York: Routledge, 2014.)

Harvard Law Review (Ed.). *Sexual Orientation and the Law*. (Cambridge, MA: Harvard University Press, 1990.)

Heatherly, G. E. (1985). "Gay and Lesbian Rights: Employment Discrimination." *Annual Survey of American Law*, 901.

Howarth, J. W. (2004). "Adventures in Heteronormativity: The Straight Line from Liberace to Lawrence." *Nevada Law Journal*, *5*, 260.

Irwin, J. (2002). "Discrimination Against Gay Men, Lesbians, and Transgender People Working in Education." *Journal of Gay & Lesbian Social Services*, *14*(2), 65–77.

Jackson, J. M. *Unmasking Identities: An Exploration of the Lives of Gay and Lesbian Teachers*. (Lanham, MD: Lexington Books, 2007.)

Jennings, K. *One Teacher in 10: Gay and Lesbian Educators Tell Their Stories*. (Los Angeles: Alyson Publications, 1994.)

Jennings, K. (2004). "LGBT Case Studies." Retrieved from http://www.NAIS.org

Jennings, K. *One Teacher in 10, LGBT Educators Share Their Stories* (2nd ed.). (Los Angeles: Alyson Publications, 2005.)

Johnson, B., Down, B., Le Cornu, R., Peters, J., Sullivan, A. M., Pearce, J., & Hunter, J. *Conditions That Support Early Career Teacher Resilience* (Doctoral dissertation). Presented at the Australian Teacher Education Association Conference, Townsville, QLD, July, 2010.

Katz, J. N. *Gay American History: Lesbians and Gay Men in the USA*. (New York: Harper & Row, 1985.)

Kennedy, A. (2003). *Lawrence v. Texas*. 539 U.S. 558, 123 S. Ct. 2472, 156 L. Ed. 2d 508.

King, K. P. (2003). "Changing from the Inside Out: Transformational Learning and the Development of GLBT Sexual Identities Among Adults." In B. Hill (Ed.), *THE AERC Lesbian, Gay, Bisexual, Transgender, Queer & Allies (LGBTQ&A) Caucus Preconference: Queer Histories: Exploring Fugitive Forms of Social Knowledge*, 63–72.

Kissen, Rita M. (1993). "Voices from the Glass Closet: Lesbian and Gay Teachers Talk About their Lives." Paper presented at the American Educational Research Association, Atlanta, April. (ERIC Reproduction Document No. ED 363 556).

Kissen, R. M. *The Last Closet: The Real Lives of Lesbian and Gay Teachers*. (Portsmouth, NH: Heinemann, 1996.)

Kudler, B. A. (2007). *Confronting Race and Racism: Social Identity in African American Gay Men* (Master's thesis). Smith College School for Social Work, Northampton, MA.

Ladson-Billings, G., & Tate, W. (1995). "Toward a Critical Race Theory of Education." *Teachers College Record*, 97(1), 47–68.

Lauritsen, J., & Thorstad, D. *The Early Homosexual Rights Movement* (1864–1935). (Ojai, CA: Times Change, 1974.)

Lugg, C. A. (2003). "Sissies, Faggots, Lezzies, and Dykes: Gender, Sexual Orientation, and a New Politics of Education." *Educational Administration Quarterly*, 39(1), 95–134.

Marcus, E. *Making History: The Struggle for Gay and Lesbian Equal Rights*, 1945–1990. (New York: HarperCollins, 1992.)

Maxwell, J. A. *Qualitative Research Design: An Interactive Approach* (Vol. 41). (Los Angeles: Sage, 2013.)

Mayo, J. B. (2008). "Gay Teachers' Negotiated Interactions with their Students and (Straight) Colleagues." *The High School Journal*, 92(1), 1–10.

Meezan, W., & Martin, J. I. *Handbook of Research with Lesbian, Gay, Bisexual, and Transgender Populations*. (New York: Routledge, 2009.)

Miles, M. B., Huberman, A. M., & Saldaña, J. *Qualitative Data Analysis: A Methods Sourcebook*. (Los Angeles: Sage, 2013.)

National School Climate Survey. (2013). Retrieved from http://glsen.org/nscs

Palmer, P. J. *The Courage to Teach: Exploring the Inner Landscape of a Teacher's Life*. (San Francisco: Jossey-Bass, 2010.)

Patterson, J. T. *Brown v. Board of Education: A Civil Rights Milestone and its Troubled Legacy*. (New York: Oxford University, 2001.)

Plant, R. *The Pink Triangle: The Nazi War Against Homosexuals*. (New York: Holt, 1986.)

Poole, W. L. (2008). "Intersections of Organizational Justice and Identity Under the New Policy Direction: Important Understandings for Educational Leaders." *International Journal of Leadership in Education*, *11*(1), 23–42.

Portwood, S. G. (1995). "Employment Discrimination in the Public Sector Based on Sexual Orientation: Conflicts Between Research Evidence and the Law." *Law and Psychological Review*, *19*, 113.

Powell, B., Quadlin, N. Y., & Pizmony-Levy, O. (2015). "Public Opinion, the Courts, and Same-Sex Marriage: Four Lessons Learned." *Social Currents*, 1–10.

Rasmussen, M. L. (2004). "The Problem of Coming Out." *Theory into Practice*, *43*(2), 144–150.

Ravitch, S. M., & Riggan, M. *Reason & Rigor: How Conceptual Frameworks Guide Research*. (Los Angeles: Sage, 2011.)

Richardson, B. K., & Taylor, J. (2009). "Sexual Harassment at the Intersection of Race and Gender: A Theoretical Model of the Sexual Harassment Experiences of Women of Color." *Western Journal of Communication*, *73*(3), 248–272.

Richardson, D. (2007). "Patterned Fluidities: (Re)imagining the Relationship Between Gender and Sexuality." *Sociology*, *41*(3), 457–474.

Riddle, B. (1996). "Breaking the Silence." *Independent School*, *55*(2), 38.

Robinson, T. L. (1999). "The Intersections of Dominant Discourses Across Race, Gender, and other Identities." *Journal of Counseling Development*, *77*, 73–79.

Rofes, E. (2000). "Bound and Gagged: Sexual Silences, Gender Conformity and the Gay Male Teacher." *Sexualities*, *3*(4), 439–462.

Rubin, H. J., & Rubin, I. S. (Eds.). *Qualitative Interviewing: The Art of Hearing Data* (3rd ed.). (Los Angeles: Sage, 2012.)

Russell, V. (2014). "Coming Out, Rolling Over, and Playing Model: Possibilities Beyond the Trope of Queer Students 'At-Risk.'" *Teaching Education*, *25*(2), 142–155.

Sanlo, R. L. *Unheard Voices: The Effects of Silence on Lesbian and Gay Educators*. (Westport, CT: Bergin & Garvey, 1999.)

Schneider-Vogel, M. (1986). "Gay Teachers in the Classroom: A Continuing Constitutional Debate." *Journal of Law and Education*, *15*, 285.

Sears, J. T. (1989). "The Impact of Gender and Race on Growing Up Lesbian and Gay in the South." *National Women's Studies Association Journal*, *1*(3), 422–457.

Sfard, A., & Prusak, A. (2005). "Telling Identities: In Search of an Analytic Tool for Investigating Learning as a Culturally Shaped Activity." *Educational Researcher*, *34*(4), 14–22.

Shorter-Gooden, K., & Washington, N. C. (1996). "Young, Black, and Female: The Challenge of Weaving an Identity." *Journal of Adolescence*, *19*(5), 465–475.

Smith, J. A., Flowers, P., & Larkin, M. *Interpretative Phenomenological Analysis: Theory, Method and Research*. (Los Angeles: Sage, 2009.)

Sumara, D. J. (2008). "Small Differences Matter: Interrupting Certainty About Identity in Teacher Education." *Journal of Gay & Lesbian Issues in Education*, *4*(4), 39–58.

Takatori, S., & Ofuji, K. (2007). "My Coming Out Story as a Gay Teacher in Kyoto." *Journal of Gay & Lesbian Issues in Education*, *4*(2), 99–105.

Tribe, L. H. (2004). *Lawrence v. Texas*: The "fundamental right" that dare not speak its name. *Harvard Law Review*, *117*(6), 1893–1955.

Troiden, R. (1989). "The Formation of Homosexual Identities." *Journal of Adolescent Health Care*, *9*, 105–113.

Walther, C. S. (2015). "The Marrying Kind?: Debating Same-Sex Marriage Within the Lesbian and Gay Movement." *Contemporary Sociology: A Journal of Reviews*, *44*(1), 35–37.

Warner, M. (Ed.). *Fear of a Queer Planet: Queer Politics and Social Theory* (Vol. 6). (Minneapolis, MN: University of Minnesota, 1993.)

Weiss, A., & Schiller, G. *Before Stonewall: The Making of a Gay and Lesbian Community*. (Tallahassee, FL: Naiad, 1988.)

White, A. *Ain't I a Feminist: African-American Men Speak Out on Fatherhood, Friendship, Forgiveness, and Freedom*. (Albany, NY: SUNY, 2008.)

van Dijk, L., & van Driel, B. *Challenging Homophobia: Teaching About Sexual Diversity*. (London: Trentham, 2007.)

Yoshino, K. *Covering: The Hidden Assault on Our Civil Rights*. (New York: The Random House Publishing Group, 2007.)